ALL JANGLE AND RIOT

A BARRISTER'S
HISTORY OF THE BAR

by

R.G. HAMILTON

PROFESSIONAL BOOKS LIMITED
1986

Published in 1986 by
Professional Books Limited,
Milton Trading Estate, Abingdon, Oxon.

Typeset by Clifford-Cooper Limited, Farnham
and printed in Great Britain by
Biddles, Guildford.

ISBN: 086205 0839

CONTENTS

FOREWORD

It is sometimes an unwelcome chore to have to read a book with a view to writing the foreword. On this occasion it was pure pleasure. The author has done an immense amount of research. There is a welter of good anecdotes, some well-known (and none the worst for it) but mostly fresh, such as will delight every plagiaristic after-dinner speaker.

It is eminently readable, indeed hard to put down. It treats the Bar neither with adulation nor with disdain but with just the right degree of benevolent cynicism. It should be compulsory reading for every Bar student and is assured of an honoured place on the bookshelf alongside other legal classics.

LORD CHIEF JUSTICE LANE

ONE

In Ancient Rome

From this tomb let all fraud and all lawyers be absent
A Roman epitaph

How shall a History of the Bar begin? In darkness, surely, lit with a gleam of light. At a distant window, a young man of sixteen is working late, straining his eyes by the light of a lamp lit with olive oil. In ancient Rome, few people are about. A watchman passes through the quiet streets, but the young man takes no heed, deep in his study of Roman law.

A faint hint of dawn appears in the sky. The household starts to stir, and onto the streets some figures come from doorways. They are poorly dressed, and blow on their fingers to keep away the cold. Warm handshakes must be offered when they reach their journey's end, for the Clients are on the move.

Some seek out patrons little better than themselves, to win their help in puny enterprises, for the mainspring of all social life in ancient Rome is to help someone worse off than oneself, and feel better for doing it.

If the client has a special need, the patron might arrange for an expert to be called in to help. "Called in to help" in Latin, is *advocatus*, the origin of the advocate's profession.

The advocate could be an inexperienced layman. Scipio, when *praetor*, offered a man an advocate in the shape of the man's own landlord, who was a rich oaf. "Let him act for my opponent, my lord," said the man; "I'll defend myself."

But there were full-time lawyers, who would put their life's experience to work in the service of the client. Such was a young man named Marcus Tullius Cicero who literally burned the midnight oil, studying his future profession. Even at school he was made to learn the Twelve Tables off by heart. Not the "Twelve Times" tables or arithmetic, but the system of laws which was written down in about 450 BC. It was a great step forward at the time. Until then only the priests had known the mysteries of the law; but a man of the people wrote them up in the Forum, for all to read; or so the legend goes.

If someone was assaulted, he was entitled to threepence in damages; a fair sum, at the time of the Twelve Tables. But the value of money fell, and there was actually a Roman citizen in Cicero's time who strode the streets followed by his slave. If he met an enemy, he slapped him across the face, and his slave gave the man his threepence. Then the buffeter strode off in search of another victim.

Some of the words in the Twelve Tables became absurd, although you had to use them if you brought an action. It was no good claiming that someone had stolen a bull and a goat; you had to describe them as a "leader of the herd" and a "browser upon leeks".

Cicero learnt these rules off by heart, though they were ceasing to apply. He would also learn rhetoric, an important part of general education. It included "declamatory exercises", debating topics which sprang from logic rather than real life. One was called The Horns: "Everybody possesses what he has not lost. You have not lost horns, therefore you have horns." Then there was the well-known problem of the Constant Liar:

"A man who always tells lies, says that he always tells lies. That is *true*, so he is telling lies when he claims to be always telling lies. On the other hand, as it is false he is still telling lies."

This preyed so much on the mind of one logician that he died. There was also the "Crocodile problem.":

"A crocodile seized a woman's son. 'I'll give him back', it promised her, 'if you'll tell me the truth about his fate.'

'You *won't* give him back,' said the woman, looking the crocodile straight in the face.

This meant that the crocodile would either give the mother the child back, in which case she would keep the child, or it would not give the child back, in which case she was right, and would be entitled to be given it back in any event."

This shows a brilliant grasp of logic, but a profound ignorance of crocodiles.

"This is a truly tragic dilemma," a real crocodile would say, sobbing its heart out. "I will announce my decision — boo-hoo! — after the lunch adjournment."

Cicero had no time to think about crocodiles, when being punctual for his pupil master, Quintus Mucius Scaevola, one of the best advocates in Rome. Cicero, only 16, had, like the clients, to leave the house at dawn to wait upon Scaevola, who was 84.

Dawn was the time for clients and consultations. As the poet Martial put it, in one of his many Latin verses about Roman lawyers,

"In the first two hours of daylight, anxious clients seek their patrons;
In the third hour, advocates shout themselves hoarse."

Cicero would probably have joined his master in a light breakfast of bread with cheese or honey, or dipped in wine. Then he would follow him down to the Forum going from court to court, as he conducted his legal business.

He was almost old enough to start in practice on his own account. Crassus was only 18 when he conducted his first big case; Julius Caesar, whose speeches were noted for their simplicity and irony, was 20.

The Forum lay in a hollow at the foot of the Capitol hill. It was so packed with courts, shops and offices that it was difficult to force a way through the crowd. At one end stood the Rostrum, the open-air platform from which orators addressed the crowd; that needed good lungs. There were several courts, halls roofed with colonnades, that stood open during daylight hours. Such was the life of the Forum, and the word for "of the Forum" is "forensic".

If you turned off the Via Sacra (Sacred Way) and climbed seven steps, you would come to the Basilica Julia with its marble portico, and pass straight into the huge hall which was divided into three naves by columns of brick. This was where the *centumviri* decided cases. Not just a jury of "one hundred men", as the name implies, but 180 or more.

The huge court was usually packed with litigants, advocates, jurors and the general public who enjoyed listening to a good case. It took stamina to address a court like that; no wonder Martial spoke of advocates shouting themselves hoarse. So did Juvenal:

> "There's no money in it. Argue yourself hoarse before some clown of a judge — and what do you get? A couple of bottles of plonk. And you've still got your clerks to pay. The only way to make a name is to live like a lord; that's how clients pick their counsel. But you soon get through your money that way, in Rome."

Juvenal was right; the advocate got nothing out of it, absolutely nothing, except gratitude. Cicero was once paid by Catullus with a poem, a handsome present indeed.

> O most eloquent of Romulus' descendants,
> However many advocates there are, or have been, Cicero,
> However many there shall be in later generations,
> Catullus now extends to you his very warmest gratitude.
> His poetry, I grant you, may be absolutely awful,
> But even so it cannot be more absolutely awful
> Than you are quite the very best of all the patrons.

"Patrons" could include "advocates", whose clients owed them only gratitude. Even that could not be taken for granted. Domitius Afer, a most successful advocate, passed his client in the street; the man cut him dead. Afer sent him a message. "I hope you're *grateful* to me for not having seen you", he said.

Not being entitled to payment, lawyers were proverbially poor; all the Roman satirists said so. As Martial wrote:

> Diodorus has gout, and goes to law,
> But pays no counsel's fees; gout's in his paw!

Cicero certainly did his share of representing people for nothing. As soon as he heard that Tuccius was being unfairly prosecuted, he went of his own accord to the defence benches. "I got on my hind legs," he wrote, "and without a syllable on the matter in hand, I made a thorough job of Sempronius, who was conducting the prosecution."

Yet Cicero, Crassus and Hortensius, three leading advocates, were all rich, and had large houses on the Palatine Hill. This they managed by representing someone who was grateful enough to mention them in his will. The poet Horace explained it in his *Second Satire*.

4

"So tell me, sir, with your prophet's insight, how to rake in piles of cash."

"I've told you and I'll tell you again. You must fish cunningly around for old men's wills. If one or two are clever enough to nibble the bait off the hook and escape your clutches, don't give up hope; you mustn't abandon your craft out of disappointment. If a case, of whatever size, is being fought in the courts, find out which party is rich and childless; then even if he's a crook and actually has the impudence to indict a better man, you take his side."

When Cicero did this, he was only following the established practice of his time.

But his real success came from merit. He was about 25 when he conducted his first case, and soon afterwards conducted a case of a property dispute for Roscius, the great actor. It may well have been done as a favour, because Roscius had taught him a good deal about stage techniques and making his voice carry — a necessary lesson for any advocate who had to speak in the open air.

Cicero was against Hortensius, the leading orator in Rome, who had a sumptuous house on the Palatine Hill, and fed his pet fish on rich food — a sure sign of luxury. It is not surprising Cicero was nervous:

"I am somewhat embarrassed that the eloquence of Hortensius will put my efforts to shame . . . but the fact of the matter is that I am inexperienced, and by no means a match for the talents of a most persuasive advocate."

Advocate: his Latin word was "patron" again. He continued to act for those who needed his help.

Soon afterwards, in the year 80, Cicero defended another Roscius — Roscius of Ameria — on a charge of murdering his own father. It was the first murder trial since the proscriptions had ended; the public thronged to the court, glad to see that law and order had been restored.

Cicero had good reasons for taking up the defence:

"The approach to myself came from men whose friendship I regard as carrying enormous weight. I cannot forget all the services I have received from them, not to speak of the high positions they occupy in the state. The kindness they have done me, as well as the importance of their rank, seemed to me too great to disregard; and so I felt that I could not possibly ignore their wishes."

It is easy to see him, through modern eyes, as toadying to the rich. But Cicero meets that charge:

"Those are the reasons why I agreed to undertake Roscius' defence. It is not a question of having been singled out as the most talented pleader. No, the point was that I was the person left over, the person who could plead with the least danger. To say that I was chosen in order to guarantee that Sextus Roscius should have the best possible defence would not be the truth. I was chosen in order to ensure *that he had any defence at all!*"

Cicero stood up for Roscius against one of Sulla's vicious henchmen, who prosecuted him in the hope of laying hands on a rich estate. "Out of all his large inheritance," said Cicero in court, flaying him with his tongue, "that infamous robber had not even left him the right of way to his father's tomb!"
It took courage to speak like that against a powerful bully. Roscius was acquitted, and Cicero was recognised as a leading advocate.
He was not content to rest upon his laurels. In the following year he went abroad upon a two years' sabbatical. He wrote:

"I was in those days very slender and far from robust, my neck long and thin, that type of physique which is commonly thought of as incurring risk of life itself if subjected to the strain of hard work and heavy demands upon the voice and lungs."

He continued to study oratory, and to exercise his voice and body:

"Thus I came back after two years' absence not only better trained, but almost transformed. My voice was no longer overstrained, my language had lost its froth, my lungs had gained strength and my body had put on weight."

He was ready now to begin a brilliant career in public life. Of course he continued his ordinary work as a lawyer. Quintilian, a famous teacher of law, explains how advocates would argue out the issues of justifiable homicide:

"You killed the man."
"Yes, I did. It is lawful to kill an adulterer with his paramour."
"They were not adulterers."
"They were."
"Even if they were, you had no right to kill them, because you had forfeited your civil rights."

Thus the issues came to be defined. It has been said that only
the Bible has had more influence than Roman law in civilising
the Western world. Even in a violent and troubled world, it
managed to reduce many knotty problems in life with calm and
reason. The *Digest* of Roman Law, compiled long after Cicero,
set out many problems, and the answers given by learned jurists.
I pose two of them in question and answer form:

Q: A pregnant woman gives birth to a child during a voyage. Is
the ship's captain entitled to charge an extra fare for the child?
A: No. The child takes up very little room, and uses none of the
facilities available to the other passengers.

Q: It is well-known that if you buy a slave and then discover that
he has a hidden bodily defect, you can return him and claim your
money back. Does this apply if you find he wets his bed?
A: It depends why he does it. If he wets his bed when he is fast
asleep, or dead drunk, or because he is simply too lazy to get up
during the night, you cannot return him. But if he has a weak
bladder, which is a bodily defect, you may do so.

Though Roman law was intensely practical, Roman lawyers
were amazingly superstitious. Pliny the Younger, who began
to practise law at about the time Cicero was murdered, was asked
by Suetonius, the famous author of *The Twelve Caesars,* to apply
for an adjournment because he had a nightmare, and thought
it was a bad omen for the case.

Pliny quite understood; early in his career he dreamt that his
mother-in-law came and begged him on her knees to give up
an important case in the Centumviral Court. He considered it
earnestly, but went on with the case. It was the right decision;
he won the case, and was launched upon a successful career.
So he advised Suetonius to consider further. His dream might
have a favourable interpretation. But if not, he would see what
he could do.

At the height of his career, Cicero was elected a member of
the College of Augurs, those important religious officials who
took the omens upon all important occasions. He was not swayed
from his duty even by real-life nightmares.

He was thirty when he held his first important public office as quaestor in Sicily. He established such a reputation for honesty that, a few years later, in 70 BC, he was asked to prosecute Verres for extortion in Sicily. It was a mammoth undertaking; he had to gather all his evidence rapidly before the season of Roman festivals began on August 16th. You could call it their "Long Vacation".

The case began on August 5th. If Cicero had made a long opening speech, Hortensius, who was appearing for the defence, would have been entitled to reply at even greater length. But Cicero made the briefest of introductions, and plunged straight into the evidence. It was so devastating that Hortensius could not answer it. Verres fled from Rome. The date was August 14th; Cicero had forced the case to a conclusion just in the nick of time.

He was not simply a windbag. People can be forgiven for finding him repetitive; the fashion now is for much shorter speeches. But in his day he was far and away the best advocate. After the Verres case there was nobody to touch him.

He had a sense of humour which was quite delightful. Everyone knows the joke "Julia is 29. I know she must be, because she's been saying so for years." It can be traced back to Cicero.

He liked making puns. Verres was a blackmailer and embezzler, and his name meant "a wild boar"; Cicero had a field day with that. Then he defended a man call Cluentius on a murder charge, prosecuted by a man who had already escaped justice by getting Staienus, his henchman, to bribe the jury. Two of the corrupt jurors were Bulbus (which means "onion") and Gutta (which means "a drop of something" like olive oil or vinegar; dressing, perhaps.) Cicero told the jury:

"And so, ridiculous though it was, and putting the cart before the horse, Staienus had Onions for a starter." (Laughter). "Staienus gave him a little nudge. 'How are you?' he said. 'Can you help me, so that we don't have to do our jury service for nothing?' As soon as Onions heard the words '*for nothing*', he said, 'I'll do whatever you like. How much are you offering?' Staienus promised him a mint of money if Oppianicus was acquitted. He asked him to summon on the other jurors he knew. Thus Staienus added Dressing to

8

Onions." (Laughter) "*He cooked up the whole business*" (More laughter).

The Romans loved it.

Cicero's talents were not confined to humour, because he was the greatest writer of his time. It was in his First speech against Catiline that he used the phrase which now belongs to literature, *O tempora, O mores!*

Catiline, who dabbled in murder and looting, wanted to become a Consul. Having been defeated in the elections, he planned to murder the successful candidates, and march on Rome with a large mob of ex-soldiers. He meant to murder Cicero, who called an emergency meeting of the Senate, in the Temple of Jupiter the Founder, upon the Palatine Hill. Catiline attended the meeting; Cicero rounded on him with these words:

> "How far, then, Catiline, will you try our patience? How long, indeed, can your insanity last? Is there no limit to your blatant impudence? Are you undeterred by the nightly guard on the Palatine Hill? And the city patrols? And the people's fear? And these worthy people here assembled? And this place for the Senate, now armed to the teeth? And the words and faces of those Senators? Do you not realise that your plans are now exposed? Do you not know your plot is understood, bound tightly by the knowledge of these people here?
>
> Which of us do you think is not aware of what you did last night, and the night before? Of where you were, and whom you called together? The sort of plans you formed?
>
> What times are these, what standards we maintain! The senate knows it all, the consul sees it, too, but *this man* still lives on. Lives, do I say? He even comes into the senate-house, takes part in our debates, heeds everything, and with his eye singles us out, one after another, for slaughter!"

We can read this speech in the calm of a book-lined study. Cicero hurled it into the teeth of a murderer. The speech had its effect; Catiline left Rome to regroup his forces, but the opportunity had passed. The plot went sour; he and his men were all killed off.

Cicero was awarded the title "the Father of his Country", and continued to strive mightily for the standards of honesty and liberty which meant so much to him.

The First Catiline speech shows one of Cicero's techniques; he used no difficult words, but embellished them with subtle variations. Often he said the same thing in slightly different ways. In the same speech he said to Catiline, "There's nothing that you do, nothing that you plan, nothing that you *think*, which I not only hear, but also plainly feel."

He repeats his pattern three times. So did Winston Churchill on the 13th May 1940, one of the darkest days of the Second World War.

"You ask what is our aim? I can answer in one word. It is victory. Victory at all costs — victory in spite of all terrors — victory, however long and hard the road may be."

Cicero seldom wearied his audience. Other advocates were not as fortunate. Pliny the Younger was briefed with Tacitus (the famous historian and advocate) to prosecute Priscus, who governed Africa corruptly. It was his first big case, and he was understandably nervous; the Emperor Trajan was presiding.

"I managed to pull myself and my thoughts together and began to speak, meeting with a warm reception to make up for my fears. My speech lasted for nearly five hours, for I was allowed four water-clocks in addition to my twelve of full size; thus all those difficulties I had anticipated in my path were dispelled when I came to speak."

There was a point at which the Emperor kindly suggested that he should spare his voice and lungs. Trajan may have wanted to give his ears a rest, too. But from Cicero's time water-clocks were regularly used in Roman courts.

Pompey, who brought a handsome water-clock back from Egypt, decreed that prosecuting counsel should address the court for six hours, and the defence counsel for nine.

From then on clocks were kept in court, three or four of them to the hour. The Romans divided their daylight hours into twelve; at midsummer an hour might be 75 minutes long, and in the depths of winter, 45 minutes. They could be adjusted to the seasons by adding or removing wax to the inside, which altered their capacity. Some water-clocks were so elaborate that they could chime, or play the flute, trumpet or drum; they could show not merely the hours, but the minutes and signs of the Zodiac. In court, however, they were probably as simple as hour-glasses, marking the time as the water trickled from one vessel to the other.

Advocates who ran out of time had sometimes to bring their speeches to an abrupt close, which could be something of a mercy. As Martial explains in a poem written to a vehement advocate:

> When seven water-clocks' more time you loudly said you'd need,
> The judge, Caecilianus, most reluctantly agreed.
> You never pause except to swig warm water from a flask;
> Your spate of words seems endless. There's a favour we would ask.
> You'd find you'd slaked your thirst, and your allotted time had sped,
> So why not leave the flask, and drink the water-clock instead?

One could certainly work up a thirst making oneself heard in an angry court. Pompey was once defending a man in court when Clodius, one of Cicero's arch-enemies, tried to shout him down, with the support of his gang. Then Clodius rose to speak. Cicero wrote:

> "Wishing to return the compliment our side gave him such an uproarious reception that he lost command of thoughts, tongue, and countenance."

After an hour and a half of uproar, Clodius gave up trying to make a speech, and turned to personal abuse. "Who's starving the people to death?" he shouted.

"Pompey!" replied his gang.

"Who wants to go to Alexandria?"

"Pompey!" they shouted again.

Soon they were spitting at their opponents, and a free-for-all broke out; Cicero beat a prudent retreat.

Some ten years after Catiline threatened Rome, Cicero gave evidence against Clodius on a charge of sacrilege. Clodius bribed the jurors, and sought his revenge. As tribune of the people, he proposed a bill which would deprive anyone of his citizenship who had put a Roman citizen to death without a trial. It sounds innocent enough, but Catiline had been killed

11

without trial, and Clodius aimed this proposal at Cicero.

When Clodius seemed to be gaining ground, Cicero left Rome hastily, and spent 18 months in Greece, in exile. His property was confiscated in his absence. But in 57 BC, Pompey and others were able to have his decree of banishment repealed. Cicero returned in triumph. Clodius was later murdered; Cicero escaped an enemy's vengeance once again.

He was always anxious to maintain peace in Rome if he could. Quintus Ligarius fought in the Civil War against Caesar, and lost. He was tried for this not by a jury, but by Caesar himself. The result was a foregone conclusion. Still, Cicero was defending him. Plutarch relates what happened:

> " 'We might as well hear another speech from Cicero', said Caesar affably; 'why not? There is no question but that Ligarius is a wicked man, and an enemy.' But when Cicero began to speak, Caesar was moved to an amazing degree; his speech contained such a variety of pathos, and such a delightful choice of language, that in Caesar's face the colour came and went. It was obvious that he was in the grip of violently conflicting emotions. When Cicero eventually touched on the Battle of Pharsalus, Caesar was so affected that his body trembled, and some of the papers he was holding fell from his hands. Thus he was persuaded against his will, and acquitted Ligarius.''

Cicero could call upon a wide variety of emotions when he chose. He stood halfway between two traditions of oratory; there was the florid, Asian style, practised by Hortensius, with elaborate phrases and turns of speech. After Cicero came the crisper style of Tacitus, who wrote almost one hundred and fifty years after Cicero's death:

> "The public in those olden days, being untrained and unsophisticated, was quite well pleased with long-winded and involved orations, and would even bless the man who would fill up the day for them with his harangues.''

Cicero, for his part, had a good deal to say about the deplorable practices of the younger generation. They had no respect for their seniors. To one young upstart he acidly remarked "You and I were practising our declamatory exercises together before you were even born!''

They accepted money before the case was heard, despite an

edict which forbade it. They ate and drank in court to sustain their efforts, and sank back into the arms of their friends at the end of a speech to show how much effort they had put into it. They hired spectators at threepence apiece to come and cheer them on.

Domitius Afer was addressing a court in his usual masterly style when he heard the sound of cheering from an adjacent court. On learning which third-rate hack was being applauded, he gave up his speech in disgust. "Gentlemen," he said, "this means death to our profession."

Every aspect of oratory was closely studied in Rome — even how to wear one's toga. Quintilian had definite views on the subject.

"The left arm should only be raised so far as to form a right angle at the elbow, while the edge of the toga should fall in equal lengths on either side . . .

The ancients used to let the toga fall to the heels, as the Greeks are in the habit of doing with the cloak . . . Cicero was in the habit of wearing his toga in such a fashion to conceal his varicose veins, despite the fact that this fashion is to be seen in the statues of persons who lived after Cicero's day . . .

When a speech draws to its close, more especially if fortune shows herself kind, practically everything is becoming; we may stream with sweat, show signs of fatigue, and let our dress fall in careless disorder and the toga slip loose from us on every side . . .

On the other hand, if the toga falls down at the beginning of our speech, or when we have only proceeded by a little way, the failure to replace it is a sign of indifference, or sloth, or sheer ignorance of the way in which clothes should be worn."

Pliny the Younger spoke of Cicero's "lavish colouring"; nobody could call his advocacy colourless. His colleagues used phrases like "Dread Africa Trembled with Terrible Tumult", "The Capitol drips with my brother's blood", or even a line and a half of verse:

Why, my very brother bids me miserably masticate
Mine own children . . .

Quintilian certainly approved of forensic melodrama:

"Actions as well as words may be employed to move the court to tears. Hence the custom of bringing accused persons into court wearing squalid and unkempt attire, and of introducing their children and parents, and it is with this in view that we see blood-stained swords, fragments of bone taken from the wound, and garments spotted with blood . . . and scourged bodies bared to view. The impression produced by such exhibitions is generally enormous, since they seem to bring the spectators face to face with the cruel facts.''

But a reaction set in. As Martial complained, to his advocate:

My simple claim's about three goats,
Not Civil War, or Poisoned Throats.
My neighbour stole them, so I sue;
The Judge thinks that's the issue too.
But you describe Rome's Darkest Hours,
The Tyrants who Abused their Powers;
You wave your arms about, and shout
How Hannibal's Campaigns turned out.
There's just one favour you can do:
Mention my goats, I beg of you.

Quintilian gives several examples of dramatic gestures which fell flat. Advocates often produced children for pathetic effect; Cicero ended one speech with a baby cradled in his arms.

One advocate turned to a boy who was crying. It was the boy's chance to say he was weeping for his murdered father, or his ruined mother, as the case might be.

"Why weepest thou?" he inquired, in tragic tones.

"My tutor's pinching me," replied the lad.

Another advocate asked a rhetorical question of his opponent. "Why do you look at me so fiercely, Severus?" he inquired. He was probably going to follow it up by saying, "Because the truth of your client's guilt is staring you in the face!"

But Severus was an unmitigated cad, and sprang to his feet.

"I wasn't looking fiercely at all, as a matter of fact; but if it says in your script that I do, then I shall."

And he gave the most frightful basilisk glare.

Another advocate waved a blood-stained sword. His opponent, an even more unmitigated cad, uttered a shriek of terror and fled from counsel's benches. He hid his face in a cloak, and begged to know whether the man with the sword was still there.

It was not advisable to joke about things like that; in ancient Rome, you never knew where the next blood-stained sword was coming from.

Julius Caesar was murdered in 44 BC. Cicero was not one of the conspirators, but supported them. He hoped that a better order of government would follow, but his hopes were dashed. The three-man team called the Triumvirate seemed no better than Caesar had been, and Antony was the most dangerous of the three.

Antony left Rome and returned with a large army of veteran soldiers. Was he going to seize power? Cicero feared so. He made a speech at the Senate known as the First Philippic, because his speeches against Antony were later compared with the blistering attacks the Greek orator Demosthenes made upon Philip of Macedon.

His First Philippic was fairly moderate. Cicero criticised some of Antony's behaviour, to be sure, but praised him for his better actions, and urged him to continue them. Seventeen days later, Antony replied at the Temple of Concord, hardly the appropriate scene for what happened. He packed it with his soldiers, and made a vitriolic attack upon Cicero's whole career. Cicero's friends kept him away, fearing his assassination.

From that moment, Cicero and Antony were at daggers drawn.

Cicero then wrote the Second Philippic, and published it. His words were never meant to be forgiven:

"Do you want us to look at your career from the time when you were a boy? So be it; let us start from the beginning. Do you remember that while you were still in boy's clothes, you went bankrupt?

'It's my father's fault', you'll say. Granted. That excuse shows real family loyalty!

No sooner had you donned man's attire than you swapped it for drag. At first you were just 'cheap trade' — you sold yourself for cash though you rather overcharged — but later Curio led you away from a life as a male prostitute, and, just like someone giving you a dress, made you a nice steady husband. No boy who was ever purchased as a sex-object was as much in his master's power as you in Curio's. How often did his father kick you out of his house? How often did he post sentries to stop you crossing the threshold? But you still got in over the tiles. Night was your accomplice.''

Cicero had flayed Catiline, and Verres, and Clodius with his tongue, and lived to tell the tale. But his luck was running out. He ended his speech in philosophical resignation:

"I really hope for death now, members of the senate. I have finished the tasks for which I was trained, and which I have performed. I hope for two things now. That my death may leave the Roman people free, which is the highest gift the gods can grant. And that everyone may get from the state his just reward."

By November of that year, 43 BC, his name was on the list of those marked out as public enemies. The historian Livy describes the events of December 7th:

"Cicero had no illusions about the fact that he could not escape Antony's clutches. He fled first to Tusculanum [one of his estates], and then set out towards Formianum [another of his estates], with the intention of sailing from Caieta. He put out to sea several times. Sometimes contrary winds brought him back; sometimes he could not endure the tossing of the ship. At last he grew weary of trying to escape, and weary of life itself.

'I shall die', he said, 'in my native land which I have served so often.'

It is generally recognised that his servants were ready to put up a fierce fight, and would have done so loyally. But he ordered them to set down the litter in which they were carrying him, and wait patiently for whatever fate lay in store for him. He leant out of his litter, and presented his neck as an easy target; his head was cut off.

Antony's soldiers did not stop at that gross act of savagery. They hacked off his hands, which had written scathing words against Antony, and sent the head back to him. Antony had it set between his two hands on the Rostrum, where Cicero had stood as consul, where he had often acted as a statesman, and where he had delivered his speech against Anthony that very year.

No human voice was ever so admired for elloquence."

Juvenal agreed:

"That talent alone cost Cicero his severed head and hand:

What third-rate advocate's blood ever stained the rostra?''

There have been advocates as great as Cicero, writers as clear, and statesman as brave. But no-one else combined those roles so well. It was clear, long before he died, that times were changing fast. Trebatius, an able young colleague of Cicero's, went to Gaul where there was a flourishing Bar. Cicero wrote to him there, a year after Caesar invaded Britain:

"You may congratulate yourself on having got to your present part of the world, where you can pass for a man of wisdom! Had you gone to Britain as well, I dare say there would have been no greater expert than you in the whole vast island . . .

A British advocate would make a marvellous figure of fun!''

TWO

The First Barristers

"I suppose I shall learn to respect these people in time," he thought.
They all seem so much less awe-inspiring than anyone I ever met."
Evelyn Waugh, *Decline and Fall*

In Gaul, people laid great store by eloquence. They worshipped Hercules as the God of Speech, and pictured him with golden chains coming from his mouth, to bind his listeners spellbound.

The Druids carried on justice at Chartres; Julius Caesar noted in his history of the Gallic War that they did not think it right to entrust their laws to writing. Marseilles had excellent laws even before the Romans came. Then Roman lawyers arrived, of whom Juvenal spoke highly: "The Gallic faculty of law has taught the British advocates."

Fifty years later the Emperor Claudius set up speaking tournaments at Lyons; the losers had to lick their speeches off the wax tablets with their tongues.

When the Franks overran Gaul they kept most of the Roman laws, and a flourishing legal system. One of the laws of Burgundy, in about 500 AD, stated:

XXX. Concerning false witnesses and plaintiffs.
If someone gives a Plaintiff help in fighting a case, and loses, he too shall be beaten many times, as provided above.

This was rather like trial by battle in later years, where the loser was deemed to be perjured, and might have his hand struck off, or even be hanged.

Clothair, the King of the Franks, decreed in 590, "If anybody is accused of any crime, he shall certainly not be condemned unheard."

There was a system of law in England even when the Angles invaded, but it was not written down until the advent of Christianity. Its first aim was to provide fixed penalties for

18

offences. The Laws of Ethelbert, King of Kent (602-3 AD) laid down, "If a hair-pulling occurs, 50 *sceattas* are to be paid as compensation."

There was a graduated scale of penalties for gate-crashers:

> "If a man is the first to force his way into a man's homestead, he is to pay 6s compensation; he who comes next, 3s; afterwards each is to pay a shilling."

Any man with a complaint brought it at the folk-moot, and the Defendant had to answer it; if he failed to appear, he would be outlawed.

A man was entitled to have an advocate — a *forespeca* to use the Saxon word, who was the "speaker for" him. During the reign of Alfred the Great a man was accused of stealing a belt, and one of his accusers tried to claim his land. Whereupon, a writer says, the Defendant "sought me and prayed me to be his intercessor. Then I spoke on his behalf and interceded for him with King Alfred."

King Alfred listened, and ordered an arbitration to take place.

In Saxon times, Bishop Aldhelm wrote to his colleague, the Bishop of Worcester, expressing his earnest desire of learning Roman law. It was useful in church affairs. He would still need to know Saxon law, however, for everyday matters. It was used at the folkmoot, which in London, met three times a year summoned by St. Pauls' bell, at Michaelmas, Christmas and Midsummer. All the men of London could gather there. But all over the country there were the Hundred Courts, which met once every four weeks.

Roman law was highly regarded, but not as highly as the law of Lombardy. Two monks were fighting a case before the Pope at Rome in 998 AD; one, Ugo, pleaded with him:

Ugo: I beg for an adjournment because I am not yet ready with my law, and I have neither my judges or an advocate.

Pope Leo: No. I will give you an advocate who will plead for you.

Ugo: A Roman advocate, or one from Lombardy?

Leo: Roman.

Ugo: God forbid that my monastery should ever be under any but Lombardian law; no Roman advocate for me!

Leo: Whether you like it or not, you must have Roman law.

But Ugo was lucky; he got a Lombardy lawyer, in the end.

Then came 1066. At the Battle of Hastings a man in full armour rode in the thick of the fighting. HERE BISHOP ODO, says a legend in the Bayeux Tapestry, HOLDING A MACE, CHEERS ON HIS LADS. After the Conquest his brother, William the Conqueror, made him Earl of Kent, and Odo enriched himself as much as possible at the expense of nearby churches and abbeys.

He reckoned without an even more formidable figure, the Archbishop of Canterbury. Lanfranc had been a lawyer at Pavia in Lombardy, the centre of law teaching in Italy, and was a brilliant advocate from whom even his older colleagues were glad to learn. William recognised his talents when he was in Normandy, and made him Archbishop; then Lanfranc sued Odo to recover the church property.

The trial lasted three whole days; it was the most important case of William's reign. By the end he had vindicated the rights of the church so completely that "there was not a man in the whole kingdom of England who could claim any jot or tittle of them."

Furthermore, he proved conclusively that he was entitled to the ancient Saxon privileges of:

sake and soke;

toll and team;

flymena fyrrmth;

grithbryce;

forsteal;

and hamfare and infangthief.

It is some consolation to know that, in the year 1321, lawyers were not entirely sure what all these words meant:

Serjeant Scrope:	What do you understand by "team"?
Mr. Justice Stanton:	That means possession of the families by their sokeman.
Scrope:	That is "soke".
Stanton:	No. "Soke" means the right to hold a court for their tenants.

William the Conqueror made sweeping administrative changes in England — the Domesday Book illustrates that — but on the whole left the Saxon system of law alone. Although he was certainly a strong man, he was not in favour of capital punishment. One of his laws declared:

"I also forbid that anyone shall be slain or hanged for any fault, but let his eyes be put out and let him be castrated. And this command shall not be violated under pain of a fine in full to me."

There were no central courts during William's reign except for the King's Council, and no specially trained advocates. Justice was administered by Normans who did not know English. So Latin became the language of official use. No doubt there was always a steward or clerk of the court who could interpret for English people.

In Lanfanc's day, England had no entirely separate legal profession. Most lawyers were also clergymen, but gradually they came to be a specialised occupation. It is broadly as simple as that. Lanfranc conducted his own case, and it lasted three days, which was then a record.

It was common, when a man needed legal assistance, for his Lord to speak for him. In this respect the early feudal system was not unlike the relationship between a patron and his client, at Rome.

Odo brought another case against the church at Canterbury. Practically all the lawyers were involved; Lanfranc was absent; he did not usually attend unless there seemed to be urgent necessity. But he heard about the case, and found an error in the pleadings. He ordered the case to be adjourned to the following day. That night, St. Dunstan appeared to him in a dream, and told him to appear in the case. He did, and won it resoundingly.

Perhaps the first two full-time lawyers to be named in English history were Sacol and Godric. William the Conqueror issued a writ which was thought to infringe the existing rights granted to the Church at Abingdon under a charter of King Edward. The Lord Abbot resisted the claim, helped by Alfwin, a priest and rector of the neighbouring village, and the two monks, Sacol and Godric, who were very knowledgeable in these matters and in local history:

"And there were many other pleaders too, among the English at that time in the abbey whom, when they agreed, no wise man contradicted. Hence, whenever they took up the defence of the Church's interests, its aggressors were silenced."

21

Since Alfwin was specifically said to be a priest, Sacol and Godric are thought to have been laymen. Selden, the famous legal historian, says that is was common for secular persons to live in monasteries, and practice law.

Anselm was enthroned as Archbishop of Canterbury on September 25th 1093. Ranulf Flambard arrived that very day to bring proceedings against him; he has been described as "a pleader but also a perverter of justice, a debt-collector but also carrying out a scorched-earth policy".

Scorched-earth: his nick-name, Flambard, meant a torch whose flame devoured everything. William of Malmesbury, the best English historian to follow Bede, gives a devastating picture of him:

> "He was unbeaten as an advocate. He was outrageous in his words and deeds, venting his wrath equally on those who sought his protection and those who directly opposed him. Whereupon people sniggered and said that he was the only person to carry on like that; he didn't care who hated him, so long as he pleased the king."

He was not therefore the most popular Chancellor that Britain has ever known.

William of Malmesbury used a phrase which historians often quote: "every clergyman was an advocate". He was writing in withering scorn:

> "Every rich man was a money-grubber, every cleric was a barrack-room lawyer, and every single priest was, if I may coin a phrase, a rent-harvester."

Still, almost all the advocates in the courts were clerics too. Ranulph Flambard was described as a "pleader", though he was in holy orders. Many distinguished lawyers and judges had been canons of St. Paul's: Martin of Pateshull, Ralph de Hengham, and many others.

At this time the word "serjeant" began to be used. It first came from *sirviens*, a common soldier, or someone owing a special service to the King, such as bringing him a dinner of roast pork, when he was hunting in Wychwood Forest.

Henry de la Wade was a serjeant; he looked after Henry I's menagerie, which included lions, lynxes, leopards, camels and a pet porcupine. Henry de la Mare's task was to look after the Court strumpets. And in 1139, when an ecclesiastical synod sat

22

in judgement on him, King Stephen employed Aubrey de Vere as his serjeant to plead for him, which he did very well.

So the word "serjeant" gradually came to mean a senior practising barrister. The serjeants had this in common with the knights; they wore vermilion robes with white cuffs, as the Knights of the Bath used to do.

Another legal landmark was the trial of Richard de Anesty, from 1158 to 1163, which has been called "the ancient *Jarndyce v Jarndyce.*"

> "These are the expenses which I, Richard of Anesty, incurred in gaining possession of the land of my uncle. First of all I sent one of my men to Normandy to obtain the King's writ to put my adversaries on trial. This man spent half a mark on the journey.
>
> When my messenger had brought me the writ I took it to Salisbury that it might be sent back sealed with the Queen's seal; in this journey I spent 2 silver marks.
>
> On my return thence, hearing that Ralph Brito was obliged to cross the Channel, I followed him as far as Southampton to speak with him and ask him to convey the King's writ to the Archbishop for me, because I knew that the suit ought to be transferred to the Archbishop's court. In that journey I spent 22 shillings, 7 pence, and lost a palfrey, which I had bought for 15 shillings . . ."

Professor Maitland, the distinguished legal historian, refers to the plaintiff as "the heroic English litigant", and speaks of "the dogged litigiousness of that immortal Plaintiff, Richard of Anesty."

It was certainly a distinguished case. Richard was probably represented by two distinguished Italian lawyers, Master Ambrose, and Vacarius, who wrote one of the leading works of law of the age, and may well have taught law at Oxford. There were numerous hearings at Northampton, Lambeth, and Canterbury, to name but three; horses galloped with writs from France and messages from Rome, and expired with exhaustion.

But all things must come to an end. Eventually, at the end of five years, as Richard of Anesty tells us:

> "We came then to the King at Woodstock, where we remained 8 days; and at length by grace of the lord king and by the judgment of his court my uncle's land was adjudged to me. There I spent 7 pounds, 10 shillings and 6 pence.
>
> These are the presents which I gave to my counsel and to the

clerks, who assisted me in the Archbishop's court, namely 11 silver marks. In the court of the Bishop of Winchester 14 silver marks, to Master Peter de Mileto 10 marks and a gold ring worth half a silver mark. To Master Robert de Chimay 1 mark. In the King's court I have spent in gifts, in gold and silver and in horses, 17 ½ marks. To Master Peter of Littlebury I gave 40 shillings. To the other counsel from among my friends, who had come regularly to the hearings of my suit, I gave in silver and in horses 12 ½ marks.''

This case marks the emergence of the legal profession in England, and only a cynic would say that the rot had set in.

In 1178 Henry II appointed two clerics and three laymen to be a ''permanent and central court'', marking a new approach to professional judges. By the end of Henry III's reign the clerical judges were in a minority. There were fewer clerics on the bench, and the clerics who practised before them tended to disappear. A rhyming Latin couplet went:

Now every kind of clergyman's unwelcome to the law,
Today his status certainly stands lower than before.

The growth of a class of advocates under Edward I was part of the same process.

Glanville was one of those who helped Richard of Anesty in the case. Ten years later he was a Chief Justice. Walter Mapes, himself a judge, congratulated him on the speed with which he had dealt with a dispute between a poor man and a rich one:

Mapes: Considering that a poor man's suit can be put off by many dilatory expedients you did it, under heaven, very well.
Glanville: Yes, we certainly do give judgement here quicker than your bishops in their cathedrals.
Mapes: True, but if our King was as far off from you as the Pope is from the bishops, I imagine you would be as slow.
Ranult laughed and said nothing.

It might be tempting to sigh for the age of trial by battle, when two champions clobbered each other with spiked maces, and had to be finished by nightfall. But they could be very expensive. Many Bishops and large monasteries kept their own prize-fighters; it could well have been cheaper to hire an advocate.

At the abbey of Meaux in Yorkshire, there was a claim against St. Mary's Abbey in York in 1249 over some fishing rights on Hornsey mere:

"Eventually, after long arguments about the pleadings, trial by battle was ordered before the justices at York. The judicial combat was arranged, the champions put on their armour, and the fight began. But while the duel was in progress the parties came to terms; William Lasceles gave up his common right of fishing to the abbot and monastery of St. Mary's York."

Then there were further arguments, and a fresh trial by combat was ordered. The monks of Meaux wrote:

"So we hired seven champions and provided them and their horses and families with board and lodging at great expense . . . Eventually the duel was ordered to take place at York from morning to evening, and our champion was gradually weakening. But during the battle Roger of Thurkelby, one of the judges who was a friend of ours, shrewdly ordered it to be broken off, and we let the abbot and monastery at York have the fishing rights."

Then there was the lady who had a dispute over pasturage rights with the Abbot of Fountains Abbey. The Abbot asked for a short adjournment, and left the court only to return with his champion. The lady was not prepared for trial by battle. Sjt. Toudeby, who was acting for her, advised her to withdraw her claim, and she did so.

Finally, there was a trial by battle between the Bishop of Salisbury and the Earl of Salisbury. The judges always examined the contestants' clothing, in case one of the champions had a horseshoe hidden inside his glove, or whatever. They found that the Bishop's champion had his clothes padded out with sheets of paper, inscribed with uplifting passages from the scriptures. The Bishop may have called it being "fortified by prayer," but the judges thought it was cheating.

The break between the clergy and the legal profession was not yet complete, as the career of Abbot Samson shows. He became the Abbot of Bury St. Edmunds in 1182. A chronicle says:

"Less than seven months after he had been appointed Abbot, letters actually came from the Pope appointing him to be a judge in ecclesiastical cases; he was raw and inexperienced in carrying out those duties, although well versed in the scriptures and the liberal arts. His learning was well known and admired in that part of the country; he had been taught at school, and had been a master too. So he called in two clerics who had been trained in law, and kept them with him. He took their opinion in church affairs, decrees and drawing up judgments, and took a lot of trouble over their drafting, when time allowed. In a short time, therefore, as a result of studying the text-books and hearing a number of cases, he acquired the reputation of being a perceptive judge who administered the law on proper lines. This led to someone saying, "Blast your abbot's court, where my gold and silver can't buy me an unfair advantage over my opponent!"

In due course he acquired experience in secular cases. He used his common sense and had a remarkably keen mind; Osbert, the son of Hervey the under-sheriff, said of him "Your abbot is a natural debater; if he goes on as he's begun, he'll put us all in the shade."

Indeed, having made his name in this class of cases, he was appointed an Itinerant Justice, but kept himself from slips and errors."

In Abbot Samson's time, more or less all of the lawyers were clerics. However, as time went on, more and more laymen took up the legal profession. Edward I specially ordered John de Metingham (then Lord Chief Justice of the Court of Common Pleas) and the other judges of that court, that they should appoint up to 140 of the best lawyers and attorneys to follow his court around the country and transact the legal business there.

But once Henry III ordered in 1224 that Westminster Hall should be built, the legal profession became more settled. There were three great courts: on the right as you went in, was the Common Bench court for civil matters, such as land and contract. Here three, four or five judges sat with the Chief Justice, in scarlet robes, with closely fitting coifs on their heads.

At the upper end was the Kings Bench court; on the left corner, the Chancellor sat, and the Master of the Rolls.

The four law terms were then, as they still are:

Hilary; Easter; Trinity; and Michaelmas.

At this stage there were various law schools in the City of London. But in 1234 a writ of Henry III suppressed them:

"That through the whole city of London let it be proclaimed and wholly forbidden that anyone who has a school for law in that town shall teach the laws *inter alia*, and if anyone shall conduct a school of that nature there, they [the Mayor and

26

Sheriffs] shall put a stop to it at once.''

It is not clear why this was so. Was he seeking to divert law students to universities or Inns of Court? Did he intend to lessen the influence of the Civil Law, which came from Rome? Whatever the real reason, it makes it clear that law schools were flourishing at that time, and that England had an established legal profession.

Special words soon appeared for the lawyers. There was "countor", a professional barrister who "recounted" what a case was about in court; the word "narrator" meant the same.

In 1267 Robert of Colevill, a "countor of the Bench", assaulted a Justice of the Jews (who tried Jewish cases) in Westminster Hall. The usual punishment for assault inside Westminster Hall was having one's right hand struck off, but his colleagues interceded for him, and he was pardoned.

An important influence upon the developing legal profession was William of Drogheda, who published a book called *Summa Aurea de Ordine Judiciorum* in about 1239. Maitland called it "intensely practical. He is going to teach his readers to win causes and begs that a few of the fees they earn may purchase masses for his soul."

His best tip was:

"Don't be put off by clients' big promises of reward for they are often merely for show; remember the doctors' axiom: 'get your money while the patient is ill'."

In 1272, Simon Wyberd's client, Nicholas le Thogh, paid 4 marks to him in advance to appear for him in the Middleton Hundred Court. Nicholas later sued him for the return of the money on the grounds that Simon had:

"imprisoned him,
    extorted the money from him, and
    spread false rumours that Nicholas had murdered his wife."

If so, Simon was certainly going beyond his instructions.

There were other cases about counsel's fees. In 1275 William de Bolton and three colleagues were paid 10 shillings by the bakers at St. Ives Fair for their counsel, and for refraining from harassing the bakers when the bailiffs tested their bread for proper weight. Bolton was promised a further 4s to defend a man for using a false measuring-rod. He went unpaid; the Court of the fair allowed him to sue for his fee.

Many counsel were on an annual retainer. John de la Chapele had an agreement with the Abbot of Shap Abbey, in Westmorland, that he was allowed to stay at the monastery whenever he wanted, would be given a decent room and food, and could have two servants and their horses looked after as well as if they belonged to the cellarer himself!

Furthermore, if he lost his horse whilst on abbey business, the monastery would replace it for him. He was also entitled to an annual retainer, which could have been anything from 6s8d to 20s per year. He sued for arrears of the money in 1302, but the defence was that John had failed to turn up for a county court case.

One William sued the Bishop of Rochester for his arrears of fees. The barristers argued the issues of the case:

Sjt. Est (for the defendant): He had been against us at three places [he gave the names] and that is the reason he lost his annuity.

Sjt. Huntingdon (for the plaintiff): You must give particulars of when — that is, on what day and what year, to justify your whole defence, and say that we would not have lost our right to the arrears except because of the forfeiture, and furthermore t hat we would not be entitled to the arrears before that date.

Sjt. Sutton (also for the defendant): Your only right to bring an action is under the deed, and your only claim is as far as the deed allows, if there is any breach. But the basis of the deed is that you attend to our problems when you meet us, and you have often been asked to come to counsel us, and you never came.

Sjt. Gosfield (also for the plaintiff): That would be a hard thing, when we had served you faithfully and well for ten or twelve years, if we had wasted all our efforts for the sake of one single failure which occurred later.

Sjt. Malberthorpe (also for the defendant): Why should that be? Are you seeking to recover under a written contract which was broken *through your own fault?*

Sjt. Huntingdon: It is only right we should have our arrears *before* the breach, because what has already been earned, cannot be forfeited by a subsequent trespass. Therefore I ask for judgment for my clients.

Mr. Justice Metingham: What have you got to say about his

allegation that you acted against his client?

Sjt. Huntingdon: We never acted against him after the contract was drawn up, and this we are ready to prove.

Sjt. Est: You must allege that you were ready to counsel our client *at all times,* as required under the contract.

Sjt. Huntingdon: We were always ready when we were given *reasonable notice,* and this we are ready to prove. So a jury can be summoned.

This was by no means a unique case. Some successful advocates might have been retained by a number of powerful land-owners, as were monasteries. Difficulties arose if one of them sued another; the advocate could not act for them both. Or if he was required at one place when he was in the middle of a case elsewhere. That could not be helped. But the colourful career of Robert of Warwick (also known as Robert le Belleyetere) owed more to design than accident. He was often briefed by the Earl of Warwick, and acted as coroner until he was removed from office, probably for being in debt. He was fined for corrupt dealings, but was still elected Member of Parliament for Warwick in 1329. However, he was hanged for felony a year or two later.

The standards of integrity of those days were clearly looser than now. In 1286, for instance, the records of Barnwell Priory near Cambridge are quite open about their Prior's conduct of cases at Cambridge Assizes:

"The Prior acted so astutely that he lost only one case, and that by the false verdict of a Cambridge jury . . . For he had the judges well disposed, and the clerks friendly, and the ushers publicly showing him respect. He retained too as his counsel from beginning to end of the Iter [the Assizes] three wise and vigilant serjeants, viz. Gilbert of Thornton and William of Kenrou and John of Insula.

He gave them all 40s, and "gratified" the judges by frequent presents so that everybody, judges, clerks, serjeants and ushers, thanked him and his monks profusely."

He was not the only forensic adventurer. In 1275 the *Statute of Westminster I* (1275), c. xxix, recognised the ill practices of the Bar:

"It is provided also, that if any serjeant, pleader, or other, do any manner of deceit or collusion in the king's court, or consent unto it, in deceit of the court, or to beguile the court, or the party, and thereof be attainted, he shall be imprisoned for a year and a day, and from thenceforth shall not be heard to plead in that court for any man ..."

In 1280 the Mayor and aldermen complained of the ignorance and ill manners of practitioners in the civil courts. As the *Liber Custumarum* put it, (a book which set out the trading practices and customs of the period):

"In the time of Gregory Rokesley, Mayor of London in the 8th year of the reign of King Edward, it became a common practice for people to set themselves up as counters who were incompetent, not having learnt their profession. It became perfectly clear to persons of consequence in the City that through the ignorance of these people the pleas entered on either side of cases were defective, and clients were losing their cases in the Hustings Court and the Sheriff's Courts. Some people actually lost their inheritances through their ludicrous behaviour. Anyone could set himself up as a counter at his own whim, without necessarily being able even to express himself in proper language. It was a complete scandal that these courts should let them appear as pleaders, attorneys, essoiners and sometimes, in the Sheriff's Court, assessors, and judgment would be given on third parties, in open court or privately. So they were perverting the course of justice."

The Mayor and Aldermen consequently ordered that incompetent barristers should not practise. This was, however, "at the request of the serjeants and the countors who knew their business." Every profession has its small minority of rogues and incompetents. It is wrong to assume that they are typical of the whole.

A long list was drawn up of the duties of a countor, which included:

1. Not using foul language or insults.
2. Not fighting the case for a share of the damages. (This would lead to being permanently struck off.)
3. Not taking money from both sides in the case. (A breach of this led to suspension for three years.)
4. Not approaching the judge without being invited to do so.

The Husting (which means "House Meeting", and had nothing to do with elections), was once a typical Saxon court, but it had a more speical purpose by the 12th century. It met every Monday at the Guildhall, and was the recognised court for such things as debt, land, and weights and measures. It was very zealous in protecting customers. There were strict rules about selling lampreys from Nantes, and in London itself butchers were not allowed to sell meat by candle-light. People needed to see what they were getting.

In 1291 the Clerk to the Sheriff of London complained about the way Sjt. Robert of Sutton behaved in the Hustings Court, because he "caused foul contempt of him, and in contempt of our Lord the King, by saying these words *in English*, "Tprhurt, Tprhurt'."

Robert had been ordered to leave the court for some breach of the rules; it may not have been a serious case. He refused, and "uttered the aforesaid words, 'Tprhurt Tprhurt, Tprhurt' to his damnifying, and in manifest contempt of our Lord the King."

These words have puzzled scholars, because they have no discernible sex, number or gender, and do not seem to spring from Anglo-Saxon or Latin roots.

A number of witnesses testified to the outrage; an armourer, surgeon, goldsmith and so on, men of the different guilds at the Guildhall. They all declared that Robert had said in open court that he cared nothing, and, in manifest contempt, uttered those words in English, at the same time raising his thumb in contempt.

He was committed to prison immediately, and it serves him right. He must have purged his contempt, because in 1304 he was back in court complaining that another advocate had been rude to him. He was also listed in 1305 as one of the counsel practising in the Hustings Court.

Any common lawyer can guess what "Tprhurt" means. It is a resounding raspberry.

Even at that early stage, the English Bar was nothing if not robust.

THREE

All Jangle and Riot

"No. It is not a muddle. To make a muddle you must first have order."
John le Carré, *A Perfect Spy*

By the reign of Edward I the legal profession was firmly established. It is kept vividly alive in the hundreds of parchment scrolls known as the Year Books, although nobody is quite sure for what they were intended. The official records of cases were kept in the official language, Latin. But the Year Books are in Law French, a linguistic cocktail of Old French and English which the lawyers spoke in court.

Chief Justice Bereford once said to counsel, *"nous voilloms savoir si vous voillez autre chose dire, qe ceo qe vous dites n'est qe jangle et riot"*, which means, when translated from the Law French, "We want to know if you have anything else to say; for what you have said is All Jangle and Riot." The phrase meant "stuff and nonsense."

It may even have been a deliberate policy for the Year Books not to record the findings of the case, because only the official records were regarded as valid; nothing else would do. In a case in 1312 Mr. Justice Staunton said to counsel, "In support of your action you bring forth naught but wind, while he produces the charter of your father; therefore we rule that you reply to the charter."

Any second-hand record was suspect, and could lead to fraud. Serjeant Stonor once spotted someone in court making notes, and reported him to the judge:

Sjt. Stonor: Sir, see here a notary who, by the Plaintiff's procurement, has come privily to watch this law-making to our prejudice and in deceit of this Court. We pray, if it please you, that he be arrested.

Chief Justice Bereford: Where is he?
Sjt. Stonor: See him here.

Chief Justice Bereford made him come forward, hand over his note, and find four sureties for bail, so that he could be dealt with by the judges in due course.

The official records stated the result of the case: A sued B, and the result was such-and-such. But the Year Books never did; they only gave the arguments in the case. They may have been simply textbooks.

Soon after 1300 one lawyer's library is shown to have contained:

The Statutes of Edward I and II
Bracton, (a leading treatise on the law)
Britton (another such)
Hengham Magnum and Parvum (on pleading)
Mettingham on Essoins (excuses for not appearing in court)
a Register of Writs
a treatise on quashing writs
a treatise on the duties of justices
a treatise on the Pleas of the Crown (mostly criminal)
a Year Book

Once the Year Books appeared, from about 1293, other textbooks such as Bracton and Britton were no longer produced.

They were probably compiled to teach the art of pleading; and why not? Students had to learn the 30 different writs and their applications; the Year Books certainly showed them in practice. Occasionally the Year Book reporter gave his own opinion. There was a case in 1313 about pasture rights in Abingdon. At the close of the pleadings, it was decided that the ultimate question for the jury was for how long the Abbot and his predecessors had enjoyed the pasture rights. "And I am of opinion," says the Year Book compiler, "that, considering what was pleaded and admitted by the Defendants, that was *not* the issue which should have been taken."

They have a consistent style, and may have been semi-official; not very official, though. For instance:

Mr. Justice Mutford: Some of you have said a great deal that runs counter to what was hitherto thought to be the law.

Chief Justice Bereford: Yes, that is very true, and I won't say who they are! (Some people thought he meant Mr. Justice Stonor).

Chief Justice Bereford is probably the breeziest judge ever to appear in print. In a case in 1308 he said:

"I have heard tell that a man was taken in a brothel and hanged, and if he had stayed at home no ill would have befallen him. So in this case. If he was a free citizen, why did not he remain in the city?"

On another occasion:

"As the prostitute said to the fellow who asked her if she was a prostitute 'Try it, try it, try it!' So (he said to counsel) *you* try it, and if the case isn't settled, blame me."

There there was his story of the Three Gallows, in 1309. There was a question of a man who continued to possess something his ancestors had wrongly obtained. Chief Justice Bereford was very caustic on the subject:

"If you have continued the tortious estate of your ancestors, you have done all the more wrong.

Once upon a time a man lay sick in his bed, and was so weak that he fainted, and lay in a trance. It seemed to him that he came to a certain place and there saw three pair of gallows, each one higher than the last. On the shortest hung his grandfather; on the middle one his father; and he asked why this was so. Someone answered him and said that his grandfather wrongfully took someone's property, and was hanged for this trespass. His son continued in wrongful possession, and was hanged even higher; and the third and highest pair of gallows was for his own use when he died, because he stayed in the wrong even longer. So do not trust too much to that you say about your doing no wrong in keeping your ancestor's property. If they came by it wrongfully, so do you."

An interesting case arose before Chief Justice Bereford about proving a debt, partly by a document, and partly by the defendant's sealed tallies. He denied writing the document, or being liable under the tallies.

Sjt. Miggeley: (for the plaintiff) You cannot be heard to say that; for we have produced tallies sealed with your own seal, and we do not believe you are entitled to deny the validity of your own deed, sealed with your seal.

Sjt. Passeley: (for the defendant) Sir, we saw a case before Sir John of Metingham, where a tally was produced, and it was sealed; and the Defendant denied making it, but it was found that he had made it. But he was not punished for denying that he had made that deed. So it seems that we are not obliged to confess or deny the validity of this tally.

Chief Justice Bereford: Are not the tallies sealed with your own seal? What can you put forward to show you are not liable; For shame!

Sjt. Claver (also for the defendant) As to the forty shillings for which the tallies are produced, we owe the Plaintiff not a penny. And this we are ready to prove.

Sjt. Miggeley: We are not interested in that averment. Is this your deed, or no?

Sjt. Claver: We have no need to answer to that, for we will aver that we owe not a penny.

Chief Justice Bereford: Will you be content with judgment on that averment?

Sjt. Miggeley: Yes, sir, if that be the award.

Chief Justice Bereford: We award it

It was common for several counsel to appear for each party in a case. Pleadings were carried out by word of mouth; it was a little like a cricket match, with one side bowling a fast one, and the other trying to slam it over the boundary. The judge's task, as Professor Maitland neatly put it, was to answer the question "How's that?"

So the plaintiff won his case for 40 shillings at least. But five years later the same judge ruled the opposite way:

Sjt. Herle: (who was regarded as the greatest lawyer of his age) Here is a writing on the tally, with the seal appendant, which acknowledges that we lent him money on a certain day and in a certain year. So we ask for judgment against the Defendant.

Chief Justice Bereford: The tally is a dumb thing and cannot speak, and there is nothing to prevent your taking off this writing and substituting another at your will. These notches, too; we cannot tell whether they refer to bullocks or to cows or to what else, and you may score as many notches as you like, and so we hold this to be no deed which a man must answer, and therefore it is right that he should be allowed to argue its validity.

There were no law reports, and so judges could only be told what other judges had decided. They were not bound by those decisions, or even their own.

If the judges at this period were sometimes fiery, one must make allowances for their tempers. Their salaries were not high, and were often two or three years' in arrears.

Even when translated into English, the Year Books are often puzzling. For instance:

"QUERY.
One can take beasts flying from one's severalt. Query whether one can distrain flying from one's fee, for services?"

But they still enable the reader to stand in the shoes of the law apprentices who sat watching the cases inside the Common Bench court at Westminster Hall, or discussing them in the Crib, which seems to have been their common-room in Westminster Hall.

The cases were conducted by the Serjeants, the "narrators" or "countors" whose rank was roughly the same as Queen's Counsel today. Each case in Court began with a writ, claiming money owed, or damages for trespass, or whatever, and the serjeant then *explained* what the case was about.

In a typical case Serjeant Moubray recounted that in 1343, Alice, a widow living in Southwark, brought a writ of *quod permittat prosternere* — "let it be demolished" — against her neighbour. As he explained, Matilda her neighbour built a house whose privy discharged into a stream which fed Alice's fishponds. Most of the fish died, her loss being 80 shillings a year. That is why she wanted the house pulled down.

Once this statement of the claim had been made, the defence could make objections to it. No point was too small to be worth exploring, if it destroyed the plaintiff's case. There might be a spelling mistake in the writ, perhaps of only one letter. In cases when "Agnys" appeared instead of "Agnes", and "Hogheland" instead of "Hogeland", the Court ruled that it made no difference. But in other cases when "Joyosa" appeared for "Jocosa", and "Tudworthe" for "Todeworth", the writ was held to be bad. So a tiny error could be fatal.

As Pollock and Maitland put it, a pleading was:

"a formal statement bristling with sacramental words, an omission of which would be fatal... In a civil action begun by writ the Plaintiff's count must not depart by a hair's breadth from the writ or there will be a 'variance' of which the Defendant will take advantage.''

One of the sacred phrases occurred in writs of trespass: ''with force and arms, to wit, swords and bows and arrows etc.'' It often seemed reasonable enough. For instance:

''John assaulted Alan with force and arms, to wit, swords and bows and arrows etc.''

''Robert broke down William's door with force and arms, to wit, swords and bows and arrows etc.''

But there was a case in 1315 when Richard and Mary sold Simon a tun of wine, and later came and stole some of the wine. They secretly topped the barrel up with salt water, ''with force and arms, to wit, swords and bows and arrows etc.''

It must have been a tricky thing to do.

Furious arguments arose over place-names, such as ''the church of Toft Newton.''

Serjeant Grene: There are two churches in Toft Newton. One is St. Michael's and the other St. Peter & St. Paul's. The writ does not specify which church is referred to. Therefore the Defendant is entitled to judgement against the Plaintiff because the writ is bad.

Serjeant Moubray (for the plaintiff): Toft Newton is a village, and Newton is a hamlet of Toft Newton, so both churches are in Toft Newton. But one is known as Toft Newton church, and the other as Newton church; they are distinguished by these names, and it is clear which one we are talking about. We ask the Court to rule that our writ is perfectly good.

Grene: You have admitted now that both churches are in Toft Newton. As a matter of law these churches can only be distinguished by their saints' names. . .

Mr. Justice Kelshulle (trying to make things simpler): Suppose the hamlet was named Kelshulle, and in Kelshulle there was a church known as Kelshulle Church, but there was in the village another church known by the village name. Would there not be a sufficient distinction there?

Grene: No.

Mr. Justice Willoughby: Yes, there would. . . There shall be a trial, not on what the villages are called, but what the churches are called.

So a local jury was summoned to decide whether the two churches were known as Newton Church and Toft Newton church respectively. Such disputes over place-names occurred frequently. But when counsel objected that a writ against the Burgesses of Newcastle *(Burgessi de Novo Castro)* was bad because only Towns have Burgesses, and not Castles, one blushes for the legal profession.

Arguments arose on every technicality. In one case it was quite simply, bullocks.

Sjt. Denham: We took no bullocks of your plough, but four cows.
Sjt. Toudeby: Our writ says "beasts of the plough" without describing them more specifically, so you must answer our writ.
Chief Justice Bereford: If you had *cows* in your plough, it was perfectly open to you to plead that he took your *cows.*
Toudeby: What he says about cows is not relevant to the writ. But the Plaintiff's writ said that the Defendants took "bullocks of the plough".
Denham: We raise this point as a valid defence, because your writ has nothing to do with cows.
Scrope (also for the plaintiff): You will have no valid defence unless you say you were justified in what you did.
Denham: We did not take your bullocks, but four cows. And this we are ready to prove.

"This we are ready to prove" was the final phrase in the pleadings before the trial was arranged. After all the arguments, the question for the jury was finally resolved: had the defendants taken cows, or bullocks?

Once the issues in a case were settled, the parties or their attornies had to attend court upon the appointed day. But travel was hazardous and difficult. In 1306, during the reign of Edward I, John of Leicester arrived one day late, due to the floods:

The Plaintiff's attorney: Where were you held up?
John: At Cesham.
Mr. Justice Mallory: At what hour of the day?
John: At noon.
The Attorney: Then we are entitled to judgment against him. He could never have got here in time, anyway. It is 15 leagues away. He set out too late.
John: I travelled day and night.
Mr. Justice Mallory: What did you do when you came to the water and could not pass? Did you raise the hue and cry and the menee?

For otherwise the local population would have no knowledge of your difficulty.

(John should have done this. A local jury would then have been able to confirm his excuse).

John: No, sir, I was not familiar with the law. But I called and shouted.
Attorney: Then I claim judgment immediately against him, because of his default, and possession of the land he holds as tenant.
Mr. Justice Mallory: Will you accept his statement that he was held up, as he says?
Attorney: If you so rule, sir; but he has admitted he did not raise the menee, so I ask for judgement on those grounds.

Judgement was not given against John immediately; the case was adjourned. It was generally reckoned that John had been lucky.

Attorneys frequently appeared in front of the judges. By 1290 they were so regularly used that they had a professional status almost equivalent to that of pleaders, though they only argued the preliminary questions in a case, what we would call "interlocutory matters."

It was essential for an attorney to be able to prove he was authorised to act in a case, by producing a "bill of attorney." There must have been serious cases of impostors claiming to represent people when they did nothing of the sort, for disaster loomed if he could not produce his bill to the court.

An attorney appeared against a woman in a case where it already appeared that there might have been delaying tactics. He appeared in front of Mr. Justice Stanton, who was ominously known as "Hervey the Hasty."

Mr. Justice Stanton: Good friend, have you taken out a writ?
Attorney: Yes, sir.
Judge: Where is your bill, which witnesses it?
Attorney: Sir, I took out no bill, for I delivered it to my master.
Judge: What do you want, then?
Attorney: Sir, may I ask for a *postea?* [a formal record of the court proceedings].
Judge: You wicked rascal, you shall not have it! But because you, to delay this woman from her dower, have vouched and have not take out a writ to summon your warrantor, this Court awards that you go to prison.

39

Attorney: I pray that I may have bail on a surety.
Judge: We do not wish you to have any bail, but stay in gaol until you are well chastised.

Some attorneys had permanent retainers. In 1298 one William was appointed by the Mayor and the Aldermen of Grantham to act as their attorneys for an annual retainer of 20 shillings. The Courts showed mercy in special cases of hardship. When one of the litigants was a leper, the Court appointed an attorney to act on his behalf, whilst prudently leaving the leper outside court. In another case in the reign of Edward II a wife came to court and said that her husband was sick of the palsy, and could neither walk nor talk. She asked that the case should cease. Mr. Justice Stanton said to the plaintiff:

"If it be as the woman has said, let the case cease, and your claim will be dismissed. If you are unwilling to do so, and we find that the woman is telling the truth, it will be to your cost."

Another act of mercy had spectacular results. In 1329 Chief Justice Hengham of the King's Bench fined a poor man one mark, but took pity on him, and reduced the fine to half a mark out of charity. He altered the record accordingly, to show what he had done. He paid heavily for this seemingly innocent act. According to one account, he was fined 800 marks; another version says it was 8000 marks, and this is thought to be the more accurate figure. As his own salary was 60 marks a year, it was more than he could have earned in his whole life. But this was an age in which a number of judges had been found to be corrupt; it was an age in which it was all too easy to alter records without being found out. Edward III must have wished to make an example of him.

The law was very hard on offenders. A girl of 13 was burnt to death because she killed her mistress; it was not merely homicide, but "Petty Treason" for someone to kill an employer. (High Treason, of course, is plotting to kill the king).

A boy of 10 was hanged for killing his companion. He would normally have been spared the death penalty at that age of 10, but he had hidden the body, which, in the eyes of the court, showed such cunning that he deserved the full rigours of the law.

The most startling aspect of the law about children related

to dowries. When a woman got married she immediately became entitled to one-third of her husband's property, and could claim it as his widow after his death.

Thus, in the reign of Edward II, a young widow in Bodmin claimed one-third of her late husband's estate. He owned 24 shops, two water-mills, one dovecote, and a good deal of land; a very valuable dowry.

Sjt. Scrope: She cannot bring an action, for she is not old enough to be entitled to her dowry.
Sjt. Laufer: That is for the court to see.

Her age was the issue in the case. She was said to be only nine years old; how old she was when she got married, no-one knows. Girls were often betrothed when they were four or five, if not in the cradle; and, strange though it seems, provided they were nine years old when they were widowed, they were entitled to their dowry. Nine was the important age; a number of cases said so at this time.

Scrope: Permit her, sir, to come to you to be examined.
Mr. Justice Stanton: It is a matter not for examination, but for judgment.

"Examination" here means "questioning", as in "cross-examination", but when it was a matter of a person's age, the Court judged by appearances.

Scrope: Examine her, sir.
Chief Justice Bereford: No, we will *see* her, and you shall *examine* her.

So they did. "And", says the Year Book, "she was adjudged of full age, so she won her case. (And she was examined as to how she and her husband behaved in bed. But she ought not to be examined, because the justices etcetera)."

It is the most curious "etcetera" in the Year Books; it means that the judges could assess her with their own eyes, and did not need to question her. "She was seen by the justices," reports the Year Book, "and they awarded her possession of the property. Whereat many were surprised, for she did not seem to be eight years old."

Chief Justice Bereford said, in a characteristically earthy

41

comment, "If the husband were not a giant, she could deserve dower at the time when he died.

One of the Chief Justice's most violent outbursts was against the Church. "The men of Holy Church have a wonderful way!" he exploded. "If they get a foot on to a man's land they will have their whole body there. For the love of God, the Bishop is a shrewd fellow!"

Churchmen appeared very often in Court, because they were men of property and position. The Prior of Dover had the right to charge a twopenny toll on every person who landed there. The Prior of Coventry had an exclusive right to hold a market within the city, where silks and spices were sold. The Dean and Chapter of St. Paul's could try criminals and had their own gallows.

Sometimes the Church and state clashed violently over their legal rights. After the murder of Thomas a Beckett the penitent Henry II recognised certain rights of the church, the best known of which is Benefit of Clergy.

It can be traced back to ancient Rome, where scholars — those at schools or connected with them — were an important asset, and given special privileges. The Roman emperors granted them exemption from military and jury service.

The Ostrogoths, in the 5th century, recognised it. Charlemagne recognised it, and in 1130 the Council of Clermont ordered that anybody who raised his hand against a clerk should be excommunicated. Clerks were not to be imprisoned for debt, or left without sufficient food; they were not to be disturbed at their studies. A weaver could not sing loudly at his loom if it distracted a scholar, nor could sulphur be burnt nearby.

Some of these privileges may not have been scrupulously observed, but when they were extended to Oxford in 1209, it was reckoned that it encouraged students to go there. There is no question but that the privileges known as Benefit of Clergy were strictly upheld by the English law.

It was not that the clergy were religious, but simply that they could read and write, which made them so valuable. Consequently, a man had only to prove his clerical status to escape the punishment of the criminal law.

This was a form of protection which the clergy expected and

generally obtained. When William the Conqueror wanted to arrest his brother Bishop Odo for treason, Odo claimed immunity because of his clerical position. (William sidestepped that difficulty, however, by having the Earl of Kent arrested instead; it was another of Odo's titles).

Most people think of Benefit of Clergy as being the right to cheat the gallows by reciting the "neck verse"; Psalm 51, verse 1. This is what Benefit of Clergy became during the 17th century; things were quite different in the reign of Edward II. The claimant had to dress like one of the clergy and wear a tonsure; this was something the court would observe for itself.

Chief Justice Bereford: Who makes answer?
John, the Defendant: Sir, I am a clerk, and cannot answer.
Bereford: We do not see that, but what we do see is that you are accused of robbery, and so you had better think what you will say in your defence.
Sjt. Hampton: We ask for judgment of him as convicted of felony.
Sjt. Warwick: I submit that even if he was willing to stand trial by jury you could not allow him to do so, for he is tonsured and a clerk. This you can satisfy yourselves of by examining him, and his tonsure is obvious. Such a man cannot stand trial by jury even if he wants to.
Bereford: You are talking rubbish. As a matter of fact, we often allow clerks to stand trial by jury, and then, if their Ordinaries come and claim them, we hand them over to them.

The Ordinary was the bishop's officer, who would certify whether or not the man was entitled to benefit of clergy. His decision was final.

There was no limit to the number of times a man could claim Benefit of Clergy. In 1319 a man was charged with counterfeiting coins, a very serious crime; the jury found that he had been convicted of it five times before. Nevertheless, the Ordinary claimed him once again, and there was nothing the judge could do but yield him up. The Ordinary lodged the offender in the Bishop's prison until the Bishop could deal with him, probably much less severely.

The Ordinary had to be present in Court, and announce whether the claimant was a member of the clergy or not. On one occasion he only arrived after the jury had retired to consider their verdict.

"And where have *you* been sleeping?" asked the Judge, irately; but the Ordinary was allowed to take him away, all the same.

One prisoner escaped from the Ordinary's custody, and killed two men; the Ordinary still claimed him. Indeed, a convicted thief was actually on the gallows when his friends rescued him by force. He was recaptured, and brought back into Court. But the Ordinary claimed him.

The Ordinary could refuse to accept a claim for Benefit of Clergy. If the accused had committed an offence against the Church, such as Sacrilege, he would refuse.

There was once a man who was acquitted of murder, and the Court offered to hand him over to the Ordinary for his disposal. The report of this case in the Year Books is brief and brutal:

Mr. Justice Herle: We deliver this man to you as we have found him Not Guilty, and thus it matters not that he should be purged of his guilt once more, for he has been purged sufficiently before us.
The Ordinary: Goodbye.

And he was hanged.

It was perfectly normal to be acquitted of murder and then hanged for it, in the 14th century. In 1310 a man was tried by Mr. Justice Spigurnel for the murder of William the Cheesemaker, and was acquitted. He was granted the King's pardon, which was a certificate proving his acquittal. He was then tried again at Chichester for the same murder before Chief Justice Bereford, and was convicted. He told the Court that he had already been acquitted, but had unfortunately left his pardon at home. So he was hanged. Counsel later suggested that this was, to say the least, inconsistent. The argument was speedily rejected:

Chief Justice Bereford: The two things can stand together perfectly well, that he was arraigned before Sir Henry Spigurnel and afterwards before me; for it may have chanced to him as it chanced to a man who committed a felony and obtained the King's charter of peace [pardon]. He afterwards came into court and left his charter at home, and was arraigned of the felony. Because of the confession of felony and because he had not the charter to hand, he was hanged before nightfall. So I say in your case, say something else, or Good God! we shall have something else to say."

Bereford was only following the accepted practice of the Courts. To quote another judge, "you will never see the day among lawyers when a deed of the King's can simply be quoted without producing it. A man who wishes to rely on it must have it ready to hand."

Or, as the Chief Justice himself put it, "if he has not his pardon in court, *shall not he be hanged?*"

Yes, unless he was lucky. A man was accused at York of felony, and had left his pardon behind. Fortunately for him, there was a court registry at York, and he could prove his pardon. Otherwise, to use the expressive phrase in the Year Books, "he would have gone on a pilgrimage to Knaresmire" — where people were hanged and quartered.

It was clearly helpful to a man to prove that he had already been acquitted of a crime. A man called Stephen was tried and then acquitted in Essex for the murder of a man whose body was washed up on the shore there. He was then tried in Middlesex for the same murder, but the record was produced to prove his previous acquittal. So far, so good.

Mr. Justice Mallory: You were acquitted in Essex but we find that you slew the man in Middlesex. An Essex jury was not competent to decide the facts, nor had the Justices, sitting in Essex, jurisdiction to hear the cause.

Stephen (plaintively): Sir, if I had been found guilty in Essex, I should certainly have been hanged in Essex. So if they had power to hang me, why should they not have the power to acquit me?

This frivolous argument found no favour with the court.

Mr. Justice Brabazon: If you had been acquitted in the county where the crime was *committed*, such acquittal would have availed you everywhere all the days of your life. But you were acquitted in the county where the body was *found*, and that county was wrong to inquire into the crime, which occurred in another county.

So Stephen had to stand his trial in Middlesex. The jury luckily failed to arrive, and he was remanded in prison. His final fate is unknown.

It was a robust age. The Lord of the Scilly Isles had the right to punish felons within his jurisdiction. His sentence was simply that they should be taken out to a certain rock, supplied with two barley loaves and a pitcher of water, and left for the tide to drown them.

The victim of a crime could always sue the criminal, but the Crown had an independent right to prosecute him. So, even when the victim's claim failed, the Crown could continue. This often happened in rape cases.

A woman called Joan claimed that a man had lain with her, but, by an extraordinary oversight, did not say that he had done so by force and against her consent. Sjt. King, for the defendant, pointed out that the essential ingredient of rape was missing from her charge. The judge upheld his submission. "The charge fails," he ruled, "because of that omission, and Joan shall go to prison for bringing a bad charge." (This was the usual fate of those who brought unsuccessful charges). "The Defendant," he continued, "shall be acquitted as far as *Joan's* suit is concerned, but he must answer to the *King's* suit. Sheriff, put him in irons."

He turned to the defendant. "You shall answer to the King for ravishing the maid Joan, who is 30 years of age and carries a child in her arms."

But who was the father of that child?

"The Defendant," said Joan.

"This is a wonderful thing!" said the Judge, astonished. "A child cannot be engendered without the consent of both parties."

Women could not become pregnant by rape — everybody knew that, in the year 1313. So the Defendant was acquitted, and Joan probably remained in prison till someone paid her fine.

Her fate was less harsh than that of Isabel of Bury, six years later. Isabel visited All Hallow's Church in Broad Street, London. She and her maid were causing such a disturbance that the Clerk of the Church ordered her to leave; she drew a knife, and stabbed him in the chest, killing him instantly. Then she claimed sanctuary in the church.

The Ordinary was so outraged at her impudence that he wrote to the Judges, refusing to let her have the privilege of sanctuary. She was taken to Newgate, and stood her trial four days later.

She was asked her name and address, and said nothing. Perhaps she was playing for time. The Clerk of the Court declared that "Inquiry had better be made whether she is dumb or not, and when she last spoke." So a jury was summoned.

But Mr. Justice Passeley was anxious to protect her interests as far as he could. He was acting almost as counsel for the defence.

> *Judge:* You would do better to speak, for if we hold an inquiry and find that you can speak, you will not be allowed to challenge the jurors. So speak, choose trial by jury, and you may be acquitted.
> *Isabel:* Sir, mercy, for God's sake!

Then she was charged with murder, and said "Sir, he struck me."

But self-defence was no defence to homicide in those days. The judge did his best to put forward her strongest line of defence:

> *Judge:* Did you kill him or not?
> *Isabel:* Sir, I did it in self-defence.
> *Judge:* What line of defence do you wish to put forward?
> *Isabel:* Sir, it was all I could do.
> *Judge:* Then you do not wish to say that you did not kill him?
> *Isabel:* Sir, I did it in self-defence.
> *Judge:* You would do better to deny that you committed the felony.

So she denied it, was tried by a jury, was convicted, and was hanged within a week. It was thought at the time that the Judge had shown exceptional leniency towards her because she was a woman. If a man had admitted causing the death, he would have been hanged straight away, without trial by jury.

She was hanged in 1321. The reign of Edward II lasted six years more. It is during his reign that lawyers and litigants are most vividly portrayed in the Year Books. They show, in a way that nothing else in the world did at that time, how cases were fought in court, and what sort of cases they were. Professor Maitland, the great legal historian, wrote of the Year Books "they should be our glory, for no other country has anything like them."

But there is one case more vivid even than that of Isabel. It comes from the reign of Edward I, and is closer to being a full shorthand transcript of the proceedings than any other case. The judge shows patience towards a tiresome defendant which is truly modern, doing as much for him as any Counsel for the Defence could have done. I quote it almost in full.

"The jury of 12 men reported that Hugh raped a girl, and took her and Nicholas to his manor in that village of N....., and had carnal knowledge of her against her will.

Hugh was brought to the bar by Brian and Nicholas of N.....

Judge: Brian, we are given to understand that you should have put him into prison because he did not accept trial by those who accused him, and you did wrong. But since he is your kinsman, we want you to look after his interests, but not that you should act as his counsel.

Brian: My lord, he is my kinsman, and I want to disprove this charge. I would like to do what is best for him. But he could not get good advice from me to disprove this charge against the common law. So, rather than get into any trouble with the law, I will withdraw.

Judge: Hugh, it is reported to us that you committed rape, as is here set down; how do you wish to be tried?

Hugh: My Lord, I beseech you that I may have counsel; I don't want to be hauled off to the King's court through lack of counsel.

Judge: Hugh, you must answer. Here is a tenable charge brought against you, said to be your own crime. You are perfectly capable of answering without counsel whether you committed it or not. The law has to be the same for everybody; and the law is that the King is a party to this case by virtue of his office, and you cannot have counsel against him. If we were to break the law and let you have counsel, and the jury were to bring in a verdict in your favour, which God grant — then people would say that you got off through a favour done you by the judge. We dare not allow this to happen, and you should not expect it.

Hugh: My Lord, I am a member of the clergy, and should not be called upon to answer without my Ordinary.

Judge: Are you a clergyman?

Hugh: Yes, my Lord; I am the Rector of N.....

The Ordinary: We claim him as a clerk.

Hugh: He says so, too.

Judge: Our ruling is that you have lost your clerical privilege, because you are a bigamist; you married a widow. You shall tell us whether, when you married her, she was a virgin or not, and there is no problem in finding out which of the two it was. A jury can reach a verdict about it straight away.

Hugh: My Lord, she was unmarried when I was betrothed to her.

Judge: This must be checked at once.

He charged the jury with answering that question, and they

48

declared by virtue of their oath that she was a widow when Lord
Hugh married her.

Judge: This Court therefore rules that you must answer the charge
as a layman, and agree to be tried by those twelve upright men.
We know they have no intention of deceiving the court.

Hugh: My Lord, it is thanks to them that I am accused; that is
why I cannot agree to them. Well, my Lord, I am a knight, and
I have the right to be tried only by people of equal rank.

Judge: Since you are a knight, we agree you should be tried by
your peers.

(Some knights were named. And he was asked if he wished to
raise any objections to any of them).

Hugh: My Lord, I don't agree to them. You can do anything your
jurisdiction allows, but I still won't agree.

Judge: If, Sir Hugh, you are prepared to agree to them, with God's
aid they may find in your favour — so long as you agree to them.
But if you wish to defy the common law, you will suffer the
appointed penalty, namely:

"On one day you shall have something to eat, and on the next
you shall have something to drink; and on the day that you shall
have something to drink you shall have nothing to eat, and vice
versa; what you shall have to eat is barley bread without salt, and
it shall be water that you have to drink."

He explained in detail to Hugh that it was not wise to play for
time; he would do better to agree to the jury. The diet of bread
and water on alternate days was the standard punishment to induce
a prisoner to agree to trial by jury, and few prisoners endured it
for long without submitting. Others, however, died.

Hugh: I agree to be tried by my equals, but not to the twelve
responsible for my being accused. I would like you to hear my
objections to them.

Judge: Certainly; let them be read out. But if you have anything
to say why they should be removed, you have only one opportunity
to say so orally or in writing.

Hugh: My Lord, as I cannot read I would like my own counsel.

Judge: No; this matter concerns the King.

Hugh: You can have them and read them.

Judge: No, because the objections have to come from your own
mouth.

Hugh: I can't read them.

Judge: How is this? You tried to claim benefit of clergy because
you could read, and now you are unable to read your own
objections?

(Hugh stood in silence, somewhat confused).

Judge: (to Sir N., of Leicester): Would you be kind enough to read Sir Hugh's objections?

Sir N: Certainly, my Lord, if I can have the book he was holding in his own hands.

(This was arranged).

Sir N: My Lord, there are objections here against a number of people. Do you want me to read them out so that everyone can hear?

Judge: No, simply read them privately to the prisoner, because they have to be heard from his own mouth.

(Which is how it was done. When his objections were heard, they were found to be valid, and those to whom he objected were taken off the jury panel.)

Judge: We are trying Sir Hugh for rape of a woman. He pleaded Not Guilty, and he was asked how he wished to be tried. He says, By jury; whence, for good or ill, he places himself in your hands. Therefore we require you, by virtue of the oath you have taken, to state whether Sir Hugh raped the said woman or not.

Jury: (presumably after pooling their local knowledge) Our verdict is that she was forcibly raped by Sir Hugh's men.

Judge: Was he a knowing party to the crime?

Jury: No.

Judge: But I take it the men had intercourse with her?

Jury: Yes.

Judge: Sir Hugh, the Jury have acquitted you, so we discharge you."

Sir Hugh may have had a lucky escape. If he had been found guilty, and was unmarried, his victim would have had the choice of marrying him. But if she preferred not to, or if the choice was not open to her, because either of them was married already, she was entitled to tear out his eyes and cut off his testicles.

Such were the activities in court during the reigns of Edward I, II and III as reflected by the Year Books. The reign of Edward III ended in 1377; Wat Tyler's rebellion took place in 1381. According to Thomas Walsingham, who gives the best account of it:

"the rioters began to kill every lawyer, apprentices as well as old judges and all the nation's *jurators* whom they could catch, without quarter or respect of person, declaring that there could be no real liberty till they were dead . . . for his [Wat Tyler's] design was, when he had killed the lawyers, to determine all matters by plebiscite. No law was in future to be passed,

50

or, if it was, he was to make it at his will.''

The legal profession can be seen here at its worst and best, sometimes arguing the most ridiculous trifles, sometimes tackling the most serious issues with dedication and calm. But they were doing their best for their clients according to the standards of the time. Wat Tyler was bent upon anarchy, which is the worst option of all.

One final date must be mentioned: 1387, when Chaucer was writing *The Canterbury Tales*. His Man of Law had seemingly not been touched by Wat Tyler's rebellion, but sat his horse with the calmness and dignity of his senior position:

> Each case and judgment was by him well known
> Which had occurred since William held the throne.

Some of them would appear in the Year Books. The Man of Law would argue in court for three hours, from eight till eleven, when the court rose. Chief Justice Sir John Fortescue wrote:

> "The judges of England do not sit in the Courts more than three hours a day, viz. 8-11 a.m. Then parties go to the Parvise and elsewhere and consult with the Serjeants and their other counsellors."

The Parvise was a porch or portico at St. Paul's, where the serjeants were regularly to be seen. The practice may have dated back to the time when so many senior lawyers were Canons of St. Paul's. To quote Chaucer:

> A Serjeant of the Law, wary and wise,
> There was, who'd often been at the Parvise.

Long before the Pilgrims set off on their journey to Canterbury, the legal profession in England could be said to have arrived.

FOUR

Excessive Expenses of Cheese

> *"Presiding over an establishment like this, makes sad havoc with the features,"* said Mrs. Todgers. *"The gravy alone is enough to add twenty years to one's age, I do assure you."*
>
> Charles Dickens, *Martin Chuzzlewit*

By the late 13th century it was no longer necessary to be a member of the clergy in order to come to the Bar, but it was necessary to be of respectable birth and to have begun an education at a church grammar school. Lessons began at six o'clock in the morning, and continued till eight; after a two-hour break for breakfast they resumed, with an hour for dinner, until five o'clock in the evening. In winter, when darkness fell, pupils worked by the light of the candles they brought with them.

In London there was a choice between St. Paul's Grammar School, St. Martin's, and St. Mary Arch's, and for a cost of 4d or 5d a year Grammar, which included literature, and Rhetoric, based especially on Cicero and Seneca, were taught. There was plenty of practice in arguing and debating; not a bad training for a lawyer.

When ready to leave school, students would know something of arithmetic (using an abacus to count), Latin, logic, medicine, philosophy, physics, and poetry, and would be ready either for University or the study of law at the Inns of Court.

William of Tonge wrote in his will dated 1389:

"If my said two sons be well learned in grammar and adorned with good manners, which shall be known at the end of twenty years, and the elder son shall wish to practice common law, and if it is known that he would spend his time well in that faculty, I will that . . . he shall have yearly from my rents for the term of seven years, five marks. And if he should waste his time aforesaid, or if he should marry foolishly and unsuitably, I will that he receive nothing more of the said five marks.''

He would probably have sent his son to one of the Inns of Court. The first records of the Inns of Court began early in the 15th century, but they were already well established then. It is not generally realised that an "Inn" could mean a "house" as well as a "tavern". A stranger from out of town once asked Mr. Noy, a famous lawyer, if he could recommend a good inn. "Lincoln's Inn," he replied, with a straight face.

Lincoln's Inn began as a friary. Edward I gave it to the Earl of Lincoln, who rebuilt it as his own Inn or mansion. Clifford's Inn was given by Edward II to the Clifford family, who let it to law students at the rent of four pounds a year. They liked to congregate in the same place. Hereflete Inn, on the west of Chancery Lane, was closer to being a real inn. It had been a brew-house, but was rebuilt as a residence for five Chancery clerks. New Inn had been a tavern too, but housed Chancery students.

Prospective barristers often began their training at the Inns of Chancery. They had to discuss a different writ every day, and learn it off by heart. At dinner the youngest person in every mess had to pose a legal problem, or be fined fourpence. After two years in this discipline the student would enter the Inns of Court, and continue studying until be could recite the different forms of pleading off by heart; they were in Law French. After three or four years the Benchers and Masters of his Inn would choose him to be an "utter-barrister", when he could dispute before them at moots and readings. It may have been an informal way of qualifying, but it was based on the merit and experience of the student.

The students enjoyed the pleasures of city life and the country combined, for no Londoner was more than one mile from open countryside.

Sir John Fortescue wrote:

"Their place of study is situated between the places where the courts are, and the city of London; not in the City itself, where the crowd of traffic could disturb the quiet of the students, but a little further, in the suburb of the city itself, and near to those courts, so that the students can easily get there without the inconvenience of fatigue."

William Fitzstephens, a valued colleague of Thomas à Beckett, tells us how charming life could be. On summer evenings the students went out to take the air at the Clerkenwell — a well for the clerks — and to other places where the waters ran sweet, wholesome and clear. On the north of the city the mill-wheels spun merrily round, and deer, wild boars and bulls roamed the forest glades.

In winter they hurried to the great marsh just outside the city walls — Moorfields. They strapped the shinbones of animals to their feet as skates, and used poles to punt themselves rapidly about on the ice. Blocks of ice served as toboggans.

Their Inns lay to the west of the city in the suburbs, "planted with trees, spacious and fair." But even a demi-paradise has its flaws. In 1360 the Prior of St. John of Jersualem, who owned the Temple, had a common latrine at the end of the Thames, with four apertures over the water. Even in those days the Thames was considered horribly polluted with sewage and rubbish and "the fumes and other abominable stenches arising therefrom."

The young barristers, "apprentices of the Bench" as they were called, behaved no better than the other London apprentices, whose misdeeds were a byword. The Coroner's records for 1325 tell their own story.

"On a certain Sunday in November, John of Glemham, apprentice of the Bench, lay dead in a house in the parish of St. Bride of Fleet Street. It was learned that on St. Martin's Eve [November 10th] John of Oxford, clerk, at the request of William of Cornwall, went to the tavern of Edmund Cosyn in the parish of St. Bride, where he assaulted John Wolfel, Edmund's taverner, on the ground of an old quarrel. John Wolfel made an outcry, whereupon came John of Glemham and a number of apprentices of the Bench whose names were unknown. A certain William the Taverner struck John of Glemham with his sword, on the fore part of the head, inflicting a wound four inches long and two and a half inches deep. Thus wounded he returned to his chamber, where he had his ecclesiastical

rights, and after lingering until the following Saturday, died.
Many apprentices of the Court were present at the inquest.''

It was at this time that Geoffrey Chaucer, then a member of
the Inner Temple, is said to have been fined two shillings for
beating a Franciscan friar in Fleet Street. The evidence of it
is admittedly second-hand, but he was one of our liveliest poets,
and some friars needed thrashing.

Chaucer must surely have been a trained lawyer. Not only
because he belonged to the Inner Temple — though one did
not have to be a lawyer for that purpose then; or that he held
several important administrative posts during his lifetime, for
which legal training was an advantage. Rather, it is especially
so because he gives a most detailed and accurate picture of the
legal profession. No other English writer can match him in this
until Dickens, and Dickens, who spent several years working
in the law, knew it from the inside.

This is Chaucer's account of the Manciple (Steward) in *The
Canterbury Tales*, written in about 1387, and given here in
slightly modernised words:

> A gentle MANCIPLE was there of the Temple
> Of whom purchasers might take example,
> . . . Of masters had he more than thrice ten
> That were of law expert and studious! —
> Of which there were a dozen in that House
> Worthy to be stewards of rent and land
> Of any lord that is in England.

On his evidence, there were rather more than 30 people living
in one of the Inns of Court. The first direct reference in literature
to them comes from Edmond Paston, one of the famous family
of *The Paston Letters*.

His fond mother wrote on February 4th 1445:

> "To Edmond Paston of Clifford's Inn, in London, be this letter
> taken. To mine well-beloved son, I greet you well, and advise you
> to think once of the day of your father's counsel to learn the law,
> for he said many times that whosoever should dwell at Paston,
> should have need to con [know how to] defend himself.''

It was a great asset to an influential land-owning family like the Pastons to have a trained lawyer as one of their number. Other families found the same, and the numbers at the Inns of Court rose rapidly in Tudor times. In about 1468 Chief Justice Sir John Fortescue wrote:

> "The students are, for the most part, young men. Here they study the nature of original and judicial writs, which are the very first principles of the Law. After they have made some progress here, and are more advanced in years, they are now admitted into the Inns of Court, properly so called; of these are Four in number."

(He meant the Middle and Inner Temple, Gray's Inn and Lincoln's Inn, though others have already been mentioned.) He continued:

> "In these greater Inns a Student cannot well be maintained under Eight and Twenty Pounds a Year; And, if he have a servant to wait on him (as for the most part they have) the Expense is proportionably more. For this reason, they students are sons to persons of quality; those of an inferior rank not being able to bear the expenses of maintaining and educating their children in this way. As to the merchants, they seoldom care to lessen their Stock in Trade by being at such large yearly expenses."

Only persons of quality could join the Inns of Court. It is not clear why, in 1437, Lincoln's Inn had a rule that nobody born in Ireland could enter the Inn, but only fourteen years later they changed their minds, as an entry shows in their official records known as *The Black Books of Lincoln's Inn*.

> "Blonket from the country of Ireland is admitted into the Society, any act or ordinance to the contrary notwithstanding, because he has brought very many Fellows to the Society."

The Middle Temple, however, excluded Irish barristers for a longer period. It was recorded in November 1484 that "If Mr. Garlonde, who was called to the Bar to practise in Ireland, practises in England longer than a year from this day, he shall be "disgraded the Bar."

There is nothing to suggest that any Irish barristers behaved badly. It would have been quite an achievement for them to behave worse than some of their English colleagues, in any event.

Education in those days was fairly broad. At University a man could learn not only general subjects, but also such specialised sciences as the Art of Fortifications, Fireworks, Hydrography and Shorthand.

At the Inns of Court a man had to learn music and dancing, as well as various aspects of law. "Readings", as the lectures were called, were provided for the students. The Reader began by reading his text, or proposition, and eventually threw it open for general discussion.

In 1512, Mr. Richard Covert gave a lecture at Gray's Inn on the question of Nuns who have been Abducted. His theme could be stated like this:

> "A man abducts a nun. The abbess, instead of claiming damages for the loss to the convent, settles the case on the basis that she is allowed to go hunting and hawking on his land whenever she wants, free of charge.
> Is this a valid agreement?"

Mr. Covert thought not. One could put a a value on the loss of the nun — he does not say how — but not on the pleasures of hunting and hawking. So it was no true bargain.

The young lawyers discussed this for a while, till Chief Justice Fyneux of the Queen's Bench, the most senior person present, gave his own opinion:

> "It is immaterial whether the thing given in recompense is valuable or not, for it is at the pleasure of him to whom a trespass is done, what he will take in satisfaction."

The pleasure and satisfaction of the nun herself did not enter the discussion, but the law of contract was in its formative stage, and the "doctrine of part performance" did not then exist.

This startling topic raised an important point of law. In time, however, readings at the Inns of Court became too clever by half. One reading at the Middle Temple in 1619 lasted for seven hours.

"They say preachers are long," said the Reader's brother, "but sure the law is very tedious."

This was a pity, because few students owned textbooks, so that readings and moots were an essential part of a legal training.

Sometimes they were discontinued because of the Plague. To quote from the records of the Middle Temple on February 9th 1592:

"Mr. Lewknor should have read for his second reading in next Lent, but because of the sickness last summer, and because one of the gentlemen died of the plague in the House, he could not have access to his chamber, so that the reading failed. Notwithstanding, it is ordered that commons [provision of meals] shall be kept next Lent, and that the moots and exercise of learning kept in the House and in the Inns of Chancery."

Some people think that the Plague occurred only twice in English history — The Black Death in 1348, and the Great Plague in 1665. It happened only too often, and included bubonic plague, typhus, and so on.

It is hardly surprising, because the water of the Thames was polluted, and servants always emptied chamberpots out of the windows. They were frequently fined, but it made no difference. Filth lay thick in the teeming streets of London. Ravens and kites helped clear it away, being scavenging birds, and were declared a protected species as a result.

Once a man joined one of the Inns of Court, his hours were much the same as at grammar school. He usually rose with the sun; as the jingle went:

Get up at five, dinner at nine,
Supper at five, bedtime at nine,
Makes a man live to nine-nine.

At six o'clock the bell rang for Morning Prayers — not well attended in winter — and the main meal of the day was at nine or ten in the morning. In the Hall, benches stood beside long tables laid with wooden trenchers for food, and wooden or earthenware pots for drink.

In the 15th century, people usually brought their own spoons to the table. They brought their own daggers, too, for cutting their food; table knives ceased to be pointed once Cardinal Richelieu objected to the distinguished guest who picked his teeth with one. Forks, however, were an effeminate Italian fashion not introduced into England until after 1600.

Nine o'clock at night was a good time to be in bed, for, in Dick Whittington's London, the curfew rang at eight every night from the City churches. So long as the bell tolled, the city gates stood open, but when it stopped, the gates were closed and chained, not to be opened again till sunrise. At curfew time, every tavern was shut, and no more drinks were to be served. No man might walk the streets unless he carried a flaming torch, and was on an obviously honest errand.

At the Inns of Court the porter would challenge every stranger with the password, which changed from year to year. At Newgate, for instance, which was close to Holborn and the Inns of Court, typical passwords in Tudor times were:

"Green Ginger."
"Pepper is black."
"Sweet meat, sour sauce."
"Nothing has no smell."

There were too many "night-walkers", as they were called, "such as continually haunt taverns, and no man knoweth whence they come; such as sleep by day and watch by night, eat well and drink well, and have no possessions."

Those who were caught by the Watch were placed in the prison known as the Tun until morning, when they could be fined or imprisoned. Many a wild young barrister learnt that to his cost.

To reduce the risk of violence, all weapons were banned from Hall except daggers, used to eat with. But trouble still broke out. In 1509 Thomas Veer was expelled from Lincoln's Inn "for an assault and affray on the Butler with his dagger in the presence of divers Benchers; he also used contumelious words in the presence of the Governors sitting in the Hall."

He was allowed back again on payment of 3s4d. Anybody expelled from Lincoln's Inn at this time was re-admitted, if he paid the fine and said he was sorry. Even William Elys.

In 1476 William Elys insulted the Butler, and was fined 3s4d. In the next year he was made Master of the Revels, which gave him an outlet for his high spirits at feast-times. But, in 1478, he:

"was put out of the Society because he had a woman in his chamber within the Inn one night, and also because during the time he was put out the said woman went to his chamber several times. *This was in Lent.* Also it was shown . . . that William had entered the house of one Henry Quarles, a capper [cap-maker] of the City of London, and had there taken from his wife and against her will a pair of rosaries of gold, value 7 marks.''

He paid a fine of 40s, and was allowed back into the Inn. Two years later, he was in trouble again because:

"he was caught one night with a woman named Grace in a house of ill-fame near Newgate by the Constable and the Beadle of the Ward, together with many others, and he was brought to the house of the Keeper of Newgate Goal"

He was lucky to escape prison, and upon payment of 6s8d was allowed back into Lincoln's Inn. He kept out of trouble for fourteen years after this, and became senior and respected enough to be the Reader for Lent in 1502. He threw up his duties after two weeks and was fined 13s4d.

That is the last that is known of him.

Most young barristers were well-behaved. Rivalry between them was reduced by banning flashy clothing or display. They were not to wear scarves of velvet caps, or to enter Hall wearing boots, hats, spurs, Spanish cloaks or swords. Nor were they to wear doublets which were violet-coloured ("pansied") or had holes in them cut or punched — "pounced" — "ponced".

They could not have long hair or large beards, but must wear sober dark clothes and gowns, except beyond the Fleet Bridge, Holborn Bridge or the Savoy. It reduced the fights near the Temple with rival groups of apprentices.

Most young barristers chased after anything in skirts, and women were a constant problem. It was hopeless trying to keep prostitutes away. Houses of ill-fame were meant to be confined to Southwark, on the south bank of the Thames, but many shady establishments found their way into the records of the Inns of Court.

There was the Green Lattice in Chancery Lane, the Antelope, John Hazelrick's house, and many more.

Christopher Tropnell was expelled in Lent 1484:

"because he seized a woman in Chancery Lane against her will and took her into Fleet Street, where a hue and cry was made by her, and thence into Fetter Lane to divers procuresses and suspected places, and unto his chamber in Lincoln's Inn, and there they remained all night.''

Syphilis came into England at this time, and its occurrence had to be reported to the Benchers. In 1515 a man was expelled for having a prostitute in his chamber, which was nothing new, but the Butler also ''confessed that he had examined her, and said she had the French Pox, and he concealed it from the Society.''

The Benchers at this period ordered that if any member of the Inn fornicated with a woman *in his chamber*, he would be fined 100 shillings. If, however, he did so merely in the garden of the Inn, or its rabbit-warren, or in Chancery Lane, the fine would be only 20 shillings. So much for the virtues of fresh air.

Some offenders had their responsibilities literally laid at their doors. In 1642 a bastard child was left on the doorstep of Richard Dewes of the Middle Temple; he was said to have begotten it in his chambers. But Dewes vanished. The Benchers had to pay five pounds towards the child's keep.

The illegitimate son of Thomas Middleton, the famous playwright, was actually born in his chambers in Lincoln's Inn, and ballads were circulated on the subject.

Lincoln's Inn was no more depraved than the other Inns, but its records are more colourful. One can learn about its food from what the students stole.

A spit of larks went missing from the kitchen. (Larks and sparrows were usually roasted on spits, but could be made into a pie, or boiled in a pipkin with mutton broth, white wine and egg yolks). They stole a doe out of the larder, whereby the whole Inn was ''destituted of venison'' for one day at Christmas. They stole eels and a quince pie out of the oven; fruit was a great delicacy for those who did not own orchards.

They broke into the cellar, where they let out the wine. Every member of the Inn had to swear on the Bible he knew nothing of the offence; those who refused were excluded from commons.

They stole a swan out of the larder. Swans are rather tough and oily to eat, but a roast swan was an important set-piece at Banquets. Its skin and feathers were carefully removed, the bird was cooked, and they were sewn on again. Its feet and feathers were painted with gold, and a crown might be put on its head.

It certainly looked regal, in the days before the law reserved it for royalty alone.

The young men were forever stealing rabbits out of the warren. It is easy to forget that meat was a great luxury for poor people; so was sauce. Nothing sounds humbler, till one reads the Tudor recipe, than:

RABBITS IN GRAVY

Take rabbits and parboil them, and chop them in gobbets, and seethe them in a pot with good broth; then grind almonds, dress them up with beef broth, and boil this in a pot; and, after passing it through a strainer, put it to the rabbits, adding to the whole cloves, maces, pines [pine-cone kernels], and sugar. Colour it with sandal-wood, saffron, bastard or other wine, and cinnamon powder mixed together, and add a little vinegar.

"Bastard" was a sweet white wine; "Oysters in Bastard Gravy", another dish from this period, was more palatable than it sounds.

Tudor cooking is best illustrated by Mince Pies, which used to have real meat, but also included dried fruit and spices which were used instead of green vegetables. We take fruit and vegetables for granted, but they were not widely available. Leprosy was the worst of the deficiency diseases which haunted medieval England.

With all these delicacies to steal from, it is puzzling to know why there was such a passion for cheese. The Steward's accounts for 1498 show that twice as much was spent on cheese as on 25 barrels of beer. It was ordered that if any member of the Inn:

"shall hereafter cut cheese immoderately, at the time of dinner or supper, or shall give cheese to any servant, or to any other, or shall carry it away from the table at any time, he shall pay 4d for each such offence."

One cheese-addict was fined 12d for such depredations.

There had to be some limit to extravagance. Smith the Butler was dismissed in 1519 for his "manifold misdemeanours." He issued beer out of the buttery in barrels and half-barrels, instead

Of smaller quantities, and incurred "excessive expenses of cheese and candles."

But parsimony was punished too. The Reader's Supper was a special event at the Inn; the Steward was fined 40 shillings for providing "a miserable and stingy supper, to the disgrace and scandal of the Inn." For a Reader's Supper, venison was expected; the Inn contributed 30 bushels of flour for it to be baked in, and 30 lbs of pepper for seasoning. More wine was allowed too.

There were other special occasions. On Good Friday the cook used to provide a meal of calves-heads, and on Easter Day, after the communion service, eggs were served with a green sauce made from sage, parsley, pepper and oil, with a little salt, blended in a stone mortar.

The happiest time was when Grand Christmas was properly kept. The Hall was strewn with green rushes, and decked with holly, ivy and bay. The tables were spread with fine cloths of white damask, and the richest silver was brought out; spoons, salt-cellars, and candlesticks. The Hall was lit with flaming torches, and there was music — drums, trumpets and fifes, with sweet harmony of viols and sackbuts.

First was brought in a boar's head upon a silver platter, heralded by the musicians, who turned to face the top table.

After the meal was over one of the senior members of the Inn made a little speech, and led them in a carol:

Nowell, nowell, nowell, nowell,
Tidings good I think to tell.
    The boar's head that we bring here
    Betokeneth a Prince without peer
    Is born this day to buy us dear
      Nowell, nowell.

They gathered round the great hearth, with drinks in their hands. Then the Master of the Revels, and the Lord of Misrule on his best behaviour, were joined by a Court of mock dignitaries:

Sir Bartholomey Baldbreech of Buttockbury, in the County of Breakneck.
Sir Francis Flatterer . . .
Sir Morgan Mumchance . . .

Thus was the evening given over to mirth, minstrelsy, and dancing, till the company departed to their rest.

But there was a darker side to Merrie England, as Henry Machyn's Diary reveals. He was perhaps a wealthy City undertaker, and noted down many sights near to the Temple in the thirteen years from 1550:

"The 13th day of January, was put upon the pillory a woman for she would have poisoned her husband dwelling within the St. Paul's Bakehouse, and the 14th day she was whipped at a cart-tail and naked [from the waist] upward and the 18th day following she was again upon the pillory for slandering.

The 8th day of June there was stood at the pillory a man and a woman; the woman bought a piece of mutton, and when she had it, she took a piece of tile and thrust it into the midst of the mutton, and she said that she had it from her butcher, and would have him punished; for it was hanged over her head on the pillory, and so there were they both set."

The man must have been her accomplice. Another man and woman were pilloried for selling pots of strawberries, which contained less than half fruit; they were filled up with fern.

The students might have seen James Ellis, "the greatest pickpurse and cutpurse", tried at the Sessions at Newgate, and hanged at Tyburn. Some of them certainly took the law into their own hands.

"The 12th day of June (1554) was a great fray between the Lord Warden's servants of Kent and the Inns of Gray's Inn and Lincoln's Inn, and some slain and hurt."

It was a violent age. In the reign of Queen Mary, two months before Cranmer was burnt at the stake in Oxford, Machyn records that there "went into Smithfield to be burnt between 7 and 8 in the morning 5 men and 2 women; one of the men was a gentleman of the Inner Temple, his name Master Green; and they were all burnt by 9 at three posts; and there were a common agreement through London overnight that no young folk should come there, for there the greatest number was as has been seen at such a time."

When Queen Mary's reign came to an end, everybody in the Temple must surely have watched the Coronation of Queen

Elizabeth, on January 15th 1559, when the whole street at Temple Bar was laid with gravel, and a great procession took place with the figures of the two great giants, Corineus and Gog-Magog.

But, no matter who was on the throne, unpopular members of the staff were treated the same by the young gentlemen of the Inns. The Chief Butler's disciplinary duties required him to report those who came into Hall improperly dressed, and to lock late-comers out of Hall if they did not arrive promptly when the Pannierman (who carried bread in a pannier) blew his horn to announce dinner.

The Steward who handled the money, was blamed when the provisions were poor. In 1627 William Skipwith, of Lincoln's Inn, threw a dish of butter at him, and was "put out of commons" (banned from eating in Hall), but came back the next day with his brother, who threw a pot at the Steward. Both brothers were fined £10; so was the Steward, who produced a pistol in self-defence.

The Chief Cook, who received the same wages as the Chief Butler and the Steward, was in charge of an impressive array of spits and other cooking utensils, and was allowed free food, meat-dripping and sheep's kidneys.

The Laundresses had to be at least forty years of age, so as to be past the attentions even of members of the Inns of Court. They brought clean linen on Sundays, Tuesdays, or Thursdays, and emptied the hot ashes from the grates into the cellar or under the stairs, if they were not watched. It is a wonder that the Inns of Court were not burnt to the ground.

They went on emptying chamber pots out of the windows, even after the Great Plague in 1665. But when pestilence stalked the streets, the gentlemen departed, and the gates and passages were locked. A few servants stayed on — for more than half a year in 1626 — and were paid double wages for the privilege.

The Porter's most important task was to keep vagrants out of the Inn, and to patrol the courtyards and staircases by night to see that nobody was robbed, which frequently happened. As a further precaution against crime, the chambers were regularly searched to see who was in them. That is how prostitutes were sometimes discovered. Some of the them married the staff. An under-porter in the Middle Temple called the Porter's wife a whore, and was dismissed for it. A junior butler in Lincoln's Inn called the washpot's wife a whore, and was sued for it in the Ecclesiastical Court. The Benchers insisted that the case was dropped.

It was quite an event when water-pumps were installed in the Inns; Pump Court bears witness to it. One replaced the Old Well in the Front Court at Lincoln's Inn in 1622, and was soon put to bad use. Two clerks tried to douse the Pannierman; he should have kept their dining-room clean.

In 1628 young Edward Heron and thirty others seized the King's Messenger, who had a warrant to execute upon one of them, and "pumped" him, shaved him and disgracefully used him." Charles I was not amused.

Seven days later Edward Heron was disciplined by the Bench not only for pumping the Messenger, but for *boasting and glorying in it*. There was then a violent demonstration in Hall; furniture was thrown about and broken. The Lord Chief Justice held a formal inquiry, and committed Heron and the ring-leaders to the King's Bench Prison, till they were granted bail.

But pumps can suffer too. Roderic Lloyd, the cousin of Lord Commissioner Trevor, was coming home one convivial night when he collided with the pump in Chancery Lane. It could well have attacked him again, so he drew his sword, and ran it through the spout. The pump collapsed, and never drew another breath. The murderer fled from the scene of the crime, leaving his sword behind him. He was found the next morning hiding in the coal-cellar.

The greatest occasions in the Inns of Court were the feast days which started with Allhallows on November 1st, and continued through Christmas until the Feast of the Purification, otherwise known as Candlemas, on February 1st. A Master of the Revels was appointed in each Inn, to lead the dancing.

Another traditional leader of the revelry was "Jack Straw", or "the Lord of Misrule". Nobody was safe, he and his followers would break open locked doors and demand money, or would wander the streets, beating drums and blowing horns. In 1524 a Lord of Misrule even killed somebody.

Time and again he and his followers were banned from the Inns, and ignored it.

But he was a very popular institution. To quote Henry Machyn's Diary:

"The same day [4th January 1552/3], afore noon, landed at the Tower Wharf the King's Lord of Misrule, and there met with him the Sheriff's Lord of Misrule with his men, and everyone having a ribbon of blue and white about their necks, and then his trumpet, drums, Morris Dance, and tabret, and he took a sword and bore it afore the King's Lord of Misrule, for the lord was gorgeously arrayed in purple velvet furred with ermine . . ."

They had a magnificent procession through the City, and dined with the Lord Mayor and the Lord Treasurer:

…"and so down Bishopgate and to Leadenhall and through Fenchurch Street, and so to the Tower Wharf; and the Sheriff's Lord going with him with torch light, and there the King's Lord took his pinnace with a great shot of guns, and so the Sheriff's Lord took his leave of him and came home merrily with his Morris Dancing and so forth."

The young members of the Inns were obliged to stay there over Christmas for study and lectures — that was the theory, at least. But high spirits prevailed, and cards and dice were played freely. Foolish young men could gamble away their estates in a night, especially when gamesters drifted in from outside to pluck them clean. Sir John Denham, poet and architect, inherited a rich estate from his father, but he was a student of Lincoln's Inn, and gambled it all away in two days.

Such behaviour continued until the Civil War. Christmas 1637 was bad enough; in the Middle Temple "base, lewd and unworthy persons" found their way into the Hall, where there was smoking, feasting and shouting down any attempts to keep order. The pounding of drinking-mugs on the tables, and the shouting for dice, drowned the voice of reason. It was a scandal.

The Benchers acted firmly. They decided that Christmas should not be held within the Inn at all; the company was to disperse over Christmas. But their order was flouted. On St. Thomas' Eve (December 20th) a number of gentlemen with drawn swords broke into the Hall and kitchen, and pursued their usual riotous behaviour. It was not to be tolerated.

The Lord Chief Justice, at the express directions of Charles I, summoned the offenders and fined them heavily. William Best, the turnspit who gave them the key to the kitchen, was instantly dismissed.

When Cromwell came to power such amusements were stamped out, and the Lord of Misrule was banned.

But the spirit of mischief was not quite quenched. Lord Keeper Guilford, when Reader of his Inn, chose as his lecture-subject the "statute of fines", which dealt with titles and their transfer. The best lawyers of the day argued the subject with him. Then came the feast, the last great feast on the heroic scale ever given. It was reckoned to have cost one thousand pounds at least, a banquet fit for a royal coronation; but it was casting the costliest pearls before swine.

Roger North wrote:

"The profusion of the best provisions and wine was to the worst of purposes, debauchery, disorder, tumult and waste. I will give but one instance; upon the Grand Day, as it was called, a banquet was provided to be set upon the table composed of pyramids and smaller services in form. The first pyramid was at least four foot high with stages one above another."

It must have taken hours to prepare, but was deemed fair game for a sort of rugger scrum:

"The conveying this up to the table, through a crowd that were in full purpose to overturn it, was no small work; but, with the friendly assistance of the gentlemen, it was set whole upon the table. But after it was looked upon a little, all went hand over head among the rout in the hall, and for the more part was trod under foot. The entertainment the nobility had out of this, was, after they had tossed away the dishes, a view of the crowd in confusion wallowing one over another and contending for a dirty share of it.

It may be said this was for want of order; but, in truth, it was for want of a regular and disciplined guard of soldiers; for nothing less would keep order there."

After the Civil War was over, the revelling in Hall never returned to its former exuberance. People were poorer, and some of the great estates were broken up. There was an earnest need to try and recoup some of the lost time and position in life. It is true that in 1719 Robert Darwin brought his dog into

Lincoln's Inn Hall during dinner, and was ordered to remove it. He threatened to throw a pot at the Porter's head, but it was a mere shadow of the Good Old Days.

The meals were more varied; green vegetables became a regular part of the diet. This was part of the menu for 1748:

EASTER TERM

Sunday. Sirloin of beef, roasted, undressed, 7 lbs to a mess [of four people] with pickles and horse-radish; and baked plum pudding.

Monday. A neck of mutton, boiled, with proper roots and greens; a fowl, roasted, with gravy and egg sauce.

Tuesday. Necks of veal, roasted with 100 of asparagus.

Wednesday. Boiled briskets of beef, with roots and greens, 7 lb weight; 4 pigeons, roasted.

Thursday. Roast beef, as on Sundays; with pudding or asparagus.

Friday. Fresh fish in season, with proper sauce; a loin of mutton, roasted, with pickles and horse-radish.

Saturday. Boiled tongues, roots and greens; a couple of rabbits.

Perhaps the students should have been happy with that diet, but they were not. A lean student of Lincoln's Inn complained to a fat Bencher that they were starved at the lower end of the hall.

"I assure you, sir," replied the Bencher, "we all fare alike; we have the same commons with yourselves." The student replied

"I can only say we see pass by us very savoury dishes on their way to your table, of which we enjoy nothing but the smell."

"Oh! I suppose you mean the "Exceedings." [Extras]. But of these the law takes no cognisance."

By the Nineteenth Century, Readings were a thing of the past. There was no formal legal education at all; aspiring barristers learnt their craft by going into the Chambers of Special Pleaders to study the technicalities of pleading, just as the first apprentices of the Bar sat with the Chancery clerks.

Foundlings continued to be found, and people of doubtful character practised their different callings. From the *Black Books of Lincoln's Inn:*

July 7th 1802. Upon a complaint of nuisance caused by Jews frequenting the Inn — It is ordered that the porters must do their utmost to prevent any persons from crying or purchasing old clothes in any parts of the Inn, and that Boards be painted to this effect, and placed in various places.

There was no thought then of Jews, however distinguished, coming to the Bar. But the barriers of religious intolerance were about to fall. Benjamin Disraeli joined Lincoln's Inn, though did not become a barrister; in 1831 he had his name taken off the books, stating that his health did not permit him to follow the profession of the Law. In 1833 Francis Henry Goldsmid of Lincoln's Inn applied to be called to the Bar. The Benchers discussed whether a Jew could be admitted, and unanimously decided that he could.

It was a more enlightened age — by gaslight, at least, which was installed in 1817. But Charles Dickens, who joined the Middle Temple, found that things were dim enough:

"I was uncommercially prepared for the Bar, which is done, as everybody knows, by having a frayed old gown put on, and, so decorated, bolting a bad dinner in a party of four, whereof each individual mistrusts the other three."

He was never called to the Bar, but Wilkie Collins his friend and fellow-author, was. Dickens wrote:

"Having no interest in the Church, he appropriately selected the next best profession for a lazy man in England — the Bar. Although the Benchers of the Inns of Court have lately abandoned their good old principles, and oblige their students to make some show of studying, in Mr. Idle's time no such innovation as this existed. Young men who aspired to the honourable title of barrister were not, very properly asked to learn anything of the law, but were merely required to eat a certain number of dinners at the table of their Hall, and to pay a certain sum of money . . .

Never did he feel more deeply what real laziness was in all the serene majesty of its nature, than on the memorable day when he was called to the Bar, after having carefully abstained from opening his law-books during his period of probation, except to fall asleep over them. How he could ever again have become industrious, even for the shortest period, after that great reward conferred upon his idleness, quite passes his comprehension. The kind Benchers . . .

70

invited him, with seven other choice spirits as lazy as himself, to come and be called to the Bar, while they were sitting over their wine and fruit after dinner. They put his oaths of allegiance, and his dreadful official denunciations of the Pope and the Pretender, so gently into his mouth, that he hardly knew how the words got there. They wheeled all their chairs softly round from the table, and sat surveying the young barristers with their backs to the bottles, rather than stand up, or adjourn to hear the exercises read. And when Mr. Idle and the seven unlabouring neophytes, ranged in order, as a class, with their backs considerably placed against a screen, had begun, in rotation, to read the exercises which they had not written, even then, each Bencher, true to the great lazy principle of the whole proceeding, stopped each neophyte before he had stammered through his first moment. This was all the ceremony.''

Dickens was perfectly right to criticise the lack of formal legal education in those days, but he must also have known that those who achieved the greatest success in the profession did so by working themselves almost to death.

Today the students still assemble in hall to eat their dinners, an experience not always exhilarating. Nigel Lawson, Chancellor of the Exchequer, once thought of becoming a barrister.

"One of the things you had to do in those days was to eat a certain number of bar dinners. I joined the Middle Temple and went to some. They were appalling. I wouldn't have minded the bad food if the company hadn't been even worse, extremely dull and boring. So I decided the law was not for me.''

The Bar has become a somewhat overcrowded profession. It is as possible to fail at the Bar as it ever was, or to succeed, if one has talent, some luck, and much will-power.

I would like to meet the student in recent times who answered a question on Equity:

Q. What is the rule in *Shelley's Case?*
A. The same as in anybody else's case. The law is no respecter of persons.

He deserves to go a long way.

FIVE

Coke Against Ralegh

Sir Thomas More said, (whether more pleasantly or truly, I know not) That a Trick of Law had no less Power than the Wheel of Fortune, to lift Men up, or to cast them down.

Walter Ralegh, *A Discourse of War in General*

Edward Coke was born in 1557, and Walter Ralegh a couple of years later. They were both men of great wealth, ambition, and energy; they were both in the Tower of London, sent there by James I, where they wrote scholarly books; yet how little they have in common!

Walter Ralegh, at the age of 21, was a member of the Middle Temple, as befitted his position in life; so was the preacher Richard Hakluyt, whose chief interest was in maps and voyages of discovery. But when Coke joined the Inner Temple, in 1572, it was law, law and law for him. He had been to Trinity College, Cambridge at the age of 15, and came down without a degree; Ralegh had been to France to fight when he was 14, and returned four years later, after seeing Catholics and Huguenots killing each other.

"The greatest and most grievous calamity," he later wrote, "that can come to any state is civil war, a misery more lamentable than can be described."

So, when he entered Oriel College, Oxford, he was already a graduate of the University of Life. Soon he came down, and published his first poems in 1576. He loved literature; it is said he helped Spenser write part of *The Faerie Queen*. But he was a man of action as well, for the sea was in his Devon blood. His half-brother, Sir Humphrey Gilbert, was urging that a North-West pasage was to be found to Cathay, and set out from Plymouth for Newfoundland. Queen Elizabeth authorised him to discover lands not already claimed by other princes, which

meant that she could not officially approve of his taking as much
Spanish loot as he could.

However, when Gilbert and Ralegh seized a Seville boat laden
with oranges and lemons no farther abroad than Dartmouth
harbour, it was a little too near home. They were ordered to
pay compensation. They sailed out of Plymouth, and attacked
some other Spanish ships. Ralegh's ship was badly damaged,
and many of his crew killed. However, as he was neither timid
nor prudent, he was content to make his own mistakes.

In 1580 Sir Humphrey Gilbert was appointed governor of
South-West Ireland; Ralegh went with him. His life was often
in danger; he was ready to charge an enemy ten times his
number, and left behind him in Ireland a name for cruelty which
the Irish have never forgiven. In England, however, he was best
known for his extravagant clothes, which gave rise to the most
famous story about him:

> "This Captain Ralegh, coming out of Ireland to the English court
> in good habit (his clothes being then a considerable part of his
> estate) found the Queen walking, till, meeting with a plashy place"
> (a marvellous phrase for a mud puddle) "she seemed to scruple
> going thereon. Presently Ralegh cast and spread his new plush cloak
> on the ground; whereon the Queen trod gently over, rewarding
> him afterwards with many suits for his so free and seasonable tender
> of so fair a foot cloth."

Coke was involved with different suits. Even as a law student
he had shown exceptional talents. The food at the Inner Temple
was poor; Coke proved, in an argument called *The Cook's Case*,
that the cook was in breach of contract, and entitled to be
dismissed.

Soon after he was called to the Bar the parson of North
Elmham, in his home county of Norfolk, let two Puritans preach
in his church.

"Thou art a false varlet," said Lord Cromwell, son of the
famous Cromwell, Earl of Essex (not to be confused with Oliver
Cromwell), "and I like not of thee!"

"It is no marvel that you like not of me," retorted the vicar,
"for you like of those that maintain sedition against the Queen!"

That was a serious libel on Lord Cromwell, with no apparent
defence to it. The parson, knowing of Coke's reputation, chose
him to defend it. It was his first brief.

Coke's line of defence was that the libel was justified. He lost the case, but did not give up. Hours of legal research bore fruit; he discovered that the original statute of 1378, written in Law French, contained the quaint word "messoinges", which means "lies"; it is close to the French word "mensonges." Someone over the centuries misread it as "messages," and translated it back into Latin as *"nuncia."* The plaintiff therefore based his claim upon libellous *"nuncia"*, not *"messoinges"*, and Coke won the case by challenging the decision on this technical point.

Ralegh's success was due to personal charm. On a window at the palace he scratched with a diamond the words "Fain would I climb, yet I fear to fall."

Elizabeth scratched another line immediately below it: 'If thy heart fail thee, climb not at all."

It did not fail him. He said her eyes set his fancy on fire, and her red hair held his heart in chains.

A German visitor to the country observed that she was said to love Ralegh beyond all her other courtiers, because two years before he could scarcely afford one servant, whereas now, with her bounty, he could keep five hundred.

The gifts came showering in on him: monopoly rights on the retailing of wine and the export of woollen broadcloth, and Durham House to live in, one of the largest palaces in London, with a lovely view of the Thames.

He was said to wear on his shoes alone pearls worth £6000. This was probably an exaggeration; perhaps they were only worth £6000 *by today's prices.* He was appointed to a committee for restraining extravagant dress, a subject on which he was conspicuously well informed

Coke, however, was not a man for ostentatious display. He was of a handsome though grave appearance, and believed that correctness in dress reflected the tidiness of a man's mind. He sought little more. But from the time of *Shelley's Case,* in 1580, the world came seeking him. A husband died, leaving a brother and his own widow pregnant; his own father then died, before the child was born. Now the father's estate had to descend from one male to another, so who was to inherit the estate, the grandson or his uncle, who was the father's only male heir at one stage?

It was an age when lawyers were constantly in demand to settle the division of rich estates. The case excited such interest that it was transferred into the Court of Exchequer, where it was heard by the Lord Chancellor himself and twelve other judges.

Coke won the case for the boy, and made legal history and his own fortune. For the rest of his career at the Bar he was in constant demand.

Ralegh had other worlds to conquer. That year a huge chart was published of the North American coastline. St. Mary's Bay, north of the Carolinas, seemed the ideal place for a colony; if the Spanish could be checked in the Caribbean, much of King Philip's power would be lost, for the Americas were his chief source of gold. In 1584, therefore, Ralegh sent out two ships to make a reconnaissance.

A long time had passed since sailors feared they might sail over the edge of the world; captains had compasses, astrolabes, and better and better charts. Books set out details of each new discovery, and enough outlandish words from the Americas to fill *Gulliver's Travels:*

The nose:	*Hehonguesto*
The feet:	*Ochedasco*
A loincloth:	*Ousconzon vondico.*

When Ralegh's men landed the natives gathered round them, saying "Windgancon! Windgancon!" They adopted it as the name of the new territory until they found that it meant "What gay clothes you are wearing!"

Virginia, in tribute to Queen Elizabeth, was a happier name.

Elizabeth did not allow Ralegh to go to Virginia — he stayed behind as Master of the Horse. She knighted him, and made him Lord Warden of the Stannaries, the most lucrative of all her gifts. Stannaries were tin-mines, and the mines of Devon and Cornwall were the most productive in Europe.

In the years before the sailing of the Armada, he was busy at court, making friends and enemies on all sides. He used some of his money to back Sir Francis Drake when he raided Spanish ports in America, but was not directly involved against the Armada.

Coke, meanwhile, continued to make progress in the law. He

became Recorder of Coventry, then Norwich. As Member of Parliament for Aldeburgh, he noted that a thorough knowledge of Parliamentary procedure would be useful, and acquired it.

In 1592 he became the Recorder of London, and then Speaker of the House of Commons. He made as glowing a speech in honour of his Queen as ever Ralegh could:

> "For as in the heavens a star is but *opacum corpus* [an opaque body] until it have received light from the sun, so stand I *corpus opacum* [a mute body] until your Highness' bright shining wisdom hath looked upon me and allowed me . . ."

Ralegh, on the other hand, went into something of an eclipse. He made pregnant Elizabeth Throgmorton, one of the Queen's ladies in waiting, and both of them were put into the Tower for a while as a punishment. Elizabeth did not choose to be slighted in this way. To court her favour again he went in search of El Dorado, which means "the Gilded Man," for the natives of Guiana were said to have so much gold that they would bespangle themselves with gold dust.

Ralegh returned after many hard years, and published an account of the Discovery of the Large, Rich, and Beautiful Empire of Guiana.

"The country," he wrote, "hath more quantity of gold by manifold, than the west parts of the Indies or Peru."

He brought back samples of white ore with golden streaks in it, which proved to be only marcasite; but he had an excuse. "It is very true," he wrote, "that had all their mountains been of massy gold, it was impossible for us to have made any longer stay to have wrought the same."

Even one or two small nuggets of massy gold would have satisfied his critics.

Still, he claimed that he had *almost* managed to capture some canoes full of Spanish gold, and assured the reader (in case Elizabeth had her suspicions) that he and his men had entirely respected the native women; "and yet", he wrote somewhat wistfully, "we saw many hundreds, and had many in our power, and of those very young, and excellently favoured, which came among us without deceit, stark naked."

She made him Captain of her Guard, no poor thing for him

to be at the age of 40, in scarlet livery with a short scarlet cloak bearing the letters ER in gold.

He never entered into her affections as far as Essex. Flirt with her he certainly did, and flattered her not a little.

"A Flatterer," he once told his son, "is said to be a Beast that biteth smiling." But he never showed his teeth at the royal hand that patted him.

Essex, however, was not so wise. In 1598 he turned his back on the Queen in the Privy Council, and when she struck him clapped his hand to his sword. In 1599 he entered her bedroom to protest about the favour she showed to Ralegh and Cecil. But his final and unforgivable error was to raise arms in the City of London. He may merely have meant to persuade her to change some of her policies and ministers, but that in itself was treason, if backed by a show of force. Ralegh tried to dissuade him, but in vain. Thus, in 1600, Essex was tried for treason, and Coke, the Attorney-General, conducted the case.

He had held that office for six years, and had questioned many witnesses on the rack, a practice then thought perfectly normal in a treacherous age. But he had not done so in Essex' case, he was sorry to say. He declared:

> "Though I cannot speak without reverent commendations of her Majesty's most honourable justice, yet I think her overmuch clemency to some, turneth to overmuch cruelty for herself; for though the rebellious attempts were so exceedingly heinous, yet out of her princely Mercy, *no man was racked, tortured or pressed* to speak anything farther, than of their own accord, and willing minds."

Essex, however, found Coke less than fair:

Essex: Will your lordships give us our turns to speak, for he playeth the Orator, and abuseth your lordships' ears and us with slanders; but they are but fashions of orators in corrupt states.

The judges stopped him, but he soon returned to the theme:

Essex: Well, Mr. Attorney, I thank God you are not my judge this day, you are so uncharitable.
Coke: Well, my lord, we shall prove you anon what you are, which your pride of heart, and aspiring mind, hath brought you unto.
Essex: Ah! Mr. Attorney, lay your hand upon your heart, and pray to God to forgive us both.

It availed him nothing. He was found guilty, and the axe was turned so that its edge lay towards him. At the hour of his execution Ralegh approached the block. Some said he was there to answer dangerous accusations Essex might make at the last minute; others said he was there to gloat over his enemy. He was persuaded to watch the fall of the axe from a tactful distance away, inside the armoury.

He had plenty of enemies left, but was safe enough as long as Elizabeth remained alive. Now she was failing, and who was to succeed her on the throne? King James of Scotland was not everyone's choice; others looked towards the Infanta of Spain, or Lady Arabella Stuart.

Coke supported James when he came to the throne, and was knighted by him on May 22nd 1603.

Ralegh was almost the only one of Elizabeth's old courtiers not to be accepted with favour. He was definitely not one of the type of men James preferred; besides, he especially was blamed for the new habit of smoking.

"It makes a kitchen of the inward parts of man," wrote James in his famous *Counterblast against Tobacco*, "soiling and infecting them with an unctuous and oily kind of soot."

Ralegh soon felt the results of James' disfavour. He was turned out of Durham House, almost at a moment's notice.

"To cast out my hay and oats into the streets at an hour's warning," he wrote to Coke, "and to remove my family and stuff in fourteen days after, is such a severe expulsion as hath not been offered to any man before this day."

His enemies no longer had to fear his royal protection. Perhaps he had been no worse involved in intrigues than most, but some of those others had lost their heads, and his was now in question.

1603 was a year of pestilence. To flee the plague, James and his court went to Winchester, where Ralegh stood his trial on November 17th. He was charged with treason under three headings:

conspiring to deprive the King of his Government;
to raise up sedition within the realm; and
to alter religion, bringing in the "Roman Superstition" and
to procure enemies to invade the kingdom.

These charges were reflected in his dealings with the unreliable Lord Cobham.

Coke, still Attorney-General, defined treason in Latin phrases:

"There is Treason in the heart, in the hand, in the mouth, in consummation; comparing that *in corde* to the root of a tree; *in ore*, to the bud; *in manu*, to the blossom; and that which is *in consummatione*, to the fruit."

This was calm enough, but a moment later he rounded on Ralegh, in one of the most deplorable scenes ever to take place in an English court:

"I shall not need, my lords, to speak any thing concerning the King, nor of the bounty and sweetness of his nature, whose thoughts are innocent, whose words are full of wisdom and learning, and whose works are full of honour; although it be a true Saying, *Nunquam nimis, quod nunquam satis.* [You can't have too much of a good thing.]"

Then he turned to Ralegh:

Coke: But to whom do you bear Malice? To the [King's] Children?
Ralegh: To whom speak you this? You tell me news I never heard of.
Coke: Oh, sir, do I? I will prove you the notoriest Traitor that ever came to the Bar. After you have taken away the King, you would alter Religion; as you, Sir Walter Ralegh, have followed them of the Bye in Imitation: for I will charge you with the words.
Ralegh: Your words cannot condemn me; my innocency is my defence. Prove one of these things wherewith you have charged me, and I will confess the whole Indictment, and that I am the horriblest Traitor that ever lived, and worthy to be crucified with a thousand thousand torments.
Coke: Nay, I will prove all: thou art a monster; thou hast an English face, but a Spanish heart. Now you must have Money: Aremberg was no sooner in England (I charge thee, Ralegh) but thou incitedst Cobham to go unto him, and to deal with him for Money, to bestow on discontented persons, to raise Rebellion in the Kingdom.
Ralegh: Let me answer for myself.
Coke: Thou shalt not.
Ralegh: It concerneth my life.
Lord Chief Justice Popham: Sir Walter Ralegh, Mr. Attorney is but yet in the General [Outline of the case]; but when the King's Counsel have given the Evidence wholly you shall answer every Particular.

Coke, however, continued his personal attack. Another outburst was inevitable.

Coke: I think you meant to make Arabella a Titular Queen, of whose Title I will speak nothing; but sure you meant to make her a stale [a stalking-horse]. Ah, good lady, you could mean her no good.

Ralegh: You tell me news, Mr. Attorney.

Coke: Oh, sir! I am the more large, because I know with whom I deal: for we have to deal today with a man of wit.

Ralegh: Did I ever speak with this lady?

Coke: (avoiding the question, which could not be answered): I will track you out before I have done. Englishmen will not be led by persuasion of words, but they must have books to persuade.

Ralegh: The Book was written by a man of *your* profession, Mr. Attorney.

Coke: I would not have you impatient.

Ralegh: Methinks you fall out with yourself; I say nothing. . . I will wash my hands of the Indictment, and die a true man to the king.

Coke: You are the absolutest Traitor that ever was.

Ralegh: Your phrases will not prove it.

Coke: Cobham writeth a Letter to my Lord Cecil, and doth will Messis' man to lay it on a Spanish Bible, and to make as though he found it by chance. This was after he had intelligence with this viper, that he was false.

Lord Cecil: (one of the Commissioners hearing the case): You mean a Letter intended to me? I never had it.

Coke: No, my lord, you had it not. You, my masters of the jury, respect not the wickedness and hatred of the man, respect his cause; if he be guilty, I know you will have care of it; for the preservation of the king, the continuance of the Gospel authorised, and the good of us all.

Ralegh: I do not hear yet, that you have spoken one word against me; here is no Treason of mine done: If my lord Cobham be a Traitor, what is that to me?

Coke: All that he did was by instigation, thou Viper: for I *thou* thee, thou Traitor.

Ralegh: It becometh not a man of quality and virtue, to call me so: But I take comfort in it, it is all you can do.

Coke: Have I angered you?

Ralegh: I am in no case to be angry.

Lord Chief Justice Popham: Sir Walter Ralegh, Mr. Attorney speaketh out of the zeal of his duty, for the service of the king, and you for your life; be valiant on both sides.

Calm was restored, but Coke should never have spoken as he did.

Cobham had made several confessions implicating Ralegh, and these were read aloud, though Cobham himself was not called as a witness. Ralegh argued that the law required two witnesses against him, but he was out of date. The law had been changed in Queen Mary's reign: one witness was now enough:

> *Justice Gawdy:* The Statute you speak of concerning two Witnesses in case of Treason, is found to be inconvenient, therefore by another law it was taken away.
>
> *Justice Warburton:* I marvel, Sir Walter, that you being of such experience and wit, should stand on this point; for so many horse-stealers may escape, if they may not be condemned without witnesses.

It was said that Ralegh had planned to kill "the King and his cubs"; others had mentioned his name in that connection. Ralegh told the court that they were "hellish spiders", and Coke retorted "Thou hast a Spanish heart, and thyself art a Spider of Hell."

Ralegh had indeed been extremely indiscreet, and had spun himself into the centre of a sinister-looking web. He borrowed a book from Cecil which questioned the validity of King James' title to the throne, and kept it; he listened to Cobham talking of taking money from the Spaniards, without reporting it to the King, as he should have done. Finally, after Cobham had said he had been plotting with Ralegh, Ralegh threw an apple through his window with a message attached, to persuade him to change his story.

Ralegh may have been innocent, but he had done more than enough to give the opposite impression. Everything he said in Court — there was plenty — made his case look a little worse.

There was one more outburst from Coke when he said that there never lived a viler viper than Ralegh. "Viler Viper" is good; it has a hiss and sting to it which "badder adder" would wholly lack.

The evidence came to an end. The jury took less than a quarter of an hour to pronounce Ralegh guilty. Lord Chief Justice Popham seemed genuinely sorry:

"I thought I should never have seen this day, to have stood in this

81

place to give Sentence of Death against you; because I thought it impossible, that one of so great parts should have fallen so grieviously . . . It is best for man not to seek to climb too high, lest he fall; nor yet to creep too low, lest he be trodden on...

I never saw the like Trial, and hope I shall never see the like again."

He pronounced the usual sentence for traitors: to be hanged, but cut down whilst still alive; to have his heart and bowels plucked out before his very eyes, then to have his head cut off, and his body to be divided into four quarters. Such were often placed upon the walls of different towns, as a warning to others.

Ralegh then hoped for no reprieve; he had seen too many die in the same way. He watched Lord Cobham and Lord Gray of Wilton, another conspirator, brought out into the castle yard; but their lives were spared. They were imprisoned instead. "And although myself have not yet been brought so near the very brink of the grave," wrote Ralegh that day, "yet I trust that so great a compassion will extend itself towards me also."

He was sent to the Bloody Tower, where for twelve years he passed the time writing, cultivating a little allotment of favourite shrubs and herbs, and carrying out chemical experiments in a shed. He learnt to distil fresh water from sea water, and to crystallise his melancholy into verse:

As in a country strange without companion,
I only wail the wrong of death's delays,
Whose sweet spring spent, whose summer well nigh done,
Of all which past, the sorrow only stays.

The following year, James signed a treaty with Spain, yet still allowed Roman Catholic recusants to be prosecuted. This prompted the Gunpowder plotters to act, for they wished to see a Catholic government. Coke had no doubts that their prosecution was an historical event. "The eye of all Christendom is bent upon the carriage and event of this great cause," he wrote.

The indictment against the conspirators was so fulsome that it took thirty minutes to read: they had not merely plotted "suddenly, traitorously and barbarously" to blow up the palace,

but "most barbarously and more than beastly" to destroy it.
Yet he described treason in terms of a charming fable:

> "The cat shaved its head, and addressed the mice formally and
> fatherlike. O brothers, I am no more a cat — *non sum quod fui sed
> tonsum frater!* [I am not what I was, but a tonsured friar!] See my
> habit and my shaven crown!"

The point of his fable is that the mice were not deceived.
Coke was ceaselessly active in the case, riding backwards and
forwards to the Tower to interrogate Father Garnett, and to
prosecute him thereafter. He was hanged, and Coke was more
than ever the ferocious mastiff of the state, ready to set his teeth
into its enemies. Triumphant in his ferocious prosecutions, he
seemed to have less than ever in common with the gallant and
foolish Ralegh, now languishing in the Tower.

But Coke was to be made a judge, and in the midsummer
of 1606 rode home to Norwich as Chief Justice of the Court
of Common Pleas. His way of life was totally transformed. "I
must therefore," he said, "as the young Roman did, take leave
of all former acquaintance, and do that which is just unto all
estates and degrees, without partiality."

There is no telling what sort of judge a man may become.
Francis Bacon said that judges "must be lions, but yet lions
under the throne, being circumspect that they do not check or
oppose any points of sovereignty."

Lions who were royal watchdogs, in other words. But Coke
would have none of it; he proclaimed, as nobody else did, that
the King was under God and the law, and from that moment
on he became one of the greatest judges ever to adorn the Bench.

Nobody could have foreseen it, least of all King James.

James claimed that his royal prerogative was divine, and
worshipped it accordingly. He called the judges to him in
November 1608, declaring magnanimously that he would ever
protect the common law. Coke, begging to differ said "The
common law protecteth the King," to which James replied:

> "A traitorous speech! The King protecteth the common law, and
> not the law the King! If the judges interpret the laws themselves
> and suffer none else to interpret, they may easily make of the laws,
> shipmen's hose!"

Coke then observed that this Majesty was not learned in the laws of his Realm of England; "after which", wrote an eye-witness:

> "his Majesty fell into that high indignation as the like was never known in him, looking and speaking fiercely with bended fist, offering to strike him, etc.
>
> Which the Lord Coke perceiving, fell flat on all fours; humbly beseeching his Majesty to take compassion on him and to pardon him if he thought zeal had gone beyond his duty and allegiance. Whereupon the Lord Treasurer [Lord Cecil] knelt down before his Majesty and prayed him to be favourable. To whom his Majesty replied, saying "What hast thou to do to intreat for *him?*"
>
> 'In regard he hath married my nearest kinswoman,' replied Cecil. [She was Coke's second wife]."

The storm passed over. In being called a traitor, Coke was repaid for his treatment of Ralegh. Nevertheless, though he begged the King's pardon, then and thereafter, he never withdrew his opposition to James' dogmas. Most other judges of that time would unhesitatingly have done so; Coke chose, with unvarying courage, to lay his head almost literally on the block.

His opposition sometimes took colourful forms. In *Edwards' Case*, the defendant said that a bishop was suffering from syphilis, and drew a picture of a horn, which was pointed, to say the least of it. But it was an age when the courts went to absurd lengths to give innocent meanings to offensive phrases. Someone once said "Fie, I wonder you will sit with him, he hath the pox"; the court held that this was not defamatory, as it might merely have meant *smallpox*.

That is why the Court of High Commission sought to clarify Edwards' words: "We require you upon your oath to set down whether you meant not that he was a cuckold, and what other meaning you had, to the dislike of the dignity and calling of Bishops."

Coke disliked the High Commission, and was as jealous of it encroaching upon the common law as a dog is of others approaching its bone. He ruled:

"The Ecclesiastical judge cannot examine any man upon his oath, upon the intention and thought of his heart. *Cogitationis poenam nemo emeret:* for it hath been said in the Proverb, THOUGHT IS FREE."

He issued a prohibition against the Court of High Commission, refusing to allow it to interfere in Edwards' case, and in several others beside. He was ordered to appear in the Privy Council, where for three days he was virtually on trial for his behaviour. He said:

"I think this to be the first time that ever any judges of the realm have been questioned for delivering their opinions in matter of law according to their consciences in public and solemn arguments."

He refused to back down, and three months later James announced that he would reform the High Commission, confining its jurisdiction to certain ecclesiastical cases. It was a promise he never meant to keep. He even appointed Coke to be one of its Commissioners, hoping to draw his teeth in that way, but Coke continued to issue prohibitions.

Meanwhile, in the Tower of London, Ralegh continued his researches. He wrote the *History of the World,* his greatest work, though it spoke of no events later than 67 BC. Ralegh expressed the view in it that God punished wicked Kings. This displeased James, and was intended to do so.

Prince Arthur, James' son, went swimming in the Thames, and caught a chill; one of Ralegh's medicines was tried to revive him, but he died. Ralegh lost a useful friend then.

In 1613 the Lord Chief Justice of the King's Bench died, and Coke was transferred to that office. It was thought that he might become more cooperative. In the following year James devised "benevolences", those enforced donations of cash which wealthy citizens were required to make to him. Coke refused to endorse this practice.

Ralegh, however, had another scheme for making money: he begged to be allowed to return to Guiana, to find El Dorado again. He was released from the Tower on March 19th, 1616, aged 63, and lame in one leg. His seamen were "the very scum of the world," and his officers seasoned pirates; even his ship had an ominous name, the *Destiny.* After many difficulties the ship reached Guiana. He remained on board, whilst an expedition went ashore; he was too weak to join it. When the survivors finally rejoined him, he learnt that they had fought with the Spanish, and his son had been killed.

Fighting with the Spanish was against the express orders he had been given. He returned to London and was placed back in the Tower. James, who oscillated rapidly in his foreign policy, was once again seeking friendship with Spain; there were hopes that Prince Charles would marry the Infanta.

But there was a price to pay for Spanish cooperation. Their ambassador had only one word to say to James: "Pirates, pirates, pirates!" He wanted Ralegh to be handed over to them for execution, or at least be executed in London.

James sought the opinion of the Judges. Were there new charges on which Ralegh could be tried? Could it be said, for instance, that fighting the Spaniards was a treasonable defiance of his instructions? The Judges thought not; nevertheless, he was still under the sentence of death passed fifteen years before.

On October 28th 1618 he was brought to the bar in the King's Bench Court. Had he anything to say, why execution should not be awarded against him?

He said "My lords, my voice is grown weak, by reason of my late sickness, and an ague which I now have; for I was even now brought hither out of it." Lord Chief Justice Coke replied "Sir Walter, your voice is audible enough."

Ralegh naturally pleaded that he should not now be executed upon so old a sentence, but Coke interrupted him: he had been condemned for treason. Only an explicit pardon could set that sentence aside, and it had never been granted to him:

"I am here called to grant Execution upon the Judgement given you fifteen years since; all which time you have been as a dead man in the law, and might at any minute have been cut off, but the king in mercy spared you. You might think it heavy, if this were done in cold blood, to call you to Execution, but it is not so; for new Offences have stirred up his majesty's justice, to remember to revive what the law hath formerly cast upon you ...

You must do as that valiant captain did, who perceiving himself in danger, said, in defiance of death: 'Death thou expectest me, but maugre thy spite, I expect thee.'

86

Fear not death too much, nor fear not death too little; not too much, lest you fail in your hopes; not too little, lest you die presumptuously. And here I must conclude with my prayers to God for it; and that he would have mercy on your soul.

Execution is granted."

Coke was administering the law as it stood, without rancour. He was certainly not toadying to James.

On the following morning, at nine o'clock, Ralegh was taken by the Sheriffs of London to a scaffold in the Old Palace-Yard at Westminster. There he smoked a pipe — why not? — and, as so often in his lifetime, made a lengthy speech from notes to justify his actions. Nobody tried to stop him. Then he said, "I have a long journey to go, and therefore I will take my leave." He took off his doublet and gown, and asked the headsman to show him the axe.

"I prithee let me see it," he said; "dost think that I am afraid of it?"

He ran his finger along its edge. "This is a sharp medicine," he said to the Sheriff, "but it is a physician that will cure all diseases."

After a short prayer, it was time to lay his head upon the block. The headsman asked which way he would like to place himself. "So the heart be straight," he replied, "it is no matter which way the head lies."

With two blows of the axe the headsman struck off his head. He was 66 years old.

It was not an age when statesmen lived secure. Coke was dismissed as Lord Chief Justice, and retired to the country. He was called back to take part in a commission of inquiry into the allegations of corruption against Bacon, the Lord Chancellor. Coke was incorruptible.

"Make what law you will," he told the House of Commons, "inflict what punishment you will, little good will come of it if offices be bought and sold. He that buys must sell."

His career lay in Parliament now, bitterly attacking James' Spanish sympathies. "The first plague among our sheep," he said, "was brought by a Spanish sheep to England. So also *morbum Gallicum* [the Gallic disease — syphilis] by Spaniards from Naples."

Parliament was now in open conflict with James, refusing him the large grants of money he demanded, and insisting upon a petition for their rights. Coke, at the age of 69, was in their forefront. The Privy Council sent for him, and told him he had forgotten the duty of a servant of a Councillor of State, and of a subject.

"I hope I have failed in none of these," he replied, "but God's will and the King's be done."

He was placed in the Tower, in the quarters that Lord Cobham had once occupied at the time that he conspired with Ralegh.

At first he was deprived of all books, the harshest possible sentence upon a great scholar. Confined to his rooms, with no friends to see him, he scrawled Latin verses on the wall with a piece of coal.

He was accused of being a traitor.

"If the King desire my head," he replied, "he knows whereby he may have it." A few months later, however, he was set free.

"Throw this man where you will," declared James, "and he falls upon his legs."

Nothing came of the Spanish Match between Charles and the Infanta, and there was talk of a war with Spain. James decided that he had special need of Coke's services for a commission in Ireland. This was not the honour it might seem, being a form of exile. Coke, now seventy-four years of age, took leave of his friends, never thinking to see them again. But James changed his mind. Coke's influence in Parliament was still decisive; the King's right to grant monopolies was abrogated, and Coke declared that no man could be exiled save by Parliament or the law.

James died, and Charles I came to the throne. Coke and Parliament were just as hostile to his demands for money. The Commons drew up four resolutions:

> No free man to be imprisoned without cause shown, even at the King's command
>
> *Habeas corpus* not to be denied
>
> A prisoner brought to court upon a *habeas corpus* was to be bailed or freed.

No taxes or levies were to be made by the King without Parliament's consent.

Four members of the Commons were chosen to put forward these resolutions, and Coke was one of them.

Charles put forward all sorts of compromise proposals, asking Parliament to trust to his goodwill and discretion, but Coke would have none of it. He insisted upon the proposals being properly enacted. He asked:

> "What is that to Acts of Parliament? I was committed to the Tower, and all my books and study searched, and thirty-seven manuscripts were taken away. Thirty-four were restored, and I would give three hundred pounds for the other three."

Charles made more promises, but they were not accepted. So he summoned Parliament once again, and after reading the Petition of Right once again, uttered the formal words which passed it into law: "*Soit droit fait, comme il est desiré.*"

The bells rang out the victory, and bonfires blazed.

Only then did Coke retire, with three striking careers behind him: as an advocate, as a judge, and as a doughty champion of Parliament. His greatest career lay ahead of him, as an author: he began his *Institutes* with the work for which he is best known, *Commentary Upon Littleton*, which deals with the law of property, a difficult book on a very difficult subject. It is not for the casual reader, despite a charming opening sentence about Littleton:

> "Our author, a gentleman of an ancient and a fair-descended family de Littleton, took his name of a town so called, as that famous chief-justice Sir John de Markham, and divers of our profession, and others, have done."

Next he waxed poetical in favour of Queen Elizabeth:

> "Of this queen I may say, that as the rose is the queen of flowers, and smelleth more sweetly when it is plucked from the branch, so I may say and justify, that she by just desert was the queen of queens, and of kings also, for religion, piety, magnanimity, and justice; who now by remembrance thereof, since Almighty God gathered her to himself, is of greater honour and renown than when she was living in this world. You cannot question what rose I mean; for take the red or the white, she was not only by royal descent and inherent birth-right, but by roseal beauty also, heir to both."

When he turns to his main subject, his attention to detail is astonishing. Most textbooks on the rights of heirs would consider only the males and females, but Coke goes further:

"Every heir is either a male, or female, or an hermaphrodite, that is both male and female. And a hermaphrodite (which is also called *Androgynus*) shall be heir, either as male or female, according to that kind of the sex which doth prevail. And accordingly it ought to be baptised. See more of this matter Sect. 35."

His flashes of ignorance are as delightful as they are rare. He asserts, for instance, that the Druids spoke Greek. He plunges into the derivation of words with as much pleasure as Dr. Johnson. Of "robbery", for instance, he says "It is called robbery, because the goods are taken as it were *de la robe*, from the robe, that, is, from the person; but sometimes it is taken in a larger sense."

He has it the wrong way round; the French word *robe* comes from the Germanic word *rauben*, meaning "to rob." *Robe* was originally any form of booty, before it came to mean "clothing."

These are tiny criticisms of a gigantic work. Its last words are as charming as the first:

"And for a farewell to our jurisprudent, I wish unto him the gladsome light of jurisprudence, the loveliness of temperance, the stability of fortitude, and the solidity of justice."

Coke deserved a dignified departure from the world, but it was denied him. On the first day of September 1634, as he lay dying, King Charles' men searched his house and removed the manuscripts of his *Institutes*, together with notes for two volumes of reports. He was buried at the church of St. Mary's, Tittleshall, in Norfolk, in a vault with his first wife. In the words of Seneca, which he quoted in his *First Institute*, "Certain it is, that when a great learned man (who is long in making) dieth, much learning dieth with him."

Coke had little in common with Ralegh save his greatness. Coke's verse is justly forgotten, and is to be found summarising the cases in his law reports:

Cawdry: 'Gainst common prayer if parson say
     In sermon aught, bishop deprive him may.

Ralegh, however, upon the night before he died, inscribed these words upon a candle-snuffer:

Cowards fear to die; but Courage stout,
Rather than live in Snuff, will be put out.

It is an apt epitaph for both of them.

SIX

Excommunication and Costs

They neither hold them to the sincerity of God's service,
nor to the mere toys and fooleries of the heathen: but
frame to themselves a mingle-mangle out of both.

Sir Henry Finch, *Nomotexnia*

The churchmen were always a race apart. One of the laws of King Canute, in about 1020 AD, said "If a man in holy orders commits a capital crime, he is to be seized and kept for the bishop's judgment, according to the nature of the deed."

William the Conqueror granted to the bishops the right to hold their own courts, where ecclesiastical cases were tried. He ordained:

"If therefore, anyone has so high an opinion of himself that he thinks himself too important to come to the bishop's court, and is not prepared to do so, he shall be summoned once, twice, and three times. If he does not then submit himself to correction, he shall be excommunicated."

The church courts had a lot of work to do. People made their wills when they contemplated death - the church courts therefore tried probate cases. Likewise questions of adultery and divorce, which raised moral issues. All professional people were trained by the church in those days; even in the reign of Henry VIII, a man could only be a surgeon with the licence of the Archbishop of Canterbury.

As the legal profession developed, the barristers ceased to be clergymen. Some of them specialised in Canon law (Church law) or the "Civil law" (we would call it International law), which they studied at famous foreign universities such as Bologna and Padua.

Such men, who spoke several European languages and were learned in the system of law practised on the continent, made excellent ambassadors. Henry III and Edward I both employed Italian civil lawyers; one had the quaint name Accursius, from Bologna. He acted for the King of England in disputes with the King of France; he was sent to inquire into allegations that the sheriff of Oxford had been making extortionate demands on the Jews living there, and he went to Rome on the King's business too.

In the 14th and 15th centuries such men, even if born in England, were trained in the civil law either abroad or at Oxford and Cambridge; after rendering distinguished service to the King they were sometimes rewarded with the rank of bishop, or Master of the Rolls. As time went on these "civilians" tended to be laymen, but at first they were members of the Church.

One of the most important church courts was the Court of Arches in London, named after the arches which supported the steeple of the church of St. Mary-le-Bow, where the cases were heard. John Lydford was admitted as an advocate of that court in 1370. His official notebooks, discovered in 1960, give a vivid impression of the work of an ecclesiastical lawyer. He was, as the need arose, someone who would plead his client's cases, travel to Rome to negotiate for him and draft the necessary documents; someone who would sit as a judge when called upon to do so; and someone who would carry out important church duties.

When he became Archdeacon of Totnes, he had to carry out Visitations, which might be described as Administrative Inspections of the work of the Diocese.

The Bishop of Lincoln in 1236 gave his archdeacons strict instructions:

"Cause strict prohibitions to be published in every church, forbidding certain parishes to fight with their banners for precedence over other parishes, seeing that such fights are wont to result not only in quarrels but even in cruel bloodshed."

The Bishop of Ely, an hundred years later, issued much the same instructions, save that he said "this is wont to result not only in fights but in deaths."

Things were little better even at Exeter Cathedral in 1330. As a report showed:

"those who stand at the upper stalls in the choir, and have lights within their reach at mattins, knowingly and purposely throw drippings or snuffings from the candles upon the heads of the hair of such as stand at the lower stalls, with the purpose of exciting laughter and perhaps of generating discord, or at least rancour of heart and silent hatred among the ministers (which God forfend!) at the instigation of the enemy of mankind...''

Three years later things were little better there:

"We have learned from the lips of men worthy of credit, not without grave displeasure, that certain Vicars and other Ministers of our Cathedral, to the offence of God and the grievous hindrance of Divine Service, and to the scandal of our Cathedral Church itself, fear not irreverently and damnably to exercise disorders, laughter, gigglings, and other breaches of discipline, even with masks on their faces, by which obscene orgies of gesticulations they make vile the honour of the clergy before the eyes of the people.''

John Lydford was, for much of his life, the Official appointed by William of Wykeham to carry out his work. On several occasions between 1370 and 1375 he went to the papal court, then at Avignon, and obtained the Pope's permission to found New College, Oxford. When Winchester College was founded, in 1382, John Lydford's signature was on the foundation deed. He was an expert on heresy, and acted as an assessor at Blackfriars in 1382 when Wyclif and others were condemned.

A clerk was accused of stealing a horse, and was lodged in the Marshalsea prison; John Lydford went and claimed him on behalf of William of Wykeham, then Bishop of Winchester, and put him in the bishop's prison at Wolvesey Castle.

He also had the devil's own job with the wayward villagers of Hook, in Hampshire. People were not allowed to put up a chapel, still less one with a belfry, to summon people to church, unless they had official permission. It was a question of money and authority; the parishioners were under a duty to attend the mother church, and *pay the Rector their tithes*. This is the origin of Mothering Sunday; not a cuddly occasion for maternal love and a bunch of flowers, but a disciplinary occasion when the outlying parish had to attend the Mother church as rigorously as if on an inspection parade.

In 1377, William of Wykeham ordered John Lydford to visit the people of Hook, and tell them to stop using their chapel and belfry. This he did, but they appealed to Pope Gregory XI, who ordered the bishop to inquire into the matter.

Meanwhile, the people of Hook went on holding services, and even baptisms, which made things worse, although under the bishop's interdict. John Lydford punished them in the only way he could; he excommunicated them. The arguments went on for years, and perhaps the people of Hook were never brought to heel.

One of John Lydford's most colourful cases concerned a rogue named John Bentley, who was charged in 1370 with stealing a horse, and with two burglaries of houses and stealing linen and woollen cloth there; such luxury items were particularly attractive to thieves in those days.

Bentley claimed Benefit of Clergy. John Lydford collected him and lodged him in the bishop's prison. A panel of three was convened to hear the case: the Prior of Winchester Cathedral, the Abbot of Hyde, and John of Wormenhale, a Doctor of Laws, and Canon of Sarum.

It often happened that witnesses failed to come to such a hearing, and the criminal escaped justice. At any rate, John Bentley must have been set free, because some years later he killed a man, and took sanctuary in the parish church of Overton, twelve miles from Winchester. He was entitled to remain there for forty days, and could then go into exile rather than face trial; but some of the local inhabitants called him out of the church, and then dragged him from the churchyard. They put him into the stocks, for safe keeping, and then took him to Winchester gaol.

John Lydford was not concerned with John Bentley now, but with the culprits who violated his right of sanctuary, and an inquiry was ordered. The result is not known.

Those guilty of ecclesiastical offences were excommunicated, a serious blow to their rights, and might also be required to perform public penance. These sentences were not as strict as the common law would impose, but the Church was more concerned with the reformation of souls than with the physical punishment of bodies.

To quote another case from the same period: "William Freebody, who lived in the New Forest, cut off another man's virile members against his will, and this was the penance imposed upon him: that on a Sunday before next Whitsunday he should walk at the head of a procession round the parish church, with head bared, carrying a wax candle weighing half a pound, and offer it at the altar, after repeating the Hail Mary and the Lord's Prayer five times on his knees.''

Some people thought that such penalties were not enough. There was an extraordinary case in the reign of James I when a man dug up four bodies, and stole the winding-sheets. This led to a deep legal argument as to whether one could steal something which had been buried with a corpse. It was held that one could.

The man was charged with *petty* larceny of *one* of the sheets, a misdemeanour and less serious offence; he was convicted and whipped. But he was also charged with the *felonious* taking of the other sheets, which was a more serious charge carrying the death penalty. It also gave him the right to claim Benefit of Clergy, which he successfully did. As Coke noted in his report of the case, he thus escaped the sentence of death, which he well deserved.

Part of John Lydford's duties were to try cases, as his terms of appointment made clear:

"William, by divine permission Bishop of Winchester, to our beloved clerk, master John of Lydford, professor of civil and of canon law.

Trusting greatly in your faithfulness and overall diligence, we appoint you by these presents to hear each and every civil and criminal case, or civil and criminal case combined, coming validly within the jurisdiction of our city and diocese or otherwise...

Let pure justice therefore walk before you, and thus place your steps in the right way, that having God alone for your eyes, you shall with fair balance carry out what is right to each and every person."

He had to correct and deprive a vicar of his office who was accused of "spiritual incest" with two female parishioners. He also had to arrange for the excommunication of "two unknown sons of iniquity" who stole two old swans from the Thames near Bermondsey priory. He heard divorce cases, and claims for tithes.

He was the Archdeacon of Totnes when he died in 1407, after

thirty years loyal service to the church and to the law. He lived to see Bishop Bateman of Norwich found Trinity Hall, Cambridge, for the express purpose of training members of the clergy in the law.

> The doctors of Canon law and Civil law naturally gathered together when in London, and this is how Doctors' Commons came into existence. "Commons" is an old-fashioned expression for food at a common table. It certainly existed on January 8th 1496, when three men from Cambridge stopped there for a meal, perhaps as guests of one of its members. A Latin entry in their accounts says: "To breakfast in Paternoster Row with the Doctors of Arches, 22d."
>
> Breakfast was served immediately after the third stroke of the bell for High Mass in St. Paul's, and dinner on the stroke of five in the afternoon. The accommodation was not lavish to a fault, according to Andrew Ammonio, one of its members. He wrote in Latin to the great Dutch scholar Erasmus, inviting him to stay there: "The college is near St. Paul's, as you know. People say they live in the lap of luxury; I think it's more like dwelling in a sewer."

In 1511 Doctors' Commons had 113 members, most of them practising lawyers, with not a few abbots and bishops as well. When Thomas More joined them in 1514, he was already a bencher of Lincoln's Inn, and the Under-Sheriff of London.

In 1568, Doctors' Commons left their rather cramped accommodation and moved to Mountjoy House in Knightrider Street, then described as "a great house builded of stone, in the form of a college." It had a large garden.

Members were expected to dine there when in London. During the law terms, the Bible was read aloud at meal-times. One elderly doctor, who had been a member for almost sixty years, was given special leave of absence because of his great age and want of teeth.

Erasmus and More are merely the best known of the scholars who gathered there. There was John Colet, the Dean of St. Paul's; Polydore Vergil, the historian; and many others. They tended to favour the existing order of things rather than Luther's outrageous new teaching, or the translation of the Bible into English.

When Henry VIII came to the throne, many of them advised him upon his divorce problems. Some of them advised his wives, and it was whispered that their advice had rather more of Henry's interests at heart than that of their own clients.

The dissolution of the monasteries was vigorously helped by members of Doctors' Commons, such as John London, who persecuted Lutherans in Oxford. He imprisoned one of them in the steeple of New College till he died "half starved with cold and lack of food."

Another Lutheran escaped; London was seen in the streets "puffing, blustering and blowing like a hungry and greedy lion seeking his prey."

He often left the monasteries with nothing more than their bare walls. It was said he solicited the chastity of nuns; he was eventually proved to have committed perjury, and was made to ride through the streets on a horse sitting backwards and facing its tail.

He died in the Fleet prison.

Some members of Doctors' Commons are numbered among the saints. John Story persecuted the Protestants in Flanders, and was seeking them out on an English ship which had docked in Antwerp, when it set sail, forcing him back to England, where he was executed for treason. He is one of the Catholic martyrs.

Some of his colleagues steadfastly refused to accept the validity of Henry's divorces, or the succession of Queen Elizabeth, and lost their titles, their liberty, and sometimes their lives.

Henry Cole was a fervent Catholic, but did not show himself as such until Queen Mary's reign. The first that Cranmer knew of being burnt at the stake was Cole's preaching a sermon at him urging him to recant, and comparing him to the thief on the cross. It must have been intolerable; Bishop Jewel used to say that he never heard anyone rant in a more solemn and dictatorial manner than Cole.

Cole was later sent to Ireland with a commission from Queen Mary to suppress heresy. On the way there he stayed a night in Chester with the Mayor, whose wife stole the commission and replaced it with a pack of cards, the Knave of Clubs face uppermost. She was a Protestant. When Cole reached Ireland he found that he had, so to speak, been trumped, and before the Queen could send him a new commission, she died.

"And thus," says an historian, "God preserved the Protestants in Ireland."

Doctors'Commons had its less dramatic duties to perform. In 1571 the Rector of Old Alresford claimed that John Norton owed him tithes of ewes' milk. The pleadings were set out in Latin in numbered paragraphs, and the witnesses gave their evidence in writing. This is what one of the women in the village had to say:

> "Midsummer last she being requested did three or four times help milk Mr. Norton's ewes, which were at every of the said times in number about 7 score ewes or thereabouts, and that was the uttermost. And she further says that every of the said times aforesaid all the said ewes did give a gallon and a half of milk and no more, and that is all she can say."

As to the value of the milk:

> "Every gallon of the milk was worth a penny and no more, and that is all she can say."

A lawyer must have taken her story down in formal style, and told her where to put her cross at the end of it, because it is simply signed "Johanna Wene, her mark." Some member of Doctors' Commons decided the case on the evidence thus obtained. It may seem a cumbersome way of dealing with a simple case, but it is not the worst, and perhaps in days when travel was far from easy, by no means inconvenient.

This method was also used in Admiralty cases.

Doctors' Commons was not immune from politics. The Civil law derived from Rome, and John Lydford had often gone there for his clients. When Henry VIII abolished all appeals from English courts to Rome, that caused crises of conscience in his reign. Similar problems occurred in Elizabeth's reign, for few people could with impunity question her right to reign.

David Pole, the Bishop of Peterborough, did so, but he was treated with the respect due to "an ancient and grave person and very quiet subject." He was allowed to end his days on parole, rather than in the Tower.

Queen Elizabeth abolished the right of the clergy to be tried by their own courts for the lesser crimes. They had already lost the right to be tried by church courts for murder, felony and robbery. She was a strong enough queen to dissuade Parliament from questioning her royal prerogative. With James I, however, it was different. He had been born and bred to the Scottish law, which was very similar to the civil law, and so the members of Doctors' Commons naturally looked to him for favours. After all, the Civil law proclaimed that "whatever pleaseth the Prince is law."

Parliament was not in a mood to agree. The Stuarts had more liking for Romish practices than the Puritans could tolerate, and so members of Doctors' Commons found themselves joined in the struggle.

One of them, Sir Thomas Ridley, wrote a book called *A View of the Civil and Ecclesiastical Law* in 1607, which pleased James I so much that Sir Edward Coke, the leading common lawyer, thought that the common law was seriously threatened. Then another member of Doctors' Commons, Dr. Cowell, wrote *The Interpreter* to similar effect. These books told James precisely what he wanted to hear, that he was entitled to do what he liked, and that Parliament ought to bow and scrape to him.

Coke was stung by personal spite against Cowell, whom he called "Doctor Cowheel"; people said Cowell was far the better lawyer, and that Coke knew it. Besides, Coke's most famous book was his commentary upon Littleton's treatise on Land Tenure, and Cowell dared to say that Littleton's work was confused, absurd, and inelegant.

Coke would have resented it less had Cowell merely bitten him in the leg.

So Parliament impeached Cowell and had him arrested. His book was burnt by the public hangman. The common lawyers had a more powerful weapon against the members of Doctors' Commons, namely the writ of Prohibition, which banned ecclesiastical and Admiralty courts from hearing the sort of cases which had been their speciality for several hundred years.

Were Admiralty cases usually heard by the Admiralty courts? Obviously; but the common law courts claimed that Marseilles was in the parish of Marylebone, and therefore that a case which arose in French waters came within the common law jurisdiction.

Did a claim for tithes (of ewes' milk or otherwise) come under

Church jurisdiction? Certainly, because they were owed to the vicar. But the common lawyers now claimed that tithes came within their own jurisdiction.

This is how the writ of Prohibition worked. In 1601 a Mr. Harris was excommunicated, for some offence or other. A record of this sentence was sent to Mr. Harris' parish church, where the curate had the duty of reading it out. But the curate scratched out Mr. Harris' name, and inserted a Mr. Kenton's name instead. On hearing himself proclaimed in church as excommunicated, the outraged Mr. Kenton sued the curate for damages.

The curate tried to stop the common law court from hearing the case by issuing a writ of Prohibition against it, because he said that excommunication was entirely a matter of ecclesiastical law. So it was, but Mr. Kenton was seeking the more worldly remedy of damages, and the common law court was the proper place to do it. The curate failed.

The tug-of-war between the two systems of law was fiercest in cases of defamation. Certain decisions of the courts could be summed up in question and answer form:

Q: A man says, "Thou art an impudent brazen-faced Beelzebub." Should he be tried by the spiritual court?
A: No. "Beelzebub" may be a Biblical word, but the insult is general abuse.
Q: What about "You are an old rogue, and a thief, and I will prove you so, and a bastard-getting old rogue?" The last part clearly shows immorality.
A: True, but taken as a whole it is still general abuse, and belongs to the common law.
Q: Does the same apply to "You are a brandy-nosed whore, you stink of brandy"?
A: No. This is closer to immorality than intemperance, and therefore belongs to the spiritual court.

These cases gave clients ample scope for litigation, and in Stuart times people sued each other right, left and centre.

Two rich young heiresses came to London to pursue various lawsuits; one summer's evening they were visited by a young graduate from Oxford and his friend from the Middle Temple, whose attentions were so unwelcome that the girls emptied a chamber-pot over their heads. The young men fled.

The girls then pursued them with actions in the Star Chamber for

defamation

conspiracy

unlawful assembly, and

forcible entry.

These young Amazons even sought a writ of *ne exeat regno* ("he is not to leave the kingdom") to make sure the young men did not escape their clutches.

Any plaintiff with a genuine claim might find himself outflanked by a defendant bringing a counter-action, and if all else failed impeaching the plaintiff's witnesses by charging them with perjury, fraud, forgery and so on. Such actions could be prolonged almost interminably, and life was made almost intolerable for the opposite side.

Thomas Parry, of Carmarthen, had sixteen suits running at the same time concerning the rectory there and its tithes.

The professional lawyers, for their part, developed ingenious tactics known as Special Pleading; William Hudson's own masterpiece in this line was when, in 1614, he persuaded the Court that it "would not examine what coloured hens the said John Taughton hath bred, nor whether she hath bred any, nor whether a hen were bred of her own proper goods."

Complexity for its own sake killed off litigation, because cases became almost impossible to win.

The battle between the common lawyers and the civil lawyers raged on. The Puritans hated the Star Chamber as a court of intricacy and privilege. They also hated Archbishop Laud for his ritual practices.

He had an important part to play in divorce cases. Divorce petitions were petitions addressed to him personally, not only from rich people, but ordinary citizens as well.

A glover's wife complained that her husband nailed her foot to the ground, and beat her so ferociously that she was crippled. A felt-maker's wife complained of her husband's lewd practices, and a sailor's wife complained that after four days of marriage her husband went to sea, and stayed away for almost three years without paying her a penny. She claimed maintenance from him; after all, he was a gunner's mate, earning 28/- a month.

Laud referred all these cases to Sir John Lambe, the Dean

of Arches, who heard them within a few days. Modern justice is never as rapid.

The Puritans hated the crookedness of the church courts most of all; this discontent is said to have been one of the chief reasons for the departure of the Pilgrim Fathers for America.

People were constantly brought before the courts for minor offences. A man was fined 40 shillings at Canterbury for ploughing on St. Bartholomew's Day. Another man was fined 54 shillings for wearing a dirty ruff in church, and another for sitting in the same pew as his wife.

It is easy to sympathise with the defendant who was held in contempt of court by declaring "All the Court is caterpillars in the market place", and another who was summoned for not attending church and then, according to the words of the charge, "unreverently and contemptuously farted unto them and said, "Present *that* to the Court.""

As long ago as Chaucer the Summoners of the ecclesiastical courts had been blackmailing adulterers, and in Elizabethan times a number of apparitors (as summoners were then called) were put in the pillory for such offences.

The corruption even spread to the judges. Sir John Lambe took bribes, and pursued the Puritans ardently.

"I confess," he wrote to Laud in 1641, "I have been for the conformity of the church and for St. Paul's, and I have been a High Commissioner."

(The Puritans hated the Court of High Commission as much as the Star Chamber.)

"If they forgive me these offences," he continued, "which I account none, I will desire none of their favour for my bribery or corruption, nor for my injustice nor for any other of my grievous crimes."

Only the dissolution of Parliament saved him from being impeached; Sir John Bennet was not so fortunate. As Judge of the Prerogative Court he had to administer the estates of those who had died without making wills, and it was proved that he had found in favour of those who made him the biggest offer. He was fined £20,000, the same sum that had been imposed on Francis Bacon, Lord Verulam, the Lord Chancellor. It was an age in which corrupt judges were not altogether rare.

During the Civil War, Doctors' Commons suffered a blow

from which it never fully recovered. Its members were no longer employed in diplomatic missions. It barely existed during the struggle, with only a handful of members in residence, and very little work for them to do.

In 1660, when Charles II came to the throne, many ageing members of Doctors' Commons petitioned the King, explaining how they were imprisoned during the Civil War, and had their estates confiscated. Some of their claims were rewarded, but Doctors' Commons was no longer the powerhouse of talent it had been. Clergymen were no longer admitted there as members, and the work was largely confined to Admiralty cases and divorce.

In 1682 the Court of Arches was troubled with a Nonconformist, who showed so much zeal that he refused to take his hat off. A court official did it for him; the zealot sued him at common law, and recovered 20 marks in damages.

In this period there were still distinguished lawyers at Doctors' Commons, to be sure, but the mixture was rather more diluted. Sir Leoline Jenkins, for instance, was a famous Admiralty judge, and did much to modernise the law, with such measures as the Statute of Frauds. But nobody now remembers his colleague Sir Timothy Baldwin, a clerk in the House of Lords, who encouraged an Oxford apothecary to sell "coffee publicly in his house against All Souls College," perhaps the world's first coffee-shop.

At the same time William King was an Admiralty judge in Ireland, but probably not a very good one; he neglected his duties, and was described by Dean Swift as "a poor starving wit."

Pope recalled him too; "I remember Dr. King would write verses in a tavern 3 hours after he could not speak," because he was so drunk.

After the rebellion of 1745, a number of the rebels were tried and executed in Carlisle. Dr. Burn, another member of Doctors' Commons, had to advise the Bishop of Carlisle whether the rebels should be buried there. When a member of Doctors' Commons advised on a case, he often quoted authorities and decisions which were as old as church history itself. This was his advice:

"It is certain, that after execution, the bodies being at the king's disposal, are, for the public example, and for the greater terror unto others, never admitted to Christian burial; and this seemeth to have been the law of the church of England from the ancient canons."

He went on to quote the First Council of Braga in 563 AD, which forbade the burial service being read over those who died violently by their own hands. Then there was the ruling of Egbert, Archbishop of York in 750 AD, which added the clause "if they do it by the instigation of the devil", and the further reservation added in 960 A.D. in King Edgar's time, "if they do it *voluntarily* by the instigation of the devil." The final result was a merciful one; the rebels were given Christian burial.

In the 18th century some of the most interesting cases in Doctors' Commons arose from that great social evil which is now hopelessly overlaid with romance, the runaway marriage.

The daughter of a senior official of the Bank of England ran away to France at the age of 15, and married a man not openly in church, but privately, which was unlawful. The Romish priest who conducted the secret ceremony was paid five guineas for the deed, and the two witnesses to the ceremonies were ruffians; one had come from the galleys. The court had no hesitation in declaring the marriage invalid.

"This affair has been prejudicial to Miss Jones, who is a lady of good character," said the Judge. He awarded her £400 damages, and hoped she would find a man who deserved her better.

Before the Marriage Act 1753, a marriage performed without banns or a licence, performed at any hour, in any building, and without a clergyman, was yet valid.

There were many undesirable marriages inside the "Rules of the Fleet", as the notorious Fleet Street area was called. Francis Place, "the Radical tailor of Charing Cross," describes what it was like:

"In walking along the street in my youth, I have often been tempted by the question 'Sir, will you be pleased to walk in and be married?'

Along this most lawless space was hung up the frequent sign of a male and female hand conjoined with 'Marriages performed within' written beneath. A dirty fellow invited you in. The parson was seen walking before his shop, a squalid profligate fellow clad in a tattered plaid night-gown, with a fiery face and ready to couple you for a dram of gin or a roll of tobacco. Our great Chancellor Hardwicke put these demons to flight [by the Marriage Act 1753] and saved thousands from the misery and disgrace which would be entailed by these extemporary thoughtless unions."

Unusual marriage cases continued into the 19th century. Dr. Lushington, one of the most famous members of Doctors' Commons, appeared for the Earl of Portsmouth in a nullity case which had all the eccentricity of the Regency period. The Earl was pronounced insane in 1809, and was thereafter induced to marry the daughter of his keepers; it would have made her a wealthy heiress, if the court had not decided that he was incapable of the firm state of mind necessary for a valid marriage.

He used to flog his horses unmercifully, from a sadistic turn of mind.

Sir John Nicholl, the Dean of Arches, said: "As further proofs of his insanity may be added his propensity for bell-ringing, not, as sometimes young men will do, for exercise, but to share the money. [Bell-ringers received a modest wage.] This too by a nobleman of 40 at his own parish church, and near his own residence... A still more decided delusion of his own is that relevant to lancets, and tapes, and basins in women's pockets.."

In 1829 Dr. Lushington, as Chancellor of the Diocese of London, tried the case of *Hoile v Scales* in his consistory court. It arose from a vestry meeting at the church of St. Mary's, Stratford, Bow, when Mr. Hoile alleged that Mr. Scales was "quarrelling, chiding, and brawling by words."

Many affidavits were filed on both sides. The Hoilians swore that the ruffianly Mr. Scales resorted to fisticuffs, and uttered words which came as near to blasphemy as a man can do without actually blaspheming, namely "We want no lawyers here."

The Scalesites, on the other hand, stoutly maintained that their hero had reasoned with the overbearing Hoile in such terms as "Do go, you had better go", until he tried to push Mr. Scales into the fireplace.

Dr. Lushington, who was well aware that in parish squabbles a certain bias creeps in, sifted the evidence minutely, and gave judgment that Mr. Scales was not guilty of "brawling by words", but was guilty of "smiting." Accordingly, under an ancient statute, he passed upon him the terrible sentence of Excommunication and Costs.

Truth is often stranger than fiction, but the above case has a certain distinct literary flavour. The case was heard in 1829, a significant date; the young Charles Dickens, newly trained in shorthand, was reporting cases in Doctors' Commons that year.

Sure enough, the case appears in *Sketches by Boz* under the name of *Bumple v Sludberry*. Dickens writes as an eye-witness, so it is highly probable that he wrote the official law report as well. It is to be found in the English Reports, Volume 162, at page 958.

It is fascinating to compare the two versions. Sir W.S. Holdsworth, the great legal historian, gave a series of lectures on Dickens as a Legal Historian, and acknowledged his pictures of the law as being unrivalled for their accuracy. Dickens hated Doctors' Commons even more than he hated the delays and futility of Chancery proceedings; this is his description of the judge hearing the case:

"At a more elevated desk in the centre, sat a very fat and red-faced gentleman, in tortoise-shell spectacles, whose dignified appearance announced the judge..

The red-faced gentleman in the tortoise-shell spectacles had got all the talk to himself just then, and very well he was doing it, too, only he spoke very fast, but that was habit; and rather thick, but that was good living...

And when some very long and grave speeches had been made *pro* and *con*, the red-faced gentleman in the tortoise-shell spectacles took a review of the case, which occupied half an hour more, and then pronounced upon Sludberry the awful sentence of excommunication for a fortnight, and payment of the costs of the suit. Upon this Sludberry, who was a little, red-faced, sly-looking, ginger-beer seller, addressed the Court, and said, if they'd be good enough to take off the costs, and excommunicate him for the term of his natural life instead, it would be much more convenient to him, for he never went to church at all.

...We retired too - pondering, as we walked away, upon the beautiful spirit of these ancient ecclesiastical laws, the kind and neighbourly feelings they are calculated to awaken, and the strong attachment to religious institutions which they cannot fail to engender."

Dickens returned to the attack in *David Copperfield*, who was advised by Steerforth to practise there:

"On the whole I would recommend you to take to Doctors' Commons kindly, David," he said. "They plume themselves on their gentility there, I can tell you, if that's any satisfaction."

Dickens described the judge further as "an old gentleman whom, if I had seen him in an aviary, I should certainly have taken for an owl."

There may have been some error here. "The red-faced gentleman in the tortoiseshell spectacles" was not Dr. Lushington, but Dr. Jenner, the distinguished ecclesiastical lawyer whose son was Bishop Henry Jenner.

There was certainly plenty about Doctors' Commons which deserved criticism, but if Dickens had known Dr. Lushington better, he might have respected him not only as a man of great learning, but someone who was anything but owlish.

He was an MP for Great Yarmouth in 1806, and spoke out against the Slave Trade when it was by no means a fashionable thing to do. "At a Reform Dinner in 1821", the Dictionary of National Biography states, "he was said to have distinguished himself by the vigour or rather violence of his language."

He spoke in favour of civil rights for the Jews, and pressed for an inquiry into the Peterloo Massacre. He was in favour of ballots for elections to Parliament, instead of corrupt practices. He was against capital punishment, and was one of the junior counsel who appeared for Queen Caroline in her famous trial.

He was also one of the Select Committee who sat in 1840 to consider a new system of law courts, and revealed his own turn of mind in a question he asked:

"But is it not desirable that the Judge, provided he does not form an opinion upon the case, should be as accurately informed as possible, both as to the points of law likely to arise, and the evidence which is publicly discussed; will he not be able more easily to comprehend the arguments of Counsel from such previous preparation?"

John Hope, (Dean of the Faculty of Advocates in Edinburgh) replied "I would fairly say that I think that may be carried too far."

Sir John Nicholl, Dean of the Arches, and of the Prerogative

Court of Canterbury, which dealt especially with wills, was asked
"What are the duties of the Judge of the Prerogative Court?"
He replied:

> "They are extremely laborious; for all contested cases must come
> before him for his decision; those contested cases are principally
> questions of fact, and are involved in very large masses of written
> evidence, and the duties of the judge are to prepare himself for
> the decision upon that evidence, and the number of days exercised
> in Court are few in comparison to the number of days that the judge
> is occupied in preparing himself for the hearing of the case; I might
> say that I work three days at home for one day I work at Court."

It was the volume of paperwork, and the intricate procedure,
which especially attracted criticism. When a Royal Commission
reported upon the Ecclesiastical Courts in 1830, the days of
Doctors' Commons were numbered.

In 1857 the Probate and Divorce Courts were set up, and the
Admiralty Court in 1859. Most of the work of Doctors'
Commons was now open to the legal profession as a whole. The
building known as Doctors' Commons was sold in 1865, and
its proceeds divided among the remaining Doctors. The last of
them, the learned Dr. Tristram, died in 1912.

This was not, of course, the end of ecclesiastical law. As long
as there are churches there must be principles to govern them.
In 1869, for example, a furious dispute arose about the proposed
election of Frederick Temple as bishop of Exeter Cathedral.
His opponents claimed:

> "The said Frederick Temple is not a prudent and discreet man
> and is not eminent for his knowledge of the holy scriptures, and
> is not, and cannot be greatly or at all useful and necessary to the
> cathedral church of Exeter."

He was an advanced thinker; one of his books had been
reprinted eleven times, but his opponents urged that he should
publicly recant.

Sir Travers Twiss, the Vicar-General of the Archbishop of
Canterbury, heard these objections, but ruled that as Temple's
appointment was approved by the Crown, it was not for him
to disapprove of it.

"I think", he said, "it is their duty if they think the choice
of the Crown has been erroneous, to go to Her Majesty and

beseech her, or humbly request her, not to issue her mandate
for the confirmation of the election.''

Frederick Temple became Bishop of Exeter, and later
Archbishop of Canterbury; his son, Archbishop William
Temple, brought even greater lustre to the church.

In 1934 an attempt was made in Liverpool to wrench the clock
back to mediaeval times,

The Dean of Liverpool, Dr. Dwelly, was a man of great gifts,
but could be very prickly if rubbed up the wrong way. Bishop
David, who had his own decided views, was an ailing man;
Archdeacon Twitchett, who had a flair for organisation, was
sometimes supposed to be the power behind his throne. The
Bishop insisted that the Dean should install the Archdeacon as
a canon of the Cathedral, and the Dean resented it. He refused
to obey.

This was what his critics had been waiting for. Dr. Dwelly
had been so wicked as to allow Unitarian preachers into the
Cathedral pulpit; people had been burnt at the stake for less,
in the good old days.

The Bishop proceeded against the Dean for the ecclesiastical
offence of *scandalum magnatum* ''offence to the authorities'' and
the critics rubbed their hands. Dean Dwelly would be shown
up for all his iniquitous deeds and thoughts.

Mr. Gamon, on their behalf, rose to his feet before an
ecclesiastical tribunal presided over by Judge Chaloner Dowdall
KC, the Chancellor of the Diocese of Liverpool. He was
savouring in his mind the stinging onslaught he would make
upon the Dean, but his opponent interrupted him.

Vaisey KC, who appeared for the Dean and Chapter, was one
of the greatest lawyers of his day. It is not often that a member
of the Bar can almost with a single breath demolish a case, like
a house of cards, but this was one such occasion. Vaisey pointed
out that the Dean could only have disobeyed the Bishop if he
had been given official notice of the Bishop's command with
due warning; it had arrived only ten minutes before the service
at which the Archdeacon should have been installed, which was
far too late.

The point was unanswerable. The case collapsed, and the
Dean's critics retired in confusion. The *Guardian* commented
that the point at issue seemed singularly trivial, and the

Church Times wondered why the dirty linen had to be washed in public.

Shortly after this Bishop David went on holiday to Australia. When he returned, the Dean and Archdeacon were there to meet him, and hands were shaken amicably all round.

The Church is no longer the power in the land it once was; the current of ecclesiastical law is something of a backwater. It matters a great deal to the churches and congregations involved in a dispute, but the course of history is not greatly affected by questions as to whether candles which burn North Sea Gas should be allowed on the altar, nor (to quote from my own experience) whether it should be the widow or mistress of the deceased who should be entitled to erect the tombstone in his memory.

Are the ecclesiastical lawyers now, as Charles Dickens described Doctors' Commons, "a cosey, dosey, old-fashioned, time-forgotten, sleepy-headed little family party"?

I trust not. We gather together once a year from different parts of the country to discuss the latest developments, in a room where learned stiff-backed books rise high on shelves to the ceiling, and the noise of the outside world is never very intrusive.

SEVEN

Masques and Anti-masques

*Whereat and with the noise of our trumpets they seemed
greatly to rejoice, skipping, laughing, and dancing for
joy. And hereupon we made signs unto them, holding
up two fingers...*

Hakluyt's *Voyages*

The best time was always winter, for feasting and fun. In pagan times there was the Feast of Lights, to brighten dark days. Christmas replaced it, but the tradition was much the same, and lights on the Christmas tree proclaim it still.

In the Fourteenth century, when Prince Richard, son of the Black Prince, kept Christmas, a torchlight procession of mummers rode through London to greet him, some visored, and all richly arrayed. They came into the Prince's presence, and diced with him, making sure that he won jewels, a ring and a cup of gold; and after a banquet they all danced together.

In the Fifteenth century, the citizens of Dick Whittington's London had to hang a lantern outside their houses all Christmas through. Mumming and disguising had to be kept indoors, however, lest masked robbers stalk the streets.

In the 16th century, Henry VIII loved such fun. He dressed up as Robin Hood, and Katherine of Aragon was dutifully surprised; he and his courtiers on another occasion appeared as Turks, Russians and blackamoors. In the year 1512, for instance: "The king with ll others were disguising after the manner of Italy, called a 'mask'; a thing not before seen in England..."

This is said to be the first "masque" in England, though it meant little new:

"...They were apparelled in garments long and broad, wrought all of gold, with visors and caps of gold, and after the banquet [was] done these Maskers came in with 6 gentlemen disguised in

112

silk bearing staff torches, and desired the ladies to dance. Some were content, and some that knew the fashion of it refused, because it was not a thing commonly seen. And after they danced and communed together, as the fashion of the Mask is, they took their leave and departed, and so did the Queen and all her ladies."

"Masque" was the French spelling, and may seem ornate and perhaps pretentious; but that is not wholly inapt. It gave the Court a glitter intended to enhance the royal image; an important matter. Some such images are imprinted indelibly on our minds. Louis XIV was "Le Roi Soleil", and Elizabeth I the "Virgin Queen"; she posed for portraits in that very role. She naturally liked pageants which paid her the same tribute. In *Cynthia's Revels*, performed in 1600, Ben Jonson included the lovely lines beginning "Queen and huntress, chaste as fair."

She was pleased to have her chastity and beauty appreciated. But the words "Queen and huntress" would have been even more welcome to her successor, Anne of Denmark, Queen to James I. She esteemed herself highly as a huntress, though the only beast she ever shot was James I's favourite hound, and she killed it.

On her inaugural journey from Scotland to London, a masque was performed for her in the open air. It was midsummer; Ben Jonson's *Masque of the Fairies* enchanted her. From then on he was her favourite poet, and masques were a regular part of Stuart life. That very year, as a courtier wrote:

"both the king and the queen's majesty have a humour to have some masques this Christmas-time: the young lord and the gentlemen took one part, and the queen and her ladies the other. As there was great ingenuity in the ballet, Mr. Sanford had the drilling of the noble dancers."

She was a young and spirited girl, and took the fancy to appear in a masque black-faced. Ben Jonson wrote the *Masque of Blackness* for her, and so, on Twelfth Night 1605, she appeared at the Banqueting-House on a throne like a scallop-shell, black of face and hands, and arms as far as the elbows. When the Spanish Ambassador bent to kiss her hand, there were those who wished the black would rub off on him.

This was the plot: Twelve negresses, tired of their dark colour, see in the waters of an African lake a luminous face and

mysterious words which suggest that they should reach a
northern land whose name finished with the letters "..tania".
There they would receive the white colour they wished. The
Moon informs them - or they might never have guessed - that
the land is Britannia.

It is easy to curl the lip at folly such as this; Sir Dudley
Carleton thought it very unbecoming. "Who," he wrote, "can
imagine an uglier sight than a troop of lean-cheeked Moors?"

Nevertheless, the *Masque of Blackness* was an event of
immense artistic importance. It was the first collaboration of
the greatest production team the world has ever seen, Ben
Jonson as writer, and Inigo Jones as designer and producer.
They worked together for almost 30 years, and their masques
were astounding in their beauty and spectacle. It was such a
privilege to attend them that when the Spanish and Venetian
ambassadors were invited, and the French ambassador left out,
he was simply furious.

They can yield much pleasure for those prepared to see them
as they then appeared. But for those who are not - to use Ben
Jonson's words:

> "where it steps beyond their little, or (let me not wrong 'em) no
> brain at all... I am contented, these fastidious stomachs should leave
> my full tables, and enjoy at home their clean empty trenchers."

Barristers had an important part in the development of the
masque. They staged their own shows at Christmas from time
to time, electing their mock Prince and courtiers. Gray's Inn,
for instance, built on an old Port-pool of London, hailed its
Prince of Purpoole. Lincoln's Inn, built on a Grange, its Prince
de la Grange. The Inner Temple, an Emperor; the Middle
Temple, its Prince d'Amour.

It was not only fun, but good training. They reigned,
according to a handbook:

> "during the whole time of Christmas, and are to behave themselves
> in that Port (Bearing), Gravity, and Authority, as if they were in
> the King's house, that so thereafter they may know the better to
> behave themselves, in case they should be promoted to that
> honour."

Francis Bacon of Gray's Inn was equally aware of their value.
He wrote:

"If it be made a part of discipline, it is of excellent use... an art which strengthens the memory, regulates the tone and effect of the voice and pronunciation, teaches a decent carriage of the countenance and gesture, gives not a little assurance, and accustoms young men to bear being looked at."

A Prince of Purpoole was therefore someone of consequence, who would move in the highest circles. There is good reason to think that William Hatcliffe, who held that position in 1587, was the Mr. W.H. of Shakespeare's Sonnets. The first performance of *Love's Labour's Lost* may have been at Gray's Inn the next year, on Twelfth Night; and *Twelfth Night* itself was first performed at the Middle Temple in 1602. The link between the Inns and the arts was clearly very strong.

Shakespeare, as a professional actor, did not belong to an Inn of Court. Nor did Ben Jonson; his acquaintance with the law included being twice in prison for outspoken criticism of the authorities. When, in 1599, he dedicated *Every man out of his Humour* to "the Noblest nurseries of humanity and liberty in the Kingdom; the Inns of Court", he may have had his tongue somewhat in cheek. Yet almost all the other poets and dramatists who wrote masques were aspiring barristers, at least in name.

The poet Thomas Campion was at Gray's Inn with William Hatcliff, and took part in one of their productions. His masques give a particularly vivid picture of Inigo Jones' stagecraft. In *The Lord Hay's Masque* (1607) there was a pastoral scene. Campion describes it:

"Presently the Sylvans with their four instruments and five voices began to play and sing together the song following, at the beginning whereof that part of the stage whereon the first trees stood began to yield, and the three foremost trees gently to sink, and this was effected by an engine placed under the stage. When the trees had sunk... they cleft in three parts, and the Masquers appeared out of the top of them; the trees were suddenly conveyed away, and the first three Masquers were raised again by the engine."

This interesting effect was somewhat marred by the carelessness of one of the stage-hands, who had forgotten to attach some of the trees to the engine. In *The Lords' Masque* (1613) Campion had a scene in which the celestial stars appeared on the stage.

115

> Advance your choral motions now,
> You music-loving lights

began their song. Whereupon "the stars moved in an exceeding strange and delightful manner." Campion had never seen such superb stagecraft. "About the end of this song, the Stars suddenly vanished, as if they had been drowned among the clouds, and the 8 Masquers appeared in their habits, which were infinitely rich..."

The scene is the more magical because he does not explain its technique.

On February 18th 1613 a Masque at Court was presented by the Middle Temple joined with Lincoln's Inn; masques were often joint ventures. A splendid procession rode to Whitehall. First came 50 gentlemen, richly attired. Then came baboons, or rather boys dressed as such; in great ruffs, riding on asses and ponies, and throwing sweetmeats or confetti to the crowd. Next came the chief performers in the Masque, dressed in cloth of silver, embroidered with golden suns; and the rest of the cast besides, with torch-bearers so that none of the splendour should be lost.

The streets were thronged. When the performers entered Whitehall, the scene was already set for them in the royal Banqueting Hall. It was a huge artificial rock, almost as high as the hall itself, with crags and hollow places from which might appear all sorts of surprises, including baboons. On the top stood a silver temple bearing the words *Honoris Fanum*, the Building of Honour.

It would have been a wonderful thing to see. But we should probably not have seen it, thanks to female fashion of the time. Anne of Denmark was very fond of farthingales, skirts widened with whalebone hoops, rather like crinolines. She even wore them when out hunting. One farthingale is all very well, in its way; but several get in each other's way. Four or five ladies got stuck in the passage, and even in the Banqueting Hall they took up more than their fair share of the seating space. Next day a wrathful James banned the "impertinent garment" from Court, but the ladies took no notice whatever.

When he was called the wisest fool in Christendom, it was not a compliment paid him by any woman.

Yet James enjoyed the show. When it was over he made the Masquers kiss his hand, and gave them many thanks; "I never saw so many proper men together," he said, and feasted them royally.

It only remained to pay the bills:

"To Mr. Anton, mercer, for divers parcels of cloth of silver, £182 13s...
To John Dowland [and two others] for playing of Lutes, each one of them £2 10s...
To a porter for going home with horses, 1s..."

Two days later the Inner Temple and Grays Inn presented their masque. They set out on the Thames in a blaze of light, carried in the King's royal barge, and a line of others. Loud music went with them, and cannon salutes greeted them. They were welcomed by the Lord Chamberlain. Some were dressed as the Gods from Olympus; there were nymphs, Cupids, and stars; and country bumpkins for comic relief.

The masque was written by Francis Beaumont, of the Inner Temple. He cannot have applied himself very diligently to the law, for he had been writing plays since 1604 with John Fletcher.

Most masques had some message, if only the glory of the King and Queen, and the blessings their reign conferred; *The Triumphs of Peace* speaks for itself. *Britannia Triumphans*, in 1640, proclaimed the virtues of the Ship-money tax; not very successfully.

The Inner Temple's masque in 1613 was to honour an important marriage. In it Jupiter and Juno give their blessing to the marriage of the rivers Thames and Rhine. The parallel is obvious, though parallels (like the Thames and Rhine) never meet. In the Banqueting Hall, the scene was already set.

"The Fabric was a Mountain with two descents, and severed with two Traverses."

A Traverse is a curtain to be drawn back sideways, discovering something unexpected; "discover" as a stage direction heralds some new delight:

"*At the entrance of the King*, the first Traverse was drawn, and the lower descent of the Mountain discovered; which was the Pendant of a hill to the life, with divers boscages (woods) and Grovets upon the steep or hanging grounds there, and at the foot of the Hill,

117

four delicate Fountains running with water and bordered with sedges and water flowers..."

After some dialogue in verse between Mercury and Iris, "Four Naiads arise gently out of their several Fountains, and present themselves upon the stage" in charming sea-green costumes, with little bubbles of crystal powdered with silver to look like drops of water. They dance.

Mercury soon ushers in another favourite device. The Hyades are the five stars of the constellation Taurus, said to bring rain; they have not yet appeared on stage, but Mercury speaks to the sky:

> You maids, who yearly at appointed times,
> Advance with kindly tears, the gentle floods,
> Descend, and pour your blessing on these streams.

Descend: the key word. Inigo Jones built a framework around his stage, from the top of which a platform was lowered into view. It was always a cloud, but a cloud with side-panels to be drawn aside, so that from out of the cloud personages could appear. Thus:

> "Five Hyades descend softly in a cloud from the firmament, to the middle part of the hill, apparelled in sky-coloured Taffeta robes, spangled like the Heavens, golden Tresses, and each a fair Star on their head."

They danced, then Cupids and Nymphs, and finally four Statues from Jove's altar. Many of Inigo Jones' designs for these masques still exist; most of the texts; and some of the music. But the choreography is only preserved in a phrase or two.

When the Statues entered, the music changed to soft oboes and cornets, suitably slow; "and the Statues placed in such several postures, sometimes all together in the centre of the dance, and sometimes in the four utmost Angles, as was very graceful besides the novelty."

The audience loved it, and James called for an encore, "but one of the Statues by that time was undressed." He was probably changing into his next costume as a country bumpkin.

This was one of the anti-masques, an essential part of the

entertainment, as a contrast to the main theme. It was an opportunity for boisterous humour; the rustic dance somehow included two baboons. It provided "such a spirit of Country jollity as can hardly be imagined, but the perpetual laughter and applause was above the music."

Every masque ended with "Revels", when the leading actors in the masque, who were sometimes the King and Queen, danced with the audience. It was the climax of the evening. In this particular masque they danced "Galliards, Durets, Corantoes &c." And the masque was over.

It ended in applause and joy. But the Inns of Court were to produce an anti-masque writer of a very different kind. He became the most prolific author of his age; he had a sallow, saturnine complexion with a narrow face; some said he looked like a witch. His name was William Prynne.

His was not a subtly persuasive style, coaxing the reader to accept his arguments, but like a steamroller, crushing everything before him with the weight of quoted authorities. His titles are enough to make the heart sink:

The Quakers unmasked
A Gag for long-hair'd Rattle-heads
Health's Sickness: or a compendious and brief discourse proving the drinking and pledging of healths to be sinful and ... unlawful unto Christians.

It was his habit of quoting countless chapters and verses at the side of the page which defied the reader to hold any different opinion, and earned him the nickname "Marginal" Prynne.

He was only 24 years of age, a member of Lincoln's Inn not yet called to the Bar, when he started to write "*Histriomastix*, The Player's Scourge." He was not the first Puritan to despise stage plays, but he scourged them in a book 1000 pages long. He was given a licence to print it in 1630, and it appeared at Christmas in 1632. A copy of it lay in Lincoln's Inn library, and nobody there thought it objectionable until 6 weeks later.

In 1633 there was a Royal masque called *The Queen's Pastoral*. One of its aims was to improve the Queen's English, since Henrietta Maria preferred to speak French. Mr. Wingate, a learned barrister from Gray's Inn, was appointed to coach her in her lines. She complained bitterly; her part was as long as a whole play, she said, and might last eight hours.

Ben Jonson was not prepared to write it, because he had broken permanently with Inigo Jones two years before, and all because his name was given second place on a title page. So it was written by one Walter Montague, and lacked merit.

But William Prynne's anti-masque certainly made an impact. Archbishop Laud pointed out, with relish, that his *Histriomastix* scourged not only the acting profession. Women often played courtesans in anti-masques, and even in classical scenes Inigo Jones' designs show nymphs and goddesses bare-breasted. But Prynne also stated that dancing "even in Queens themselves and in the very greatest persons" was "always scandalous and of ill report among the Saints of God."

The Inns of Court were not at all abashed by this. They proceeded to mount the most expensive, and perhaps the most suggestive, masque ever seen. It was called *The Triumph of Peace*, by James Shirley of Gray's Inn. It has been said of him that if he had been alive today he would have been writing for the glossy magazines. Shirley sarcastically dedicated one of his works that year to Prynne; it was called *The Bird in a Cage*, which proved prophetic.

The Triumph of Peace was presented, as usual, at the Banqueting-House at Whitehall, and Inigo Jones surpassed himself:

> "The curtain being suddenly drawn up, the scene was discovered, representing a large street with sumptuous palaces, lodges, porticoes, and other noble pieces of architecture, with pleasant trees and grounds... Over all was a clear sky with transparent clouds, which enlightened all the scene."

Enter several cheerful characters.

FANCY: How many anti-masques have they? Of what nature?
...Give me a nimble anti-masque.
OPINION: They have none, sir.
FANCY: No anti-masque! I'd laugh at that, i'faith.

Of course there were anti-masques; lots of them. There was

a tavern scene in which a bawd and two wenches "express their natures." There was the woodland glade with four Nymphs, and three Satyrs did "attempt their persons"; only one Nymph escaped.

The most charming episode began with cries of panic behind the scenes, followed by a ghastly crash, as if the stage machinery was falling to pieces; after which the stage hands came in and danced a fegary.

At the end of the performance the Queen and her ladies danced with the masquers until morning, when they banqueted. She was so delighted with the whole entertainment that it was re-staged for her 10 days later.

Prynne's point of view had some justification, but not in the eyes of the law.

He was brought before the Court of Star Chamber and fined £5000; this colossal sum can be compared with the cost of the masque, £21,000. He was also sentenced to the pillory at Westminster, where he had to stand with a paper on his head admitting his offence, and have one ear cut off; then to Cheapside where the other ear was cut off. This must have been humiliating, to say nothing of the pain. Perhaps the hardest thing to bear was that a cartload of his beloved books had to be sold to pay the fine.

His room in Lincoln's Inn, (Garden Court) first staircase, second floor up), was given to another tenant, and he was expelled from the Inn. He was sent to the Tower.

It was not enough to silence him. From the Tower he wrote more pamphlets, attacking the Bishop of Norwich, amongst others.

Prynne's chief enemy was Archbishop Laud, whose attempts to break away from the austerity of church services he saw as sheer popery.

He was brought before the Star Chamber; Sir John Finch, the Chief Justice, noticed his appearance.

"Is this Mr. Prynne?" he asked. "I had thought Mr. Prynne had no ears, they being adjudged to be cut off by the sentence of this Court. But methinks he hath ears..."

So he had, though now somewhat curtailed.

"My Lord," said Prynne, "there is never a one of your honours but would be sorry to have such an ear-mark, and to have your ears cropped as mine are."

"What doth he say?" said Sir John.

Prynne said it again.

"In good faith, my Lords, he is very saucy!"

Prynne was fined a further £5000, his ears were savagely hacked off in the pillory, and he was branded on the cheeks, as all Seditious Libellers were, with the letters SL. Prynne said they should stand for *Stigmata Laudis*, or "Laud's Stamps", as he put it.

He was sent to prison again, without books, pen or ink. During the next few years he produced a quantity of verse which has been tactfully described as having none of the qualities of poetry, save that of rhyme. But when Parliament prevailed over Charles I in 1640, they ordered his release. He was given back his room in Lincoln's Inn, and marched in a triumphal procession into London. He wore a long rusty sword which tripped him up as he ascended the steps into Parliament, causing much merriment.

During the years that followed Prynne prosecuted Archbishop Laud with the greatest vehemence; he was executed. Yet Prynne was not as extreme as some of those who marched under Cromwell's banner. The Levellers would have abolished the Monarchy; Prynne disagreed, and brought his literary steamroller against them in *The Levellers levell'd*.

At the Restoration, therefore, Prynne was not out of Royal favour. The golden age of masques was over, though some were still presented.

"I am glad," wrote someone in 1662, "of his Majesty's dining at Lincoln's Inn with the Prince de la Grange; to have some comedy after so many tragedies."

Prynne had no comments to make.

Charles II appointed him to be Keeper of the Records in the Tower. He was as happy as a sandboy, grubbing about amidst ancient parchments with his obsessive passion for detail. If any young man came to consult him about research, he was particularly pleased.

There let us leave him, an angular peg snug in his angular hole.

EIGHT

The Bar Clerk's Tale

Little is known about barristers' clerks.
John A. Flood. *Barristers' Clerks*

Samuel Romilly was rushed off his feet. Ten years earlier he had been called to the Bar, and decided to go the Midland Circuit. He chose Beckers, the husband of a servant girl who had been with his family a long time, to be his clerk, valet and groom. He went the Circuit seven or eight times, and much good Beckers did him. He often got drunk, and was hopeless at copying papers for his master. During that period Romilly hardly got a brief.

The time came when he realised that he would do far better to stay in London. Ten years after his call to the Bar, his fortunes had completely changed. He wrote to one of his friends:

"Lincoln's Inn November 22, 1793
Dear Dumont,
    You would perhaps set some value on this letter, if you knew how many things I have to do at the moment I write it. And what excuses I must make tomorrow to some stupid attorney for having devoted to you the time which I ought to employ upon an appeal in Chancery."

Cicero would have known exactly how he felt. He wrote a similar letter to his brother, late in August of the year 54 BC:

"When you get a letter from me in the hand of one of my *secretaries*, you can reckon that I didn't have a minute to spare; when you get one in *my own*, that I did have *one* minute! For let me tell you have I have never in my life been more inundated with briefs and trials, and in a heat-wave at that, in the most oppressive time of the year. But I must put up with it."

He had many things in common with Samuel Romilly,

123

but one which is never considered is the role of the clerk.

There have always been different kinds of clerk. Even in Rome, shorthand writers were used to taking down speeches word for word. They were slaves, and were sent to such places as Egypt to learn the mysteries of the Art. Cicero's speeches, which still exist in large quantities, were re-dictated by him after his cases were over, and have become classics of literature.

He must have revised them carefully, because they do not suffer from clumsy transcripts.

Quintilian, another highly successful advocate, complained bitterly about shorthand writers. They mangled his speeches almost beyond recognition, and sold them for publication without paying him! Eighteen centuries later, the shorthand-writers were no better, because they insisted on putting all the verbs into the present tense. Thomas Erskine, who prided himself upon his precise use of English, was disgusted with them.

"If the speaker is speaking of a transaction as ancient as the Flood, it is still the present tense," he wrote: "Noah ENTERS into the Ark."

Edmund Burke, in the same era, was astonished to find himself quoted as having said in the trial of Warren Hastings, "Virtue does not depend on *climaxes and trees.*"

It suggests a sultry afternoon in the Forest of Arden. What he really said was, "Virtue does not depend on *climates and degrees*"- meaning that it was not affected by fluctuations in temperature.

The original Bar clerk is not to be found among shorthand-writers, nor among the Roman "scribes", a professional class of civil servant not unlike our Permanent Parliamentary Under-Secretaries.

Perhaps his fore-runner was present when Servius Galba, another excellent advocate, prepared himself for the final day of an important case.

On that day, Cicero tells us, someone went early to Galba's house to remind him of the hearing, and to escort him to the court. He was in a vaulted room with his slaves, dictating notes to them right, left and centre. He left the room with a flushed face and flashing eyes, ready for the case, and fought it magnificently; but the slaves were completely worn out.

124

Cicero, perhaps the busiest advocate in ancient Rome, must have needed a skilled slave to arrange dress-rehearsals with key witnesses before they gave evidence in court. This was thought perfectly proper, but "planting" one's own witnesses amongst those of one's opponent, so that he called someone whose evidence ruined his case, was frowned on.

That slave, in arranging his master's career, comes nearest to a modern Bar clerk. Licinius, the clerk to Gracchus, another famous orator, made it his duty to watch his master's performance.

He stationed a man with a little ivory flageolet at the side of the court. If Gracchus seemed to be flagging, the man blew a low tootle; if he got over-excited, and risked straining his high-pitched voice, a shriller tootle, carried a different warning. Cicero often heard this happen.

In Norman England, it is not possible to say precisely what the clerks did.

The first advocates were certainly members of the clergy, because "clerk", "cleric" and "clergy" are all the same word. Even the Lord Chancellor was once the King's law-clerk. The advocates' clerks must have been monks, recording their masters' affairs as diligently as if they had been priory accounts, sacred manuscripts, or chits for wine in the cellar.

As junior servants they would accompany their masters wherever they went throughout the land. Perhaps they were like Samuel Romilly's clerk, acting as valets, grooms and clerks for their masters.

In 1302 John de la Chapele, an advocate with a retainer from Shap Abbey, sued the abbot for arrears of its payment, and quoted in his claim the terms of his contract. He had to represent the Abbey when called upon to do so, and was allowed to stay there when he wanted, with decent food and accommodation. He could bring two servants and their horses with him, and they had to be treated as well as if they belonged to the cellarer himself!

It shows where the Abbey's priorities lay.

What did his clerks and servants have to do? An account-book for the year 1378 quotes prices for stationery:

2 papers covered with red leather

13 quires of paper
7 leaves of paper
6 skins of parchment
2 pencases
2 pairs of pencases with inkhorns
18 horns called inkhorns [ordinary cow's
horns, with stoppers for the ink]

His clerk must always have been ready for his master's dictation with a good piece of paper or parchment, a sharpened pen, and a well-filled inkhorn.

William Caxton's *Dialogues in French and English*, "A Book for Travellers" published in about 1483, with a character sketch of life in the 14th century, suggests how a writer dealt with his materials:

> "Jose the parchment-maker sold me a skin of parchment that was all flawed, and a covering of franchin shaved on one side, which was worth nothing; I couldn't write on it. Go fetch me a pumice and the best paper, my penknife and my shears; I wish to write a love-letter and send it to my girl friend."

The so-called "Black Books of Lincoln's Inn" are the earliest surviving records of life in one of the Inns of Court. In 1441 only the Benchers were allowed to have a servant who could eat in the Inn, for 14d a week; he is described by the Latin name *valettus* and may indeed have been only a valet or personal servant.

In Tudor times it is difficult to learn much about Bar clerks, because few people were writing chatty letters like Cicero, and the great Diarists had not yet been born. Even *The Paston Letters*, a mine of information about a wealthy Norfolk family, two of whom were members of the Bar, have nothing to say about their clerks.

But some of them worked at St. Paul's along with the serjeants and some apprentices. In 1406 there is a record of Sjt. Tremaine and an apprentice giving counsel there on a conveyancing question; in 1465 the Carpenters' Company note in their accounts a fee "paid at St. Paul's in a plea against Puncheon's wife."

To clinch it, the accounts for Canterbury in 1500 refer to a payment made "the same afternoon to the said Mr. Holton in the cloister at St. Paul's when he corrected the copy, 3s 4d. Item to his clerk there, 12d.'' This is the first specific mention of any barrister's clerk which has yet to come to light.

In 1520, however, it was ordered in Lincoln's Inn that the Benchers should be allowed to have two clerks "boarding at yeoman's commons", at the cost of 14d and 18d per week respectively; and the barristers were allowed some such privileges, too. The announcement read:

> "Each Utter Barrister may have one clerk at yeoman's commons, if he wish, at 14d a week. Hereafter no one shall have any servant in commons at yeoman's commons except the said servant be a clerk, lettered and of honest appearance and condition, under a penalty of paying 2s a week for the commons of every unlettered servant, and 12d for half commons.''

A similar ruling in 1538 refers to "any clerk, servant, page, or lackey,'' which puts clerks in the menial category in which they were certainly then regarded.

Some of them abused their positions as much as the other servants in Lincoln's Inn. In 1602 it was found that the brewers were giving short measure; the kitchen weights were dishonest, and the beer was of cheaper quality than had been paid for; the Steward's practices with the beef and butter were open to question, too. Furthermore, "some of the Bencher's clerks were fetching breakfasts in their masters' names,'' - pretending to take them to their chambers - "when their Masters are in Hall at breakfast.''

Perhaps the clerks were having a little breakfast of their own.

Clerks no doubt looked after the income and books of their masters, but Francis North, later Lord Keeper Guilford, used to do it himself. Roger North wrote:

> "His skull-caps which he wore when he had leisure to observe his constitution, as I touched before, were now destined to lie in a drawer to receive the money that came in be fees. One had the gold, another the crowns and half-crowns, and another the small money. When these vessels were full they were committed to his friend (the Hon. Roger North) who was constantly near him, to tell out the cash and put it into bags according to the contents; and so they went to his treasurers Blanchard and Child, goldsmiths at Temple-Bar.''

These accounting methods were sophisticated indeed compared to those of the frugal Serjeant Earl, who worked on the principle: "I get as much as I can, and I spend as little as I can; and there is all the account I keep."

From the days of John Scott, later Lord Eldon, we hear much more of the clerk's role. When he rode the Northern Circuit in 1775, his clerk was certainly not experienced. Lord Eldon wrote in his *Anecdote Book:*

> "At last I hired a horse for myself and borrowed another for an inexperienced youth who was to ride behind me with my saddlebags. But I thought my chance was gone for, having been engaged in discussion with a travelling companion, on approaching the assize town I looked behind, but there was no appearance of my clerk and I was obliged to ride back several miles, till I found him crying by the roadside, his horse at some distance from him, and the saddlebags still further off; and it was not without great difficulty that I could accomplish the reunion between them, which he had in vain attempted. Had I failed too in this undertaking, I should never have been Lord Chancellor."

He was at Durham when - his clerk being absent - a highwayman burst into his room and demanded the return of the two guinea fee he had paid him, on the grounds that he had not earned it. (Scott had secured his acquittal with effortless ease).

"Sirrah", exclaimed John Scott, seizing the poker, "although you escaped today, when you deserved to be hanged, you shall be hanged tomorrow for attempting to rob me, unless you instantly depart."

Luckily at that moment his clerk came in, and the highwayman slunk off.

It is the duty of the clerk to insulate his master from malefactors. Frank Lockwood QC defended Charlie Peace, the murderer. Unsuccessfully. A few weeks later, his clerk announced that some of the Defendant's relatives had come to see him. He was naturally alarmed.

"We've only come," the widow said, "to tell you how glad we are that you did not get him off!"

One of the duties of a clerk on circuit was to secure lodgings for his master. It was contrary to the etiquette of the Bar for a young man to gallop ahead of his elders and betters, and secure the best accommodation. The youngest had to wait their turn.

John Scott and Jack Lee were returning to Newcastle from Lancaster Assizes, and decided to spend the night at Kirkby Stephen. Jack Lee thought of sending his servant - his clerk, presumably - ahead of them to book their beds, but the long-standing tradition militated against it. Whilst dining somewhere along the way, two strangers asked where they would recommend them to stay.

They named an alehouse, where the strangers spent a bad night. Scott and Lee went to a much better Inn.

Scott married Elizabeth Surtees, of Newcastle; one of her family was R.S. Surtees, the sporting writer, whose novel *Handley Cross*, published in 1844, introduced John Jorrocks to the British public. In the book Charles Stobbs, a newly-called barrister, joins a set of chambers in Lincoln's Inn Square.

Bill Bowker, the fictional clerk (who had no connection with the famous Arthur Bowker, clerk to Marshall Hall and Norman Birkett) asks if he has found any lodgings. Charles replied that he had just taken lodgings in Hadlow Street.

"What, at the feather-maker's?" inquired Bowker, balancing on one leg.

"No," replied Charles, "at Mrs. Hall's a widow woman's, number twenty something."

"I know her!" exclaimed Bill, resuming both feet, "left-hand side of the way, going up - D-----d bitch she is, too (aside); pawned her last lodger's linen - Well, perhaps you'll bear *us* in mind, in case she don't suit."

Barristers certainly had to be content with humble lodgings on circuit. James Parke wrote to his wife in 1819 from "Mrs. Barlow's, York":

"I have taken my abode upstairs in the back room where I breakfasted this morning very sumptuously on some of the potatoes (which are nearly done and what are not eaten are spoiling) and some of the new marmalade."

James Boswell, riding the Home Circuit in July 1786, was also anxious to find somewhere cheap:

"So drove with my servant in a postchaise through Dartford and Rochester to Maidstone... I got small quiet lodgings at Mr. -------'s, the Organist's".

This was the year in which he got his first brief, thanks to a friendly attorney and a Bar clerk:

"*February 22nd*. This day in the Court of King's Bench Mr. McDougal, clerk to Mr. Irving, of the Inner Temple and connected with Mr. Currie, an Attorney, handed me my first brief, with two guineas. Captain Grigor Farquharson and others were prosecuting of an indictment for perjury against Thomas Jackson; and Farquharson, when a *writer* at Edinburgh had employed me, I suppose, suggested me on this occasion. I was very happy to get business the second week I was at the Bar, when many people may stand for years unemployed. I had a boyish fondness for my first brief and fee, and put up the guineas as medals."

Boswell would have done better at the Bar if he had kept his nose closer to the grindstone, and his mouth further from the bottle. One can guess how Mr. McDougal the Bar clerk felt, when his attempts to help him only a fortnight later were wasted:

"*Friday 3rd March*. I did not attend the sitting at Guildhall after this Hilary term. I am sorry I did not, as I should have learnt a good deal, and as I should have had at least one brief, as Mr. McDougal, clerk to Mr. Irving, informed me; for an acquaintance of his wanted to employ me, and did not know where I was to be found. The truth is that there is very little room for counsel at Guildhall, and besides I was as yet at a very great distance while in Portman Square. I shall henceforward attend at Guildhall."

Three weeks later Boswell rode the Northern Circuit. He was again lucky to be given a brief; barristers often went on circuit for years without getting one:

"*Friday 31st March*. Had a motion handed to me in Court with half a guinea by Mr. Cross of Preston, Pronothary of the Court of Lancaster. Bolton [a colleague at the Bar] had made me acquainted with him, and I suppose I owed my being thus launched on the Circuit to him."

His most famous brief of all would never have escaped the vigilance of a modern Bar clerk, with an eagle eye:

"*Thursday 6th April*. Last night a feigned brief had been left at my lodgings."

This was the brief, faked by some colleagues on the Circuit, which instructed him to apply to the Court for a writ "*quod adhesit pavimento.*'' ''because he stuck to the pavement'' the previous night, when he was lying there dead drunk. Boswell had never heard of such a thing, nor had the astonished judge, till a member of the Circuit explained the joke. The rest of Boswell's legal career was marked by failure and self-pity, in a profession which calls for the utmost courage and stamina.

Few great men at the Bar escaped the agony of waiting for the clerk to bring them their first brief. The future Serjeant Ballantine described how he began his legal career in the grimy edifice of 5 Inner Temple Lane. ''A mischievous little urchin cleaned my boots, and was called a clerk,'' he wrote. The chambers boasted on pair of sheets, a teapot, a coal-scuttle, and not much more.

A local tradesman finally refused him further credit even for pats of butter and penny rolls, but a solicitor's clerk arrived from heaven, bringing him three half-guinea motions, and the *cash in hand!*

That night he squandered several shillings in a wild carouse. He went to the local chop-house, and had not only two helpings of roast saddle of mutton, but more portions of jam tart than it is decent to describe.

His clerk can have been little help to him in starting his career.

Frederick Thesiger, the future Lord Chancellor Chelmsford, was in a more thriving set of chambers when he received his first half-guinea motion. One attorney was well-known there; he would storm in and complain that his pleadings were not ready. Still, he had a set of papers for young Thesiger, the very day after he had been called to the Bar, and he paid for them with a very crooked half-guinea.

Thesiger did the papers, and waited for more work from that attorney. It never came. The half-guinea was, after all, exceedingly bent.

The day had not yet dawned when Bar clerks were treated almost as emperors in their own chambers; their role was still a subordinate one, however great or lowly their masters were.

Some of them were clearly responsible, trusted men. In June 1752 there was a fire which destroyed Nos. 10 and 11 New Square, Lincoln's Inn. Mr. Wilbraham lost all his papers, including the title deeds to an estate of great value. Mr. Pickering, his clerk, lost not only £1100 in money and bank notes of his own, but securities to the value of a further £30,000. He was clearly a person of standing. The *Gentleman's Magazine* wrote:

> "When the fire was reported, most of the watch were asleep or drunk, and the wife of an upholder [upholsterer, perhaps] in Carey Street, whose husband left his bed to assist the sufferers, hanged herself in his absence."

Her mysterious fate is not explained. The fire had a serious effect upon Chancery work; the Lord Chancellor suspended all proceedings in that Court. The other losses were not quite as serious as had been feared; Mr. Pickering was able to "re-establish" most of the bank notes, which in that age were not printed mechanically, but individually drawn and recorded.

Other clerks were less methodical or respected. Sjt. Ballantine described Mike Prendergast, a shambolical figure who always arrived late for a case, and never understood it. He appeared one day at a London Sessions after his case had been called on.

He turned to his clerk. "Where's me brief, Frederick?" he inquired in some agitation.

"I gave it you this morning at breakfast, sir," said the clerk; "you put it in your coat pocket, sir."

Prendergast delved into the depths of his overcoat pocket, and retrieved not only the brief, which consisted of a single greasy sheet of paper, but also a slice of buttered toast.

I have sometimes had instructions as skimpy as that, but without the buttered toast.

Barristers were sometimes slovenly almost to a fault; but a century ago it was regularly true of their clerks.

Sir Harry Poland once pointed out to Huddleston (later Baron Huddleston, an Exchequer judge) that his clerk was remarkably dirty, and would be much improved if he would wash his face.

Huddleston agreed. "The trouble is," he said, "that I share my clerk with another barrister, so that only half of him belongs to me, so to speak."

Poland was not at all abashed. "Then why not get him to wash *your* half of his face?" he suggested.

Dirt was the accepted quality of legal premises. As early as 1729 Lincoln's Inn Fields were described as "a very receptacle for rubbish, dirt and nastiness of all sorts." They were no better a century later, when Charles Dickens was in the Temple. In *The Uncommercial Traveller* he described the squalor common both to solicitors' and barristers' chambers.

"At one period of my uncommercial career," he wrote, "I much frequented another set of chambers in Gray's Inn-square."

They belonged to the solicitors Messrs. Ellis and Blackburn, for whom he worked as a clerk in the year 1827, when he was only 17 years old. "Now," he continued:

> "they were so dirty that I could take off the distinctest impression of my figure on any article of furniture by merely lounging upon it for a few moments; and it used to be a private amusement of mine to print myself off - if I may use the expression - all over the rooms. It was the first large circulation I had."

He was also impressed by the number of insects which were definitely red, and certainly not ladybirds, which inhabited the curtains. This insect-colony was due more to the laundresses than the clerks themselves.

He was not alone in his opinion of legal premises. Anthony Trollope, whose father was a Chancery barrister, described in his novel *Orley Farm* a set of Chambers in Old Square, Lincoln's Inn. The Square had always been dingy, even when it was first built; but now it seemed more dingy than ever. So did Mr. Furnival's chambers:

> "This waiting-room was very dingy, much more so than the clerk's room, and boasted of no furniture but eight old leathern chairs and two old tables. It was surrounded by shelves which were laden with books and dust, which by no chance were ever disturbed. But to my ideas the most dingy of the three rooms was that large one in which the great man himself sat... There were heavy curtains to the windows, which had once been ruby but were now brown; and the ceiling was brown, and the thick carpet was brown, and the books which covered every portion of the wall were brown, and the painted woodwork of the doors and windows was of a dark brown."

Laundresses had enjoyed a special reputation in the Inns of Court for several centuries. In Queen Elizabeth's reign it was ordered that no laundresses, "nor women called victuallers", should enter the gentlemen's chambers of this society, unless they were full forty years of age. Nor were they to send their maid-servants, *of what age soever*, into the said gentlemen's chambers.

But at that time they seem to have been reasonably paid. Until 1602 they could not only charge 2d each time they brought clean linen, but were allowed to collect, on each visit to Lincoln's Inn at least, twelve loaves of bread, and two quarts of beer at breakfast, one gallon at dinner, and another at supper.

There was hardly any time when the Inns of Court were safe from feminine temptation; in Gray's Inn women were not even allowed into the chapel during the sermon.

But the laundresses of the Temple were a very special breed. As Sjt. Ballantine wrote about his earliest days at the Bar, at 5 Inner Temple Lane:

"My establishment was limited. I shared with some half-dozen other aspirants to the Bench what, in Temple parlance, is called a laundress, probably from the fact of her never washing anything. I fancy that her principal employment was walking from my chambers to the pawnbroker's, and then to the gin-shop. At the end of a short period my property, never very extensive, was reduced to little more than a pair of sheets, a teapot, and a coalscuttle, over which last it pleased Providence that she should tumble downstairs, and the injuries then sustained relieved me from her future attendance."

Dickens wrote even more emphatically:

"The genuine laundress is an institution not to be had in its entirety out of and away from the genuine Chambers. Again, it is not denied that you may be robbed elsewhere. Elsewhere you may have - for money - dishonesty, drunkenness, dirt, laziness, and profound incapacity. But the veritable shining-red-faced shameless laundress; the true Mrs. Sweeney - in figure, colour, texture, and smell, like the old damp family umbrella; the tip-top complicated abomination of stocking, spirits, bonnet, limpness, looseness, and larceny; is only to be drawn at the fountain-head. Mrs. Sweeney is beyond the reach of individual art. It requires the united efforts of several men to ensure that great result, and it is only developed in perfection under an Honourable Society and in an inn of Court."

Not all the laundresses were bad. Francis Place, who is known to historians as "the Radical tailor of Charing Cross," lodged for several years before 1800 with Mrs. Baker, in Star Court. He paid high tribute to her. She was a civil cleanly woman, and had the care of three or four sets of Chambers in the Temple. He wrote:

> "My landlady furnished me with occupation. She brought to me books from the Chambers she had the care of, and exchanged them for others as often as I wished...
>
> I now read Blackstone, Hale's Common Law, several other law books, and much biography. This course of reading was continued for several years until the death of my Landlady, she was a very good sort of woman and was a friend of ours as long as she lived."

The barristers may have wondered where their books had gone. Place put his education to good use; he became a member of the Corresponding Society, and was a colleague of many of the very progressive thinkers whom Erskine defended.

Henry Hawkins too had fond recollections of his laundress. He wrote of his first days at the Bar:

> "My rent at this time of my entrance into the fashionable words was £12 a year; my laundress, perhaps, a little less. She earned it by coming up the stairs; but she was a good old soul. I remembered her long years after, and always with gratitude for her many kindnesses in those gloomy days. Her name was Hannem."

If, however, most of the laundresses were as Dickens describes, there was some reason for this. They worked longer hours than perhaps any other working women. It was common for a laundress to arrive at midnight at a house, in order to work there the whole day through. In 1831 J.T. Smith wrote in *The Cries of London*:

> "Perhaps there is not a class of people who work harder than those washer-women who go out to assist servants in what is called a heavy wash; they may be seen in the winter-time shivering at the doors at three and four in the morning, and are seldom dismissed before ten at night."

For these labours they were paid half a crown.

There were good Bar clerks as well as good laundresses. Charles Lamb, in his Essay on *The Old Benchers of the Inner Temple*, drew a charming picture of Lovel, clerk to Samuel Salt. He wrote:

> "Lovel took care of everything. He was at once his clerk, his good

135

servant, his dresser, his friend, his flapper (flapping away loose powder from his wig), his guide, stop-watch, auditor, treasurer.''

Lovel loyally warned his master, who was going out to dinner, not to mention a certain Miss Blandy, who was due to be hanged that day. It might have saddened the whole proceedings, she being related to the dinner party host. But in vain. During the dinner, Mr. Salt looked out of the window and observed that it was a gloomy day. ''Miss Blandy must be hanged by this time, I suppose,'' he observed.

Some barristers are beyond the help even of their clerks.

In Lamb's day people lived in the Temple, and cared about their surroundings. But the Bar grew so rapidly that they moved away, and the Temple became more like a series of office blocks.

Rebuilding was the order of the day. What use were attractive grounds then? The London Embankment was allowed to cut a huge swathe through the famous gardens where once the White and Red roses were plucked to represent York and Lancaster.

The Temple needed a woman's touch to restore its charm and beauty. But it was wholly lacking. As one man said to Henry Mayhew, ''Those chambers in the Inns of Court are the ruin of many a young girl. There isn't a woman in London who'd go with a man to the Temple, not one.''

Too many barristers began their careers when cobwebs and grime reigned supreme. By the time they were earning a living, they took the squalor for granted.

Perhaps the Bar was too busy to care. Not only laundresses gave scandalously bad value for money. The milkman who supplied Gray's Inn was asked to explain why he overcharged outrageously.

''Well, you see, it's like this,'' he said. ''The Benchers of Gray's Inn they likes a special kind of milk; it is neither cream nor milk, and that is why we charge a bit more.''

The laundresses certainly preferred drinks which were neither cream nor milk, but rather stronger.

It was not an age in which the Bar clamoured for luxury. At the Old Bailey they were provided with one small robing room, without lockers or cupboards. A single attendant dispensed refreshment; he would, on request, serve potatoes direct from the saucepan, and gravy from a cup.

So the Bar continued to suffer from ugliness, dirt, and insects.

The Judges at their Lodgings suffered too. Sir Henry Hawkins declared that, at the beginning of one Assize visit, the fleas stood on chairs in the hall and barked at them.

At the beginning of the 20th century, the laundresses maintained their proud tradition. Henry Cecil recollected that, at 4 Essex Court in the Temple, the laundress used to come round every morning, make herself a cup of tea, and then go on to the next set of Chambers, where she repeated the process. This was the full extent of her "cleaning."

Standards improved somewhat in the Twenties and Thirties, but modern ideas of cleanliness have only set in since World War Two.

It was perhaps in late Victorian times that the Bar clerks changed from being servants to monarchs of all they surveyed. Arthur Bowker wrote:

"The wise young man at the Bar and the man who is likely to get on in the profession, is he who does not interfere in his clerk's arrangements, but goes where he is sent without question, and does pretty much what he is told."

He was one of the most famous Bar clerks this century, being in turn clerk to Marshall Hall and Norman Birkett. He started as an office-boy in the Temple at the age of 13, where he worked six days a week for a wage of eight shillings, handling the mail, copying the letters, and learning shorthand. He was only 17 when he began his career as a senior clerk at 1 Brick Court in the Temple, to Hans Hamilton, a busy junior on the North-Eastern Circuit. Bowker wrote:

"I entered into my heritage of not only the right but the duty of wearing the glossy silk hat, morning or frock coat and striped trousers, the recognised habiliments of the barrister's clerk, when without it (in those days) he was more or less improperly dressed.

To me that silk hat was the bane of my existence. I was never enamoured of it, and to this day I much prefer carrying it to wearing it."

In 1983 John Flood published a survey he carried out upon Bar clerks. He may have expected to find them persons of little consequence; they soon put him right. "In this world there are three "We's" he was told. "The Royal We - the Editorial We - and the Barrister-and-his-Clerk We."

Clerks can certainly seem formidable to a young barrister.

One newly-called lady barrister was convinced that her only hope of getting into a particular set of chambers was by sleeping with the Clerk. In my chambers, however, decisions about pupils and tenants are taken by the chambers as a whole. There is safety in numbers.

Lord Alverstone explained why the bond between barrister and clerk was so strong. "I know of no other instance," he wrote, "where the personal attendant of a professional man is paid directly by the clients. The result is that their good or ill fortune is linked together with that of their masters, and they learn in time to identify themselves with them."

A barrister expects a great deal of his Clerk; the clerk, equally, has an unswerving loyalty to his barrister. "A barrister's clerk does everything for his Governor," one said, "even sewing on his flybuttons, because the typist couldn't do it, as there was no time to take his trousers off."

I naturally raised this problem with my own lady clerk, now the most senior Bar clerk in Liverpool. She has never been faced with it, because we wear zips. But it is nothing to some of the problems she has to take in her stride.

Clerks are very proud of their masters' reputations. Farrer Herschell, a most successful QC, returned after the long Vacation to be told by his clerk that people had been asking "whether *we* were going to take a High Court judgeship."

"And what did you say?" asked Herschell.

"I said "Thank God We haven't fallen as low as that!" said his clerk.

The clerk was right; his master deserved better things, and in due course became Lord Chancellor.

To promote the special skills needed by barristers' clerks, there exists a Bar Clerks Association. Prospective Bar clerks take examinations.

One paper sets the problem of a prosecution for obscene films, to be tried at the Beddington Crown Court. It is a three-day case, and your counsel can only be free to view the films one afternoon in November, and to fight the case on three days in December:

QUESTION: "What should the clerk do?"
ANSWER: "Arrange for the films to be shown on that afternoon in November, and for the case to be tried on those three days in December."

138

Nothing could be simpler, at least in theory. There is no reason at all to assume in advance that:

(a)   the film projector will break down at the beginning of the show
(b)   counsel for the other side will be detained in a case which lasts longer than expected
(c)   vital witnesses will be delayed by fog
(d)   the case will be transferred to a different court, and listed to start three days earlier
(e)   one of the jury will turn out to be the star of the dirty films.

It is simply that something of the sort will inevitably happen.

Some situations are beyond the skill of any clerks. An eminent QC had an appeal to the House of Lords; the clerk kept the date free for his master. Shortly before the date of the hearing, the House of Lords announced that it would be postponed for five weeks. The clerk objected strongly, but the House of Lords remained unmoved. The QC had to postpone his holiday, and refuse three murder briefs. Still, he was ready for the new date.

Then the House of Lords moved the date back another five weeks. This time the QC even had to *postpone his honeymoon*.

I am sorry for him, his bride, and his clerk. Barristers' wives and clerks have a great bond of suffering between them; the chief difference is that the clerks see more of their barristers than the wives do.

It is amazing that Bar clerks can cope with the problems not just of one barrister, but of more than a dozen at once. A very few Bar clerks take to drink. John Flood spent some time in the company of one of them. I would certainly summarise his conclusions on the subject if he had reached any, but at the end of the day he was in such an alcoholic haze that he could not read his own notes.

Since barristers cannot sue for their fees, they depend upon their clerks to collect the money from solicitors. It is sometimes as popular as extracting teeth without an anaesthetic.

Young Tommy Hughes, who began his sixty-year career as a clerk in Liverpool in 1901, was sent to get fees from a particular firm of solicitors. He went round to their office. The cashier said blandly,

"I am terribly sorry, but unfortunately we had a fire here not long ago, and all our records were destroyed. We are therefore quite

139

unable to say whether we owe any fees or not. I am sure you will understand our difficulty."

"If all your books have been destroyed, it means you can't deny you owe the money!" retorted Hughes. This was unanswerable; the fees were paid over immediately.

Clerks have different ways of assessing fees for a case. The clerk to William Henry Upjohn KC used to fix his fees by picking up each set of papers, and weighing it in his hand. Then he would state a fee for it, and seldom changed his mind. The client could take it or leave it.

In the Thirties, when Norman Birkett was at the peak of the profession, a solicitor came to Bowker, his clerk, with a Defence brief of an unpleasant sexual case, to be heard in Derby, and suggested that the proper fee was 250 guineas.

Bowker refused to accept it. "We should want at least 1000 guineas," he said.

The solicitor picked up the brief. "Who are the other leaders on the Midland Circuit?" he inquired. Bowker told him, and he left. An hour later he returned, and without saying another word, wrote "1000 guas." on the brief.

Birkett fought the case, and won. Soon afterwards the solicitor came into chambers to pay the fee. Bowker asked him if he thought he had been too greedy over the fee. "Not a bit," said the solicitor; "I don't mind telling you now that my client would have gone up to 2000 guineas to get Mr. Birkett."

Bowker was once placed in a very embarrassing situation. When Crippen was tried for murder, a well-known criminal solicitor wanted to give the junior brief to Marshall Hall.

"I am prepared to mark it a reasonable fee," he said, "But I shall not be in a position to pay the fee until certain arrangements can be made, which certainly cannot be completed until the trial is over - probably some time after."

This was a very curious situation. Bowker and Marshall Hall suspected that the fee depended on Crippen being convicted, and the solicitor selling his story to the press. So they turned the brief down, important though the case was.

After Crippen was convicted and hanged, his "Confession"

appeared in the press. He had certainly not written it himself. Enquires were made, and the solicitor was reprimanded by the Law Society for Unprofessional Conduct.

Barristers can be unprofessional too. At St. George's Hall in Liverpool, where the Assizes used to be held, the Bar clerks had a room of their own where they gathered to prepare the lists of the following day's cases, a very important duty. A member of the Manchester Bar came to the courts and wanted somewhere quiet to work. The clerks' room was empty; he took possession of it, and held a long series of conferences there with clients.

The clerks did everything they tactfully could to hint to him that he was an intruder. They tramped in and out of the room noisily, and washed their hands strenuously at the wash-basin. They may even have gargled, but the barrister continued unmoved. Desperate measures were called for.

A senior Bar clerk seized a mat from the floor of the corridor, and flung it straight onto the table where the barrister was sitting. When the cloud of choking dust dispersed, some sixth sense warned the barrister that he was unwelcome. He fled from the room, and never again profaned that Holy of Holies.

A clerk can occasionally bring calamity upon his master. Not every future Lord Chancellor has been suspected of being an international terrorist, but it happened to Elwyn-Jones.

He was appearing in a case in Tripoli when his clerk informed him that an important case of his was to be heard the following week. There was no harm in that. Nevertheless, in hindsight, the sending of a telegram with the cryptic message "MURDER FIXED FOR WEDNESDAY, ERIC" could have been more prudently expressed.

My own clerk has never involved me in disaster, but another clerk did. It was Tommy Hughes, who upon his retirement in 1961 published his memoirs in the *Liverpool Daily Post:* they included the ill-omened Tibetan Temple defence.

One of his barristers was Lindon Riley, who had a large criminal defence practice in Edwardian times. He was an impressive man, and in his final speech for the defence would lower his voice to a stage whisper, as he told them of the Tibetan Temple:

141

"There was once an English explorer, Members of the Jury, who set out on a long voyage across the Ocean. Then he crossed the vast continent of India, until at last he came to the Himalayas, Majestic, Mysterious, and Immersed in Mist."

Those magic words held them spellbound.

"In a forgotten valley in Tibet, Members of the Jury, he reached a Temple in which no white man had ever set foot. Disguised in native clothing, he slipped past the Temple guards, and at last found himself before the Sacred Shrine, where incense burners sent their fragrant perfume curling upwards to the shadowy recesses of the roof. In that shrine was the image of a strange god seated upon a pedestal, and upon that pedestal, Members of the Jury -"

Here his voice sank to an even more intense whisper:

"was carved a mystical phrase in an age-old language. You are here, Members of the Jury, because of what those words said.
In English they mean,
The Truth Shall Always Prevail..."

This was far too bad to waste. Soon afterwards I defended an old lag for snatching three tins of sardines from a shop window. He was caught as he ran away, and immediately made a written statement admitting the crime. The evidence against him was overwhelming, and his own explanation sadly unconvincing. Clearly, nothing could save him but the Tibetan Temple.

I launched into it valiantly. Judge Laski QC, the Recorder of Liverpool, listened to it open-mouthed. My colleague Eric Goldrein, who appeared for the prosecution, had an expression which can only be described as quizzical. Nevertheless, by the time I got to the Mystical Phrase in an Age-old Language, you could have heard a pin drop in that court.

The jury retired for only a couple of minutes, and convicted my client.

Twenty years went by. I found myself defending another hopeless case. It may have been the one where my client was caught passing a forged £20 note, and was found to have a further £500 in forged notes tucked down the front of his underpants. He had a perfectly valid explanation - the money was there because he wanted to keep his assets unfrozen, it may have been - but it seemed to lose something in the telling.

It was time for the Tibetan Temple again.

The prosecution was conducted by Miss Inge Bernstein, who is in private life Mrs. Eric Goldrein. It struck me as unfair that Eric should be the sole beneficiary of the Tibetan Temple defence, and so, without giving her any warning, I unleashed it on the Court.

Twenty years earlier, I had been a mere tyro at the Bar. But experience counts for a lot, and I deployed the Tibetan Temple with all the eloquence at my command. Every pause, every inflection, was used to the maximum effect.

The judge listened to it open-mouthed, and even Inge Bernstein had an expression best described as quizzical. But, as I reached the Mystical Phrase in an Age-old Language, you could have heard a pin drop in that court.

The jury retired for only a couple of minutes before convicting my client.

I now bequeath the Tibetan Temple to posterity, free of all incumbrances, to have and to hold from this day onwards.

But watch out for falling masonry.

NINE

Erskine

Thou shalt not carry moderation to excess.
Arthur Koestler's last written words.

If Thomas Erskine had been the eldest son of the 10th Earl of Buchan, he would not have come to the Bar, as being unbecoming to his rank and station.

If he had been a rich son of the Earl, he might not have come to the Bar, preferring to live the life of a gentleman, and to attend to his estate.

But being the youngest and poorest son of that family, now fallen on very hard times, he could not afford to come to the Bar at all.

In 1764, when he was fourteen years of age, he went on board the *Tartar* as a midshipman, in the new blue uniform with white facings and cuffs, and brass buttons. He served four years in the West Indies, where he spent his spare time in botany, reading and drawing. He was lucky enough to avoid the scurvy, typhus, or Yellow Jack, for tropical waters were unhealthy.

Naval food was notoriously bad. There were only two ways to eat ship's biscuit: rap it sharply on the table so that the maggots fell out, or gulp it down in the pitch dark. Ignorance is bliss.

Yet he kept his health, and apart from being mildly struck by lightning once at sea, the years passed quietly enough.

Then he came into a very little money - just enough to buy himself a commission in the Army. He exchanged uniforms, married the daughter of a Member of Parliament, and was posted to Minorca.

Now he read Shakespeare, Dryden and Pope, and on his return to England, attracted attention even in the brilliant circle of Dr. Johnson. He was a very accomplished young man; his comic poem "The Jeranium" (his own spelling) was a popular party piece.

One day, in a provincial town, he went to listen to a case at the Assizes, and was introduced to the Judge, Lord Mansfield, who suggested he should come to the Bar. He made up his mind immediately. The quickest way to the Bar was by way of a university, so he went up to Cambridge, became a Master of Arts, and was soon called to the Bar.

This was the point at which many young men of slender means wandered hopefully from court to court, waiting for their first brief, until their hopes and money ran out.

His situation was even worse, having a wife and children to support. He lodged in Kentish Town, where a working man could breakfast on bread and cheese and small beer from the chandler's shop, for twopence; dine on chuck beef, scrag of mutton or sheep's trotters with two veg. and half a pint of porter for sevenpence; and for his supper revert to bread and cheese, with radishes, for threepence-halfpenny more.

Erskine used to feast as opulently upon cow-heel and tripe. He lived on next to nothing, and, according to Jeremy Bentham, had hardly a decent coat to his back. But air is free, and of an evening he would go to the working-men's spouting-shops, and talk the hours away.

"What's a spouting-shop?" you might well ask.

"A meeting of 'prentices, clerks, and giddy young men, intoxicated with plays, and so they meet in public-houses to act speeches; there they all neglect their business, despite the advice of their friends and think of nothing but to become actors."

Or barristers, or politicians.

Francis Place, "the Radical tailor of Charing Cross," and a close friend of Bentham and John Stuart Mill, recalled what those spouting-shops were like:

> "Almost every public-house had a parlour, as some still have, for the better sort of customers. In this room which was often large and well lighted with tallow candles the company drank and smoked and spent their evenings - many constantly stopped in these rooms either alone or in parties of from two to as many as a table would hold, which was generally 6, sometimes 8.
> There were several houses of this sort near Temple Bar, two of

which were famous in their time, namely the Cock in Fleet Street, and the Three Herrings in Bell Yard, Temple Bar. The latter-named house had a large detached room in which was assembled the House of Lords.

It was frequented principally by the more dissolute sort of barristers, attorneys, and tradesmen of what were then called the better sort, nobody, however, who wore a decent coat was excluded. The regular frequenters were the Lords; they who had *not* undergone the ceremony of taking a seat were the strangers whom it was pretended were admitted from courtesy. The Lords took on solemn occasions their seats according to rank, each bearing a title as nearly as possible from the place he came from. My father being a Norfolk man was Duke of Norfolk and Earl Marshall, which gave him a precedence as the first peer next to the King's family, and entitled him to take the chair in the absence of the Lord Chancellor, who was always a barrister.''

In such places Erskine acquired practice in public speaking. He may not have been elected ''Lord Chancellor'' of such an assembly - he would surely have boasted of it in later life, if that had happened. But it was marvellous practice for him, in case he ever got a practice.

He went to a coffee-house, and overheard a naval officer talking. Erskine, never one to begrudge his own opinion, launched into an indignant attack on the enemies of Captain Baillie, the Lieutenant-Governor of Greenwich Hospital. As luck would have it, he was talking to Captain Baillie himself, due to stand in the dock a few days thence on the charge of criminal libel.

It was an age of patronage, just as in ancient Rome, and politics worked on the basis of favours done and services rendered.

The Hospital should have housed only sailors, but some in high places found it convenient to pension off their civilian friends there, and, if this was not bad enough, to stint the sailors' rations. The pea soup served there cannot have been luxurious, but the pewter soup-bowls were hammered flat to make for smaller portions!

Captain Baillie complained many times of these abuses, to no avail; so he published a pamphlet criticising Lord Sandwich, the First Lord of the Admiralty. He was suspended from office, and not simply sued for defamation, but prosecuted for criminal libel, his conduct being deemed so scandalous as to be a matter of public concern.

The Captain said nothing to Erskine that night, but made certain enquiries. Thus, on the following morning, Erskine's first fee was placed in his hand. One guinea.

He pictured himself, no doubt, holding the court enthralled with his eloquence, but when the brief arrived, he found that the Captain was also defended by: Mr. Bearcroft
Mr. Peckham,
Mr. Murphy, and
Mr. Hargrave.

They were all experienced lawyers, and Erskine came bottom of the list. Very likely he would not open his mouth at all.

There were times when his colleagues were all for settling the case, for Captain Baillie's stinging criticisms seemed almost indefensible.

But Erskine held back. "My advice, gentlemen," he said, as if they were interested in hearing it, "may savour more of my late profession than my present: but I am against compromising."

"I'll be damned if I do!" said Baillie, hugging him; "you are the man for me!"

When the evidence was over, Bearcroft addressed the court, no doubt very fully; he appeared in most cases of consequence, and expected to be heard with attention.

Then it was Mr. Peckham's turn, and Mr. Murphy's; and finally Mr. Hargrave. He was terribly boring and long-winded, and he had to break off twice because of a urinary ailment. By the time he had finished, it was quite dark.

Lord Mansfield, who was trying the case, announced that they would continue the following morning, and rose from the Bench. Nobody expected Erskine to make a speech.

But he had the whole night to prepare it. He later claimed that, when he rose to his feet, he could feel his wife and children tugging at his gown, begging him to make the most of his opportunity.

"My Lord -," he said in a well-modulated voice which had no trace of a Scottish accent. The thing was now done; he was on his feet, addressing the Court. He had to go on:

"I am likewise of the counsel for the author of this supposed libel, and if the matter for consideration had been merely a question of *private* wrong, in which the interests of society were no farther concerned than in the protection of the innocent, I should have thought myself well justified, after the very able defence made by the learned gentlemen who have spoken before me, in sparing your Lordship, already fatigued with the subject, and in leaving my client to the prosecutor's counsel and the judgment of the court."

It was well said, and tactful to his colleagues. But a moment later he flung down the gauntlet.

"I cannot relinquish the high privilege of defending such a character," he said; "I will not give up even my small share of the honour of *repelling and exposing so odious a prosecution.*"

Senior members of the Bar sometimes blush for the zeal of their juniors, and wish to heaven that they would sit down. Erskine, however, had only just begun. He attacked those who controlled the running of the Hospital:

"That such wretches should escape chains and a dungeon is a reproach to humanity, and to all order and government; but that they should become PROSECUTORS is a degree of effrontery that would not be believed by any man who did not accustom himself to observe the shameless scenes which the monstrous age we live in is every day producing.

Indeed, Lord Sandwich has, in my mind, acted such a part -"

This was intolerable. Lord Mansfield intervened to remind him that Lord Sandwich was not before the Court. Erskine retorted:

"I know that he is not formally before the Court, but for that very reason *I will bring him before the Court:* he has placed these men in the front of the battle, in hopes to escape under their shelter, but I will not join in battle with them...

I assert that the Earl of Sandwich has but one road to escape out of this business without pollution and disgrace: and *that is,* by publicly disavowing the acts of the prosecutors, and restoring Captain Baillie to his command..."

He came to a thundering conclusion:

148

"IF HE KEEPS THIS INJURED MAN SUSPENDED, OR DARES TO TURN THAT SUSPENSION INTO A REMOVAL, I SHALL THEN NOT SCRUPLE TO DECLARE HIM AN ACCOMPLICE IN THEIR GUILT, A SHAMELESS OPPRESSOR, A DISGRACE TO HIS RANK, AND A TRAITOR TO HIS TRUST."

He started the speech an unknown beginner at the Bar; he ended it almost a national hero.

Even as he left the Court, the attorneys flocked around him, to catch at his gown and brief him for their clients.

He attracted the attention of Admiral Keppel, an experienced sailor with valuable new ideas. Ships sailing in the tropics could lose a quarter of their crews from scurvy and other diseases, but Keppel insisted on scrupulous hygiene, ventilating the lower decks and scrubbing them down with vinegar. All of his crews survived.

Even Lord Sandwich is now recognised as a progressive figure. When it was discovered that sheathing ship's keels with copper restricted the growth of barnacles, making them faster of manoeuvre in warfare, Sandwich acted swiftly to have the entire Fleet copper-bottomed.

Nevertheless, the Admiralty's "Permanent Fighting Instructions" dated back to Admiral Rooke in 1704, and insisted that ships should stay in line of battle, instead of following enemy ships till they were captured or sunk. Nelson later defied these rules with glorious results, but might easily have wrecked his career in doing so.

Keppel obeyed them, and lost the Battle of Ushant. He was courtmartialled for failing to win the battle, and chose Erskine to defend him.

This was no copper-bottomed guarantee of victory, for Erskine was hampered by barnacles of procedure; he had to submit his questions in writing, which is no way to conduct a masterly cross-examination. His final speech had also to be given in writing; Keppel had to deliver it himself. Still, he was acquitted, and in gratitude gave Erskine the enormous sum of £7000.

Erskine appeared now in almost every big case in the King's Bench, and earned more than any advocate had done before him. He took silk in 1783, and was also appointed Attorney-General to the Prince of Wales.

George III practised most of the traditional virtues, and a few of the faults which go with them. He ran politics, as far as he could, by gifts and appointments to steer people his way. Those who dared suggest that more people should be given the vote, were in his eyes dangerous fanatics.

It was an inflammable age; tradesmen rioted when their trade was at a low ebb, and mobs in support of John Wilkes went round shouting "Wilkes and Liberty!"

The Gordon riots in 1780 began as a protest against Popery, though any monarch less likely to favour it than George III can hardly be imagined. Young Lord George Gordon was "President of the Protestant Association", and led a crowd of 40,000 men to the House of Commons to protest against some relaxations of the stringent laws affecting the Roman Catholics. The mob got out of control, despite his efforts, and caused terrible damage in London. After five days George III called out the troops, and restored law and order.

Gordon was charged with High Treason, for levying war against the King in his realm, and Erskine had the unwelcome task of defending him. Few people in Court could be indifferent to the case, because their property and interests would have been injured or threatened.

The mob even burnt down the house of Lord Mansfield, who was trying the case.

It turned on one point: not that Lord George Gordon had not led the first demonstration, which could not be denied, but that he had never wished or encouraged the mob to go further.

Erskine made this point abundantly clear, and rammed it home again and again, though in different ways, so as not to weary the jury.

"Alas! gentlemen," he said, courting their sympathy,

"Who am I? - a young man of little experience, unused to the bar of criminal courts, and sinking under the dreadful consciousness of my defects. I have, however, this consolation, that no ignorance nor inattention on my part can possibly prevent you from seeing, under the direction of the Judges, that the Crown has established no case of treason."

He analysed treason in the simplest terms, letting each well-chosen word have its full effect:

"One observation [the Attorney-General, for the prosecution] has, however, made on the subject, in the truth of which I heartily concur - viz., that the crime of which the noble person at your bar stands accused is the very *highest* and most *atrocious* that a member of civil life can possible commit; because it is not, like *all other* crimes, merely an *injury* to society from the breach of some of its reciprocal relations, but in an attempt to *utterly dissolve and destroy society altogether.*

In nothing, therefore, is the wisdom and justice of our laws so strongly and eminently manifested, as in the *rigid -*
accurate -
cautious -
explicit -
unequivocal definition of what shall constitute this high offence..."

He pointed out that treason required PREMEDITATED OPEN ACTS OF VIOLENTS, HOSTILITY AND FORCE, and repeated it:

"Gentlemen, I repeat these words, and call solemnly on the Judges to attend to what I say, and to contradict me if I mistake the law: BY PREMEDITATED OPEN ACTS OF VIOLENCE, HOSTILITY AND FORCE; -nothing equivocal; nothing ambiguous; no intimidations, or over-awings, which signify nothing precise or certain, because what frightens one man, or set of men, may have no effect upon another; but that which COMPELS AND COERCES: OPEN VIOLENCE AND FORCE..."

The jury acquitted Lord George Gordon, and Dr. Johnson was one of many who was thankful that the law of treason had not been extended further.

1790 was the year in which Erskine became Member of Parliament for Portsmouth, and great things were expected of him in the House of Commons. He made no great impact there. Some say he was afraid of Pitt; others, that he needed an admiring and appreciative audience, or at least one which, like a jury, cannot answer back, and must listen to a speech whether wishing to or not, without interrupting.

Lord Colchester had the shrewdest analysis of it:

"His power of commanding the passions of a jury, so justly celebrated beyond the reputation of all his predecessors in

Westminster Hall, wholly fails of its effect in Parliament; perhaps the chief cause of this is the little degree of personal respect and consideration which he has established by the extravagance of his political harangues out of doors, at charity meetings, and in his professional employment.''

In short, he was a tub-thumper, and the House soon tired of him. But he was always to be found amongst those with the most progressive ideas.

So too was the Prince of Wales, who struck out in a different direction from his father. Unlike the king, who was markedly frugal, the Prince spent money like water. Disdaining his father's irreproachable morals, the future George IV consorted with actresses and with Charles James Fox, the Radical and womaniser. Fox was one of the greatest speakers in the House of Commons, and some people thought him very dangerous.

"As for Fox and Grey," said one lady at Court to another, "I wish they would utter treason at once, and be beheaded and hanged.''

But to be with Fox and Grey was an exciting gesture of defiance by the Prince of Wales. In that circle he met Erskine, and appointed him his Attorney-General, to advise him on legal matters.

In 1786, for instance, the Prince's brother William asked him to get Erskine to defend a seaman from his ship for obstructing a Customs Officer in the execution of his duty.

"The man is as innocent as I am," wrote Prince William, "and will, I am afraid, be condemned to death unless I support him, as the poor fellow has no friends.''

Prince William was also troubled by Lt. Schomberg, a junior officer who deserved to be Court-martialled.

"I have reason to expect," he wrote, "that Schomberg means to prosecute me; in this case I must have recourse again to our ingenious friend and pleader Mr. Erskine.''

But Erskine was not content to be merely a pleader. He chose to be one of the champions of liberty in an age when freedom of speech was constantly under threat.

In 1789, for instance, Warren Hastings was impeached in the House of Commons; Burke drew up the articles of impeachment, like criminal charges.

A Scottish clergyman criticised them, and Mr. Stockdale, a

Piccadilly bookseller, published the criticisms. It might seem harmless enough, but he was prosecuted for criminal libel because it was taken as an intolerable slur upon the status and dignity of the House of Commons. It needed all Erskine's efforts to secure his acquittal.

In that same year he appeared in the House of Commons for another publisher, Thomas Carnan. Lord North moved a bill to preserve the monopoly which Oxford and Cambridge had of printing certain books.

Erskine reminded the House that, when printing was introduced, the authorities were anxious to stifle written criticism:

> "The PRESS was therefore wholly under the coercion of the Crown and *all printing*, not only of *public books*, containing ordinances religious or civil, but *every species of publication whatsoever*, was regulated by the King's proclamations, prohibitions, charters of privilege, and finally by the decrees of the Star-Chamber."

Everybody believed that Lord North's bill would be passed by a comfortable majority. But when the votes were counted, it was defeated by a majority of 45.

Erskine was to proclaim the liberty of the Press again in his famous public speeches; in private he sometimes expressed a rather different opinion.

In February 1790 he wrote to Captain Payne, on the Princes of Wales' staff:

> "I beg you will take an opportunity of presenting my humble duty to the Prince of Wales, and beg his Royal highness not to listen either for himself or the Dukes of York and Clarence to any petition for mercy from Walter, the printer of the *Times*. If the Prince will be pleased to leave it *in my hands* I will be responsible for the support of his dignity and honour, and the honour and dignity of the public, which is mainly concerned in his punishment. I do not wish anything to be said about it except that the Prince has left the prosecution to its ordinary course.
>
> By this proper severity we shall get rid of Withers [a clergyman who had libelled Mrs. FitzHerbert] and all the scoundrels; they are damnably afraid of me and I will take care to justify their fears."

If they shared Erskine's high opinion of himself, they would certainly fear him. As he told Captain Payne:

> "No man living in Westminster Hall (young as I am) has conducted

153

so many cases before juries on this or upon any other subject as I have, perhaps I might add ever did..."

Erskine's vanity earned him the nickname "Counsellor Ego", and there was a joke about a newspaper which tried to print one of his speeches in full, but had not enough capital "I"'s in the type-fount.

Yet Erskine was certainly the best advocate of his day. Lord Campbell, who wrote the *Lives of the Chancellors*, watched his career with fascination, and declared him to be the greatest advocate of all time, not excluding Cicero.

Much preparation went into his success. He would arrive at a Court on the night before the trial, to study the best position from which to address the jury. He always wore a nice wig, and new yellow gloves for each occasion; he entered the Court as soon as his case had been called on, so as to give the jury a pleasant buzz of excitement.

Although harsh words were often used about his political speeches - "very feeble", "execrable", and so on, nobody ever so described him in a Court of law. He remained always on the alert, ready for the slightest mistake on the part of his opponent, and indefatigable.

No sacrifice was too great for him. In 1792 he was asked to defend Tom Paine, whose book *The Rights of Man* was the most revolutionary of its kind until Karl Marx. It kindled the American colonists into fighting for new rights. Paine wrote "All *hereditary government* is in its nature tyranny...to *inherit* the *people* as if they were flocks and herds."

It was a direct attack on the monarchy. Erskine must have realised that to defend Paine might cost him his valued position as Attorney-General to the Prince of Wales. But he proclaimed Paine's right to be defended in a passage which every barrister should know by heart:

> "From the moment that any advocate can be permitted to say that he *will* or will *not* stand between the Crown and the subject arraigned in the court where he daily sits to practise, from that moment the liberties of England are at an end."

He defended Paine with all the skill at his command; nevertheless, as soon as he had finished his speech, the jury pronounced Paine guilty.

He did not spare himself on his client's behalf. The Courts usually sat at eight or nine in the morning, and continued if need be until the small hours.

When he defended the proprietors of the *Morning Chronicle* in 1793 he told the jury that he had for the past two days been so extremely indisposed that he felt himself scarcely equal to the common exertion of addressing the Court, but he finished his task, and they retired at two o'clock in the afternoon to consider their verdict. It seemed likely that they would take some time, so Lord Kenyon, the Judge, went home to his house. At seven in the evening they announced that they had reached a special verdict, so they all went up to Lord Kenyon's house in coaches. Their verdict was that the Defendants were Guilty of publishing the matters complained of, but Not Guilty of publishing it with any malicious intent.

This was a verdict Erskine frequently sought to uphold, though the judges used to insist that if anybody published defamatory matter, it was irrelevant that he had no wrongful intent in so doing. Lord Kenyon said that he could not accept a verdict in that form, so the jury retired again, until five in the morning, when they brought in a general verdict of NOT GUILTY.

Erskine fought for his clients as if his own life was in danger; so it was, in a sense, for he went to France to see the French Revolution, and came back expressing his admiration. This was before the Terror became the order of the day. He belonged to the Society of Friends of the People, though persons had been transported in the past, and could still be brought to trial, even on the word of one drunken witness, if it was suggested they had criticised the monarchy.

In the winter of 1794 he fought three cases, one after the other; the defendants were charged with High Treason.

First came a shoe-maker, Thomas Hardy, the secretary of the London Corresponding Society, a group similar in aims to the Society of Friends of the People, which was pressing for a wider system of voting.

Francis Place, another member of the Corresponding Society, was present at the trial at the Old Bailey, and knew that one of Erskine's chief difficulties lay in the composition of the jury. They should have been made up of householders; the Sheriff should select a street or two at a time from within a parish, and order 48 of the householders to attend as jurors. This random selection would form a reasonably independent jury who were paid a shilling for every case they tried.

In practice, however, they were usually chosen from a much smaller panel of people on special lists which the Sheriffs held. Some of them had no education at all; some were servants in the houses of noblemen, whose political views were well known. They served on juries again and again for a guinea a trial, and came to be known as "guinea men," or "packed juries." They could be reasonably expected to give verdicts which the Sheriffs and the judges would like.

Erskine's uphill task was to persuade them to return verdicts which were distinctly radical. In a speech which lasted for seven hours he spoke vigorously of the need for a free press, and pointed out that reform was only to come by peaceful persuasion.

At the end of his speech, it was reported,

"so strongly prepossessed were the multitude in favour of the innocence of the prisoner, that... an irresistible acclamation pervaded the court and to an immense distance around. The streets were seemingly filled with the whole of the inhabitants of London, and the passages were so thronged that it was impossible for the Judges to get to their carriages."

Thomas Hardy was acquitted.

Then came the trial of Horne Tooke, upon a similar charge. During his speech Erskine referred to prosecutions which had taken place in Edinburgh the previous year, when Lord Braxfield had sent the defendants to prison for twelve years. Erskine told the jury:

"These judgments, instead of producing the effect that was expected from them, produced (as ever happens from perverted authority) great irritation and discontent. They were, in my mind, and in what is far more important, in some of the greatest minds in this country, ILLEGAL PROCEEDINGS. And although I do not mean, in this place, to make any attack upon magistrates in the execution of their duty-"

Lord Chief Justice Eyre interrupted him. "It should not be stated here that they were illegal."

But Erskine was quite unrepentant. "I did not say they were

156

illegal," he retorted, "I said, *that IN MY OPINION they were so, and they were questioned in Parliament as such.*"

By the end of his speech he was so exhausted that he spoke in a whisper:

"You may see, that I am tearing myself to pieces by exertions beyond my powers - I have neither voice nor strength to proceed further. I do not, indeed, desire to conciliate your favour, nor to captivate your judgments by elocution in the close of my discourse; but I conclude this cause, I concluded the former, by imploring that you may be enlightened by the Power which can alone unerringly direct the human mind in the pursuit of truth and justice."

The jury acquitted Horne Tooke, and a crowd of enthusiasts adjourned to the Cock and Anchor Tavern in the Strand, where they drank toasts to "Trial by Jury", coupled with "Thomas Erskine", and "The Swinish Multitude, and may the Honest Hogs never cease to grunt till their Wrongs are Righted."

The last case was that of Thelwall, on similar grounds. After the case started, Thelwall took the fancy to conduct his own defence.

"I'll be hanged if I don't plead my own case," he said.

"You'll be hanged if you do," said Erskine grimly. Thelwall took his advice, and was acquitted. The crown pulled Erskine's carriage all the way back to Serjeant's Inn, and he could at last relax. During the three trials he had hardly got to bed before three o'clock in the morning.

He enjoyed a well-earned holiday. He wrote to a friend:

"I am now very busy flying my boy's kite, shooting with the bow and arrow, and talking to an old Scotch gardener ten hours a day... and am scarcely up to the exertion of reading the daily papers. How much happier it would be for England and the world if the King's ministers were employed in a course so much more innocent than theirs, and *so perfectly suitable to their capacities!*"

The Prince of Wales was less innocently employed. Although by an Act of Parliament he was not allowed to marry without the King's consent, he decided to marry Mrs. FitzHerbert, who was a commoner, and a Catholic. A clergyman was procured out of a debtor's prison, and in return for the sum of £500 down and the promise of a bishopric which was never fulfilled, he married them secretly. Rumours about the marriage were heard here and there, but nobody believed so incredible a story.

When the Prince continued to run up debts of £50,000, George III decided that he must settle down and marry, no question about it. There was a shortage of suitable Princesses, but George III's sister, the Duchess of Brunswick, had a daughter Caroline who was said to be of an amiable disposition.

Preparations were made. The Royal couple were sent each other's portrait, and were pleased with them. Thus, on April 5th 1795, Lord Malmesbury introduced the Prince of Wales to the Princess of Brunswick at St. James' Palace.

He said to Malmesbury, "Harris, I am not well. Pray get me a glass of brandy!" - for she was not assiduous in her laundry, and her personal freshness left a lot to be desired. As someone put it, "She ought to have a bath *all over!*"

She said to Malmesbury, a little later, "I find him very stout and by no means as handsome as his portrait." He wore corsets to contain his stomach.

Three days later they were married, and bells rang across England to mark the happy event. The Prince got drunk, by way of local anaesthetic, but managed to father the daughter born nine months after the wedding.

He wrote at once to inform the King:

> "I have the honour to inform your majesty that the Princess is just brought to bed of a daughter, and thank God both the mother and child are quite well and likely to continue so. The Princess has had a very severe time indeed, having been upwards of 12 hours in constant labour."

So proud was he of his wife that he settled a sum of money upon her immediately in his will: "To her who is called the Princess of Wales I leave one shilling."

He insisted that the jewels he had given her for the wedding should be returned. However, as they had never been paid for, the jeweller had to sue for his money, which was paid out of public funds.

He was more generous towards Mrs. FitzHerbert, "who is my wife in the eyes of God, and who ever will be such in mine." He hoped that when he died her picture should be buried with him.

So much for domestic bliss.

From that day onwards he lived as far from the Princess as possible. George III, a devoted family man, suffered deeply from the quarrel and the constant scandals in the press.

Erskine was now back in favour. The Prince wrote to the Queen, "I have retained Erskine beside my lawyers to prosecute every paragraph, every pamphlet that could be construed into libel."

Erskine had his own disappointments. He went to France to see Napoleon, the great hero of the English radicals. He was full of excitement; what a great occasion this would be, when the famous Frenchman met the famous champion of English liberty!

They were introduced to each other.

"You are a lawyer, sir," said Napoleon indifferently, "and your laws are Norman."

He turned away.

In 1806 Pitt was asked to form a new cabinet, and included Charles James Fox. Lord Eldon refused to continue as Chancellor with him; so did two other judges, who would have been suitable choices; so Erskine was chosen. He was fifty-six years old.

George III was a little taken aback, for Erskine's politics were far from being his own. "What! What! Well! Well!" he said, "but, remember, he is your Chancellor, not mine."

Erskine went to see Lord Thurlow, and expressed the breezy hope that, if he applied his mind to it, he should understand the rudiments of Equity within a few days. Lord Thurlow congratulated Erskine with great gravity and politeness, adding drily that he was sure that with his ability he would soon understand the whole system of Equity; he himself, however, had been engaged in Equity for more than forty years, and still had not wholly mastered it.

Erskine filled the office of Chancellor as well as any common lawyer could. He listened to every case with impeccable patience and courtesy, and when occasionally he jotted down comic verses to pass the time, he concealed the fact. A rule came out that every affidavit ought to have a title, briefly describing its subject-matter.

He wrote:

In times like these when 'tis the vogue
To title every fool and rogue,
Up starts a perjured affidavit
And swears that he must also have it.

He heard cases on lunacy, and in the case of *Ex parte Cranmer* said:

"A man may have passed a useful and illustrious life, and, by the course of nature, his faculties may decay, so that he may not be fit either to govern himself or his affairs; it is unseemly that he should be put upon the footing of a lunatic, and that, in the ordinary course, a commission should issue against him."

This common-sense pronouncement appears in the Law Reports of Vesey Jr., and the index entry reads "LUNATIC, see LORD CHANCELLOR," which must be the most insulting reference of all time.

Yet, if truth be told, Erskine was a little odd. He once told a friend that he knew the King was still insane, and was in fact better informed on the matter than all the King's physicians, because he had been in all the great cases about insanity in the last 20 years, and had kept voluminous notes on the subject bound up in one great volume.

His portrait was painted by Sir Joshua Reynolds, who agreed that his face was very handsome; "but there is a wildness in his eye," he added, "approaching to madness, such as I scarcely ever met with in any other instance."

Perhaps Erskine could never have been a great advocate without an obsessive confidence in his own abilities.

In 1806 he had to conduct what was called a "Delicate Investigation" into Princess Caroline's indelicate conduct. Her manners were coarse, her dress was too revealing, and her behaviour far too frivolous: there was an occasion when she and Sir Sidney Smith danced together, she wearing his clothes, and he wearing hers! Above all, there was a young boy in her household on whom she lavished affection. If she was the boy's mother, then she had committed adultery, and the Prince of Wales could be rid of her, bag and baggage.

Lord Chancellor Erskine, the Lord Chief Justice, and a select few others, went down to the Princess' house at Blackheath, and duly reported that although she deserved to be rebuked for her "levity of manner," the child was not hers, and there was no evidence that she had committed adultery.

The Prince was furious with Erskine.

"In these circumstances," he wrote, "he acted like a poltroon, neither with the sagacity and judgment of a statesman nor with the skill, firmness nor ability of a lawyer."

He added in another letter:

"It is a most grievous disappointment to feelings like mine to say that I cannot consider him *my friend* as he has... deserted me in the most important question of my life; but the world will judge him."

George III condemned him. In 1807, thirteen months after his appointment, he was ordered to surrender the Great Seal of his office because he was not vigorous enough for the King's taste in opposing a bill to grant Roman Catholics greater rights.

Erskine had no option but to obey. He wrote:

"If I should be called out of this world as suddenly as I have been out of this place, it will be a happy thing for me if I can render as clear an account of my conduct through life as of my administration of justice during the period I have presided here."

He was now relegated to a life of leisure. He could not return to the Bar; he had lost his huge earnings by unwise investment, and had nothing but his Chancellor's pension to live on.

He was dining at Lincoln's Inn one day when he met Captain Parry, the Arctic navigator, who described how, at the Pole, his crew had nothing to live on but the *seals*.

And very good living too," said Erskine ruefully, "if you can only keep them long enough!"

He wrote a book called *Armata*, an allegory somewhat like *Gulliver's Travels*, which had a minor success at the time, but is forgotten now. He did a little farming, a topic on which he thought himself sufficiently expert to write a treatise, so that others would benefit from his knowledge.

One day he was riding through the countryside with his friend Coke of Holkham Hall (a descendant of the great lawyer), who was a noted agriculturist.

"Good God, Coke!" cried Erskine, throwing up his hands in an ecstasy of admiration. "What a magnificent field of lavender!"

It was barley.

His gift of public speaking now lay fallow. He had a vivid turn of phrase; when John Cuthell, a Holborn bookseller, was prosecuted for selling a seditious pamphlet, Erskine had told the jury what his shop was like:

"He resides in a gloomy avenue of Holborn. No coloured lamps or transparent shop-glasses dazzle the eye of vagrant curiosity, as in the places I have alluded to. As in the shops of fashion nothing scarcely is sold which the sun has gone down upon, so in *his house* nothing almost is to be seen that is not sacred to learning and consecrated by time. There is not a greater difference between Lapland and Paris, than between the shops I have adverted to and that of Mr. Cuthell. There you find the hunter after old editions - the scholar, who is engaged in some controversy, *not* concerning modern nations, but people and tongues which have for centuries passed away, and which continue to live only in the memory of the antiquary.. Whilst crowds in the circles of gaiety or commerce are engaged at other libraries in the bitterness of the political controversy, the pale student sits soberly discussing at Mr. Cuthwell's the points of the Hebrews or the accents of the Greeks."

His keen sense of humour is not often apparent in his speeches, because he did not make the mistake of distracting the jury by laughter during a serious address. But Mr. Wallace, his opponent in a breach of promise case brought by an old woman against an old man, tried to laugh the case out of court. Erskine beat him at his own game. He told the Court:

"By Mr Wallace's favour, the jury had a view of this Defendant, and the very sight of him rebutted every suspicion that could possibly fall upon a woman of any age, constitution, or complexion.
I am sure everybody who was in court must agree with me, that all the diseases catalogued in the dispensatory seemed to be running a race for his life, though the asthma appeared to have completely

distanced his competitors, as the fellow was blowing like a smith's bellows the whole time of the trial. His teeth being all gone, I shall say nothing of his gums; and, as to his shape, to be sure a bass fiddle is perfect gentility compared with it.

I was surprised, therefore, that Mr. Wallace should be the first to point out *this mummy,* and to comment on his imperfections..."

The old man let the plaintiff live with him for several months before he turned her out, and married a young woman instead, which provoked Erskine into one of the most outrageous remarks of his career:

"Without provocation, and without notice or apology, he married another woman, young enough to be his daughter, and who, I hope will manifest her affection by furnishing him with a pair of *horns,* sufficient to defend himself against the sheriff when he comes to levy the money upon this verdict."

If Erskine could have learnt from this example, he would not have become the sad figure who appeared at levees, only to have the Queen turn her back on him, from disgust. Most of his friends avoided him, such a bore had he become with stories of his own brilliance.

He was no longer respectable: he lived with a slut in Hampstead, as beautiful, he boasted, as the naked Venus in a Titian painting; he had children by her, and she in moments of temper did not hesitate to knock him down. His first wife had died long since, so he decided to marry this woman, to make their children legitimate. He crept off to Gretna Green with her, disguised in a woman's dress, for fear his legitimate son should stop him.

At this time the Princess Caroline was abroad; news of her escapades in Italy lost nothing in the telling. She was fifty now, coarser and fatter than ever; few people had a good word for her. But when George III died in 1820, after ten years' exile in his sick-room, she suddenly became a Queen, and was determined to make the most of it.

Attempts to buy her off failed; she wanted to have her place at her husband's Coronation, her name to be included in the Prayer Book, and her massive debts to be repaid. She returned to England. George IV kept her out of Westminster Abbey simply by not issuing her a ticket for the service. But she now had the support of the Whigs, more perhaps from motives of revenge than of sympathy.

It may well have been because, while he was Regent, the Prince of Wales could afford to be friendly with Charles James Fox and the other radicals. But, when he saw what the French Revolution was doing, he changed his mind. By the time he came to the throne, he was no longer on the side of the Whigs.

They made her cause their chief ground of opposition to him, and a stick to beat him with. Since she would not go away, there had to be a trial, to convict her of adultery.

She had to be stopped from asking akward questions about George IV's affairs with various actresses, and with Mrs. FitzHerbert, to name but a few. So the proceedings began in the House of Lords upon the quaintly-named Bill of Pains and Penalties, which was really a divorce case on the grounds of her adultery.

Erskine was now 72 years of age. He had only one year more to live, and died of a chill in his native Scotland.

Most of the case was fought by Henry Brougham, who defended Queen Caroline most ably. He cross-examined one Italian witness minutely about a supposed affair of Queen Caroline's, and got the same answer to each question. It became almost a national catch-phrase - *"Non mi recordo"* - ("I don't remember").

He was successful. The House of Lords voted that she had committed adultery, but by such a narrow majority that it was politically impossible to treat her as guilty. She was therefore regarded as acquitted.

The blowzy heroine of the hour left London, crossed to Ireland, and died of a sudden illness; she did not enjoy her triumph for long, but it gave Erskine his final chance to shine again.

Thomas Creevey, who had sometimes found Erskine's political speeches execrable, had nothing but praise for him upon this occasion.

"Erskine has made the most beautiful speech possible," he said.

The effort put into his final speech took all Erskine's strength. After Lord Chancellor Eldon had made his last speech on behalf of the prosecution, Erskine rose slowly to his feet:

"I am now drawing near to the close of a long life and I must end it as I began it. If you strike out of it, my Lords, some efforts to secure the sacred privilege of impartial trial to the people of this country, and by example to spread it throughout the world, what would be left to me? What else seated me here? What else could there be to distinguish me from the most useless and insignificant, among mankind?

Nothing - just nothing!

And shall I then consent to this suicide - this worse than suicide of the body, this destruction of what alone can remain to me after death - the goodwill of my countrymen? - I DARE NOT DO THAT!"

He began to discuss the evidence, and soon paused in his words. At first they thought that he had lost his place in his notes, but the pause continued, and he pitched slowly forward onto his face.

TEN

Tricks of the Trade

*To say "he hath as much law as a monkey" is not
slander, because it could mean he had as much* and
more.
1 March, pl.93; 1 Rolle, Ab. 58. (17th century law reports)

When a man's hair turns white, he is deemed to have acquired
wisdom; whilst a young barrister's wig is white, he has
everything to learn.

To a pupil, life at the Bar seems so easy. His master demolishes
witnesses with polished ease, and the pupil can see how effortless
it is. He watches other barristers flounder, and knows that he
will never be like them.

Until he does his first case, that is. Then the bottom seems
to drop out of his world.

Montagu Williams became a celebrated QC in Victorian times.
His first case was to prosecute someone for stealing a horse.
He lost it, and rushed home to his wife saying "My dear, I shall
never go into Court again. I have mistaken my profession. I
must try something else."

Sir Henry Hawkins used to say that a beginner, when faced with
a difficult case, ought simply to jump in and splash about.
Beginners look for vivid phrases to capture the newspaper headlines.

A colleague of mine began a plea of mitigation by saying "This
case reminds me of the Frozen Snake, my Lord." One could
see the headlines:

"BARRISTER'S FROZEN SNAKE IN MERCY BID"

But he was disappointed. The Frozen Snake was only the
Viper in the Bosom from Aesop's Fables. It was certainly no
chillier than the judge's reaction.

Petronius complains about purple passages at the very
beginning of his novel *Satyricon:*

166

"But are they not the same Furies that torment our public speakers?

Those who cry 'These wounds I got defending the people's liberty! This eye was lost for you! Give me a guide, lead me to my children, for my mangled limbs will not support me!'

Even *this* may be tolerated if it puts beginners on the highway to eloquence. But with such turgid themes and hollow rattling phrases, all it comes to is this: once at the bar, your tyros imagine they set themselves down in some other world."

He complained that they filled their speeches with melodramatic pictures of pirates on the beach in chains, and so on.

We live in a less colourful age. Television has brought reality too close for ham acting. It used to be otherwise.

A regular spectator at Court fondly recalled the advocacy of Sir Alexander Wedderburn QC:

"In my time, I've heard Sir Alexander in pretty nearly every part. I've heard him as an old man and as a young woman; I've heard him when he was a ship run down at sea and when he's been an oil factory in a state of conflagration. And another time he did the part of a pious bank director that would have skinned the eyelids off Exeter Hall. He ain't bad as a desolate widow with eight children, of which the eldest is under eight years of age. But if ever I had to listen to him again, I would like to see him as a young lady of good connexions who had been seduced by an Officer of the Guards!"

Sir Patrick Hastings recognised that such days had gone for ever. He wrote:

"Ponderous oratory once so popular, and based undoubtedly upon Cicero's orations, has completely disappeared. Just as Gerald du Maurier sounded the death-knell of the old-time school of thunderous declamation from the stage, so Edward Carson put an end to forensic platitudes and passionate but irrelevant perorations from the Bar."

Carson was not alone in this. Rufus Isaacs, who was his equal at the Bar in Edwardian times, was described as "the mildest-mannered man who held a thousand-guinea brief, and one of the most effective."

Patrick Hastings never forgot his first brief. It was marked "One guinea", which was as low as a fee could be; it was returned to him by another lawyer who was unable to do it. "To this day," he wrote, "I can remember the first line of his notes for cross-examination written in his own handwriting: "Now, witness, let me see if I can understand your case!"

Some experienced advocates cannot open a case if they have not written out everything - even the words "May it please you, my Lord."

A barrister's life can become hopelessly stuck in the rut. Marshall Hall found that he was type-cast as a criminal advocate. His superb grasp of scientific details made him particularly interested in a brief which turned on the intricacies of a manufacturing process. The solicitors recommended him to the manufacturer as the man for the case, but the client indignantly rejected the suggestion.

"Good God," he said, "they'll think I've committed a murder!"

Marshall Hall was devastating in cross-examination. Its techniques have changed very little over the centuries.

The oldest recorded example in world literature is the story of *Susanna and the Elders,* in the Apocrypha. Two of the elders try to blackmail her into sleeping with them, saying they will accuse her of adultery in the garden with a young man if she refuses. They bring the accusation, and she is condemned to be stoned to death as an adultress when Daniel arrives, and asks leave to question the two elders separately.

He asks them beneath what sort of tree she was committing adultery.

"A mastic-tree," says one; "a holm-oak," says the other.

On this simple conflict of evidence they are disbelieved, and put to death. Susanna is cleared of the accusation, and "From that day forth," says the Bible,"was Daniel had in great reputation in the sight of the people."

The earliest surviving example of cross-examination in English law may be an ecclesiastical case from the Diocese of Norwich in about 1200.

Who was to inherit under a will? It depended on the validity of a marriage. Canon William was present when Ralph, the Prior, married Arnold and Agnes.

I have translated the account of his evidence into direct questions and answers.

Q: Who was present at the service?
A: As far as the canons of that monastery go, only myself and Prior John of Hatfield were present at the marriage, which took place at the west door of the church. When the Prior celebrated mass, however, all three of them were there; so were Michael of Stanstead, and Robert, a knight who is now dead; but there were no other canons there.

Q: Who else was present?
A: I don't know.

Q: How many other people were there?
A: I don't know.

Q: Was any other woman there apart from the bride?
A: I don't know.

Q: What colour of clothes were the married couple wearing, and what sort of clothes were they?
A: I don't remember.

Q: What time was the service?
A: It was in the morning of the vigil of St. Peter-in-chains [July 31st], but I can't recall what day of the week it was. But it was six years ago come the next feast of St. Peter-in-chains.

Q: How can you be sure about this?
A: I was made a canon on the feast of the Nativity of the Blessed Virgin [8th September], and I will have been a canon seven years come the next Nativity of the Blessed Virgin. I had not been a canon a full year when this marriage took place. I remember that Canon John and I held the veil above Arnold and Agnes. She was on the north side, and he on the south side.

Q: Who took the kiss of peace from the prior?
A: I don't know. Once the mass was over - it was a said mass, not sung with a chant - they left without any wedding feast.

Q: Are you sure the epistle was read at the mass?
A: Yes. I can't say whether John or I read it, but one of us did.

Q: What dower was provided for Agnes?
A: Arnold assigned one third of his land to her, as was only right.

So far, so good. Then a servant gave detailed evidence about the wedding:

Q: When did they go away?
A: I don't know, because I went away immediately after the gospel was read, and after the offering was made.

Q: ...At what time was the veil held over the married couple?
A: In the secret of the mass.

When reminded that he said he went away after the gospel, not after the full mass, he hedged, and tried to change his story.

Finally, Canon John gave evidence. "He seemed, however, to speak lukewarmly, and not constantly, and to offer a premeditated speech."

The five judges appointed as examiners may have taken it in turn to ask the questions, but there is nothing old-fashioned about the way in which the questions established the truth.

A good cross-examiner is rather like an angler who feels a gentle tug on his line, and plays the fish firmly but gently, so that the line does not break.

It used to be thought that they were to be found only at the Common Law Bar. Henry Hawkins, one of the best in Victorian times, was asked to go into Chancery to hear a witness being cross-examined. This is how it went:

Counsel: Will you swear,sir, you were on board the *Bella?*
Witness: I will.

Counsel: Let me make a note of that... Do you swear you were picked up and taken to Australia?
Witness: I do, sir.

Counsel: Let me make a note of that...

The witness was the famous Tichborne Claimant. Hawkins reckoned that if he had been properly cross-examined at that initial stage, his imposture would have been revealed at once, and a great deal of anxiety and expense saved.

Hawkins often rose to his feet with no firm ideas of the way his cross-examination should proceed; he had to rely on instinct and experience.

170

In his reminiscences he quotes a brilliant cross-examination by Charles Mathews QC in a prosecution about the forgery of a will.

A witness claimed that she had seen the old lady sign the will with her own hand. Charles Mathews led her, by seemingly harmless questions, step by step towards destruction:

Q: Where was the will signed?
A: On the bed.

Q: Was anyone near?
A: Yes, the prisoner.

Q: How near?
A: Quite close.

Q: So that he could hand the ink if necessary?
A: Oh yes.

Q: And the pen?
A: Oh yes.

Q: *Did he hand the pen?*
A: He did.

Q: And the ink?
A: Yes.

Q: There was no one else to do so except you?
A: No.

Q: Did he put the pen into her hand?
A: Yes.

Q: And assist her while she signed the will?
A: Yes.

Q: How did he assist her?
A: *By raising her in the bed and supporting her when he had raised her.*

Q: Did he guide her hand?
A: No.

Q: Did he touch her hand at all?
A: *I think he did just touch her hand.*

Q: When he did touch her hand, WAS SHE DEAD?

The witness fell to the ground in a faint.

Hawkins fought a case of a will against Edwin James, who called two excellent witnesses for the plaintiff. They were sufficient to establish his case, and win the claim for £10,000. The judge suggested that he need call no further witness, but James insisted on calling a well-known Dissenting clergyman, the Rev. Mr. Faker.
Hawkins took one look at Mr. Faker, and guessed that the name was true in substance and in fact. Only his instinct told him so.

Q: Mr. Faker -
A: Sir.

Q: You have told us you acted as the adviser of the testatrix.
A: Yes, sir.

Q: Spiritual adviser, of course?

The witness bowed.

Q: You advised the deceased lady, probably, as to her duties as a dying woman?
A: Certainly.

Q: Duty to her husband - was that one?

The witness hesitated, and Hawkins knew that he had found his mark. It gradually emerged that a will had been made in Mr. Faker's favour for £5000, and that he possessed a copy of it. As to the vital original copy of the will, he rather thought he had destroyed it.
Hawkins posed one last lethal question.

Q: Will you swear, sir, that an original will ever existed?
A: No!

172

Hawkins sat down. The plaintiff's case was completely destroyed, all because Edwin James called an unnecessary witness. Hawkins wrote:

"He hurried his client to destruction, and I have never been able to understand his conduct. The most that can be said for him is that he did not suspect any danger, and took no trouble to avoid incurring it."

The ablest barristers sometimes make the classic error of asking "one question too many" in cross-examination.

In theory, the time to stop is when the witness has admitted the basic facts alleged against him. I once cross-examined the defendant in a rape case until he admitted the offence, whereupon I sat down.

The jury acquitted him. I now ask several questions too many.

It is sad when clients lives are put at risk by one question too many.

During the Trial of the Seven Bishops for treason in 1688 it was essential to prove they had signed a petition at some place within the jurisdiction of the Court. There was no evidence of any publication of the offending document in Middlesex. Lord Chief Justice Wright started to direct the jury that they must acquit the defendants, when Heneage Finch, acting for some of the defendants, offered to call evidence on their behalf.
Sjt. Pemberton, who was also appearing for other defendants, tried to shut him up.

"My lord," he said, "we are contented that your Lordship should direct the jury."

"No! No!", said the Lord Chief Justice, "I will hear Mr. Finch. The Bishops shall not say of me, that I would not hear their counsel."

Pemberton could hardly contain himself.

"Pray, good my Lord, we stand mightily uneasy here, and so do the jury. Pray, dismiss us."

It was too late. At that very moment the Earl of Sunderland came into Court to prove that the Bishops had personally presented the petition to the King at Whitehall. The technical point in their favour disappeared entirely. As luck would have it, they were eventually acquitted; but it was no thanks to Heneage Finch.

173

Barristers have always had special techniques for getting results. In 1280 A.D. the Mayor of London, Gregory Rokesley, laid down standards which advocates had to follow:

> *"These are the duties of a counter:*
> To stand and put forward pleas and count counts, and put forward arguments at the Bar without impropriety, dishonour or foul language...
> Anyone found guilty of taking money from both sides in a case, shall be suspended for three years...
> If a counter is found guilty of undertaking a case for a share of the damages, [the Americans call them contingency fees] - he shall be permanently struck off."

These rules would not have been necessary if barristers had not been in breach of them. There have always been a small minority of crooked lawyers, and a number of clients who wanted them, too. The only unfair practice of which I approve, was the mediaeval abbess who sought to influence the judge by bringing her prettiest nuns to court.

Even church lawyers were not always above reproach.

The barristers too used dubious practices, alleging in the pleadings that something happened at a non-existent town. It was done solely to hold up the proceedings. Such devices were forbidden by the Statute of Westminster I in 1275.

A number of dodges were recommended to practising lawyers. Some came from Roman law; others from Europe. They explain why attempts were made to improve the legal profession.

One of the leading and most influential textbooks was Guillaume Durand's *Speculum Juris* (The Mirror of Law) published in Provence in the late 13th century.

Some of its advice was unimpeachable: "You must not behave insultingly to your opponent, or call him bluntly a ruffian or prevaricator, or hint as much by saying *"I* am not a thief," meaning that he is.

"If he has listened to you patiently, you must do likewise; but if he has made a noise or tittered, you can do the same."

It was as well not to quarrel in court, because it could lead to drastic consequences. But it also advised counsel to go and whisper in the judge's ear while his opponenet was addressing the court; the opponent would think they were talking about him, and would be furious.

It was not prudent to lose one's temper with one's opponent.

In one case a Mr. Bellingham deliberately barged into Master Dyer in the precincts of Westminster Hall, at a time when the Courts were sitting. It was a very serious matter; the customary punishment was to cut off the offender's right hand. But Bellingham was pardoned.

It was a turbulent age. According to a 17th-Century law report, Lord Chancellor Ellesmere did a great deal to try to reform the state of the Bar.

"Blessed Lord God of Justice!" said the Lord Chancellor, exhorting the lawyers to be truthful, unprovocative, and not to share in the proceeds of any case; they were to behave pleasantly, and not pollute the fountain of justice.

Such advice was needed. There was a famous quarrel in the Court of the Exchequer between Coke, the Attorney-General, and Bacon, the first Queen's Counsel, because Bacon had made an application in a case in which he had neither a brief nor a fee:

Coke: Mr. Bacon, if you have any tooth against me, pluck it out, for it will do you more hurt than all the teeth in your head will do you good.

Bacon: Mr. Attorney, I respect you; I fear you not, and the less you speak of your own greatness, the more I will think of it.

Coke: I think scorn to stand upon terms of greatness towards you, who are less than little, - less than the least. [Here he added some other similar expressions with an insolence which cannot be expressed].

Bacon: Mr. Attorney, do not depress me so far; for I have been your better, and may be again when it please the Queen.

Surprisingly few barristers quarrel violently in Court. Silks have been known to exchange such expressions as "Cad", and even come to blows during the lunch adjournment. One such incident was reported widely by the press in 1908.

Lord Chancellor Ellesmere took a poor view of advocates who abused their roles. But this was a tradition which has continued as long as there were courts in England. In 1565 for instance, "the Plaintiff for putting in a long replication [a pleading in reply] was fined £10 and imprisoned, and a hole was ordered to be made through the replication, and hanged about his neck, and he to go from bar to bar.''

Lord Chancellor Ellesmere gave short shrift to bad pleadings. If a petition incurred his displeasure, he would ask the petitioner if he wanted his hand to it now. The petitioner eagerly agreed, expecting it to be signed immediately.

''Well, you shall; nay, you shall have *both* my hands to it.'' And he tore it up.

Some tactics called for strong action. In 1614 a defendant pleaded that he was an infant (under 21, that is), in order to delay the trial. It was found that he was 63 years of age, and an order was issued for his arrest.

It was an age of elaborate pleadings, where one false move could cost the client the case. It was essential that a barrister should be a master of technicality; but it could be its own snare.

Charles Abbott, the future Lord Chief Justice Tenterden, earned an huge income on the strength of his pleading rather than any natural eloquence. He was briefed in an important case at Hereford about the right to return an MP to Parliament. But throughout the case his energy was sapped by terrible misgivings that the proper issue had not been taken on the 7th replication to the tenth plea.

He lost the case.

After these thickets of complexity and deceit, any lawyer with a talent for frankness and simplicity should be welcomed with open arms, except perhaps by his client.

An Admiral was sued for the return of a ring; the plaintiff's evidence proved the case, and none was called for the Defence. The plaintiff was bound to succeed, but the counsel for the defendant actually admitted that there never was a clearer or plainer case, and that they had been grossly deceived by their Briefs; they would otherwise not have appeared in such a disgraceful cause.

It takes courage to throw away one's career at the Bar like that. Hawkins, after all, had no knowledge before he rose to cross-examine the Rev. Mr. Faker, that the man was a fraud. He was simply entitled to test his evidence, and he did it.

A barrister should normally obey his instructions. Mr. Clinton of the Midland Circuit once received a brief containing the remarkable phrase "There is no defence to the action, but please to abuse the Plaintiff's attorney."

He vigorously complied, and then read his instructions to the jury, saying that he knew from experience that the plaintiff's attorney was an highly honourable man. He told the jury there was no defence to the action, so that they had no option but to find for the plaintiff. Which they did.

The views of his instructing solicitor are not recorded.

A good memory is a great advantage at the Bar, and may have its tricks, good and bad.

Hardinge Stanley Giffard could read a brief without making a single note. He conducted one heavy case without taking the ribbon off the papers in court; they were later found to have but one thing written on the outside: a list of the trains back to London.

This memory served him well when defending Thomas Smethurst for murder. Smethurst married a woman bigamously - a bad start for a case in Victorian times. She died suddenly under suspicious circumstances, leaving him all her money. There was an autopsy, and Mr. Taylor, one of the leading analysts of the day, found arsenic and antimony in her body. Motive, means and opportunity were proved: Smethurst was convicted, and sentenced to death.

Then Giffard suddenly remembered that he had once heard it was very difficult to obtain copper wholly free from arsenic and antimony. He insisted that some of the copper Taylor had used should be analysed. It was found to contain exactly the same amount of arsenic and antimony as had been found in the dead woman's stomach.

This was in the days before the Court of Criminal Appeal was set up to interfere with a jury's verdict. Giffard had to work tirelessly in order to persuade the Home Secretary to pardon Smethurst. So he went free, and was never grateful enough to Giffard to pay his fees.

Laymen find it difficult to understand that barristers must inform the Court of any cases which are against his argument.

But Serjeant Maynard, when appearing in a poorly paid case, used to refrain from telling a judge he was wrong, in order to be more popular in cases where he was better paid. For such despicable behaviour, Lord Campbell thought he should have changed places with the highwayman in the dock.

He used to invent cases which never existed, and pretend to quote them from memory. I have heard of students trying to baffle their examiners by quoting false authorities in their papers; the preferred tactic was to quote a well-known firm, but reverse the names. Everybody has heard of Marks & Spencers; the student would quote the case of *Spencer v Marks,* in the hope that it would strike not too precise an answering chord in the examiner's mind.

Necessity is the mother of invention; but professional barristers should not stoop to it.

Richard Bethell, the brilliant and waspish Chancery barrister who became Lord Chancellor Westbury, was putting forward an argument when the judge asked him what authority there was for it.

"I have forgotten," said Bethell airily, "but my learned junior, Mr. Archibald, will cite the relevant authorities to your Lordship."

A little while later he finished, and sat down. But Archibald had fled the Court, leaving Bethell to pull his own hot chestnuts out of the fire.

A member of the Bar should always read his brief, and almost invariably does. Sir Frederick Pollock, a name revered for legal learning, was once appearing at the Assizes, and intended to read his brief before breakfast.

When he woke in the morning his eye fell upon a copy of Sir Walter Scott's *The Heart of Midlothian.* He opened it, and found himself on the first page in the middle of an angry mob surrounding the Edinburgh gaol. He could not put the book down, and suddenly found it was time to go to Court, with the brief unread and the opening speech to make for the plaintiff.

He rose to his feet, and told the Judge and jury that the facts of the case were best set out by the correspondence in the case. He began to read the bundle of letters, starting from the very beginning. Onwards and onwards he read, until Chief Justice Abbott could stand it no more.

He asked whether counsel intended to read the entire correspondence.

"Why not?" said Sir Frederick, innocently; "I have never read it before!"

This is not an example to follow, but briefs are sometimes thrust into a barrister's hand not at the eleventh hour, but as the clock strikes twelve.

Sometimes a barrister has to tell the Court frankly of his dilemma, and ask for an adjournment until the following day. It takes courage, but saves him from having to muddle through. But there was one silk who won a case by having to improvise.

The plaintiff was making a claim upon his insurers, and gave his evidence too quickly; the silk had to cross-examine before lunch. He rose to his feet, and asked him politely if he liked travelling abroad.

"Certainly," said the plaintiff.

"Considerable distances?"

"By all means", said the plaintiff. The time was passing pleasantly enough; he had no idea where the questions were leading. Neither had the silk.

"Have you ever been to North America?"

"Er, yes," said the plaintiff.

"Canada, perhaps?"

The plaintiff fainted. The Court adjourned, and during the lunch-hour some transatlantic telephone calls revealed that he had been convicted in Canada of making fraudulent claims upon insurance companies.

The silk, like Hawkins in the case of the will, stumbled upon something he had never expected to find.

David Maxwell-Fyfe was once defending a traffic accident claim at Liverpool Assizes. His client insisted that the plaintiff's car had swerved across the road in the most extraordinary way, for no apparent reason at all. The plaintiff denied it, and his daughter was called as a witness. She said the same thing, but she was a podgy girl. Most remarkably podgy.

Fyfe rose to cross-examine her:

"Tell me, young lady, do you like sweeties?"

"Ooh yes," she said.

"And you take some to eat in the car?"

"That's right," she said.

"Just before the car crashed, did your Daddy turn round and

179

pass you the bag of sweeties?''

"Yes, he did," she said.

Fyfe sat down again.

This cross-examination needed no powerful presence in court, flair for words, or bullying of a witness; merely sensitivity and alertness.

Richard du Cann, in his excellent book *The Art of the Advocate*, says that ridicule is one of the "Three R's" open to a barrister. So it is, provided that it is very sparingly used. A defendant should never be laughed into prison.

When every civil case was tried by a jury, it was standard practice to bully witnesses, or mock them unmercifully. One witness was insulted about his red whiskers: another was lampooned with the expression "Coppernob." He turned on his tormentor, however, and said that he would rather have a "copper nob", than a "brazen face."

Ridicule is used less often than it was.

In a case of nuisance tried at Croydon Assizes in about 1840, it was alleged that a tank on the plaintiff's premises emitted offensive smells.

One of the local rustics, whom Henry Hawkins calls "Hodge", gave evidence about it, and Platt (later Baron Platt) asked him to describe them.

HODGE: Some on 'em smells summat *like paint.*

PLATT: Come, now, that's a very sensible answer. You are aware, as a man of undoubted intelligence, that there are various colours of paint. Had this smell *any particular colour*, think you?

HODGE: Wall, I dunnow, sir.

PLATT: Don't answer hurredly; take your time. We only want to get at the truth. Now, what colour do you say this smell belonged to?

HODGE: Wall, I don't raightly know, sir.

PLATT: I see. But what do you say to *yellow*? Had it a yellow smell, do you think?

HODGE: Wall, sir, I don't think ur wus yaller, nuther. No, sir, not quite yaller; I think it was moore of a blue like.

PLATT: A blue smell. We all know a blue smell when we see it. [Peals of laughter]. You think it was more of a blue smell, like? Now, let me ask you, there are many kinds of blue smells, from the smell of a Blue Peter, which is salt, to that of the sky, which depends upon the weather. Was it dark, or —

HODGE: A kind of sky-blue, sir.
PLATT: More like your scarf?
HODGE [feeling his scarf] Yes, that's more like —
PLATT: Zummut like your scarf?
HODGE: Yes, sir.
PLATT: Were fish remnants sometimes thrown into this reservoir of filth, such as old cods' heads with goggle eyes?
HODGE: Yes, my Lord.
PLATT: *Rari nantes in gurgite vasto?* [a quotation from Virgil meaning "Lone swimmers in the vasty deep"].

Hodge rather thought they were. At this point Thesiger, who was counsel for the plantiff, objected about the way the witness was being mocked; but Chief Justice Tindal did not intervene. "This," said Hawkins, "was my first appearance on circuit, and my first lesson from a great advocate in the art of caricature."

The rules of the Courts have changed greatly over recent years, so that cases are fought on their merits, and not on sudden ambushes and stratagems.

There is less opportunity for in-fighting between barristers, but it still occurs in Requests for Further and Better Particulars.

If you ask a silly question, you can get a silly answer. In a divorce case of desertion "Sandy" Temple, of the Northern Circuit, alleged that on a specific date Mrs. Smith "absconded from matrimonial cohabitation, and has never returned thereto." His opponent asked in a Request for Further and Better Particulars "as to the precise manner of the said absconsion."

"Initially as a pedestrian," he replied, "and thereafter as a fare-paying passenger on a Ribble Motor Omnibus."

In another divorce case Glyn Burrell alleged that Mr. A and Mrs. B, during a certain period, "lived and cohabited and frequently committed adultery together", a standard phrase in such pleadings.

He was incautiously asked, in a Request, whether the period was continuous or intermittent. He gleefully replied that "the period of cohabitation was continuous. It is presumed that the adultery was intermittent."

Taking one's opponent's trousers down is not the highest form of advocacy, but is enormous fun.

High-flown advocates are ready victims:

A prosecutor at the Old Bailey: I have set the stage for you, Members of the Jury. The scenery is in place. Let me ring up the curtain and the play begin.

His opponent: And have the actors learned their lines?

Or in another case:

A.P. Marshall Q.C. for the prosecution: And you may think, Members of the Jury, that the most remarkable feature of this case was the COMPLETE and TOTAL disappearance of Mr. X.

His opponent, drily: Not half as remarkable as his *partial* and *gradual* disappearance would have been.

Perhaps the best form of advocacy is to be always right. A barrister may address a judge with a torrent of superb phrases, each one polished till it shines.

But if his opponent replies in a couple of sentences, and the judge says "Yes, I think that's right", he has won.

The use of simple and effective language is an important "trick of the trade". Norman Birkett honoured it as "proper words in proper places."

He was surely correct. Cicero took this art to its furthest possibilities. It was not only his words, but their rhythms which counted:

"But the eloquent orator who ought to win not merely approval, but admiration and shouts of applause, if possible, should so excel in all things that he would be ashamed to have anything else awaited with greater anticipation or heard with greater pleasure."

He wrote:

"I was standing in an assembly when Gaius Carbo the Younger, the Tribune of the People, spoke in these words: 'O Marcus Drusus, I call on your father.'

This was made up of two *commata*, each consisting of two feet. He followed it up with *cola* of three feet each, and finally slammed it home with a triumphant *ditrochee*.

"It was marvellous what a shout arose from the crowd at this ditrochee!"

Ditrochees are the speech rhythms which go DUM-di-di-di DUM-dum.

"I have to admit that I CANnot recomMEND them."
"To use them would be an ABsolute disASTer."
"That sort of thing is best LEFT to one's opPONent."

ELEVEN

Disbarred!

*"My dear fellow, judge not that you be not judged. I
am older than you, and have seen more of these men.
Believe me that as you grow older and also see more
of them, your opinion will be more lenient, — and more
just.*

Anthony Trollope, *Orley Farm*

In any highly specialised profession, there are always rules
which must be kept. There is no room for talented amateurs
among brain-surgeons; nor at the Bar. It is equally important
to uphold standards of behaviour.

Pliny knew one of the best advocates in Rome, Valerius
Licinianus, who was exiled to Sicily, and was only allowed to
teach rhetoric.

"All this, you may say, is pitiably sad," he wrote, "but no
more than the just fate of a man who disgraced his profession
by the crime of violating a Vestal Virgin."

"Professional etiquette" sounds a little old-fashioned today;
"Basic Code of Standards" might be better. But rules are still
needed. When complaints are made about the Bar, they need
to be investigated. In really serious cases of misbehaviour the
punishment is drastic. So when a QC was disbarred for the first
time, a century ago, it caused a sensation. The culprit was Edwin
John James, QC.

He was born in 1812, the son of a Radical MP. He looked
like a prize-fighter, which he virtually was. At first he
longed to be an actor, and studied with John Cooper, a
Shakespearean "heavy" who played Iago to Kean's Othello.
James appeared on the stage in Bath in the popular melodramatic role of George Barnwell, a young apprentice lured

MARCUS TULLIUS CICERO

He was far and away the best advocate, with a sense of humour which was quite delightful. (see p. 8)

SIR EDWARD COKE
There was one more outburst when he said that there never lived a viler viper than
Raleigh. (see p. 81)

SIR WALTER RALEIGH
His seamen were "the very scum of the world," and his officers seasoned pirates;
even his ship had an ominous name, the *Destiny*. (see p. 85)

THOMAS ERSKINE

He fought for his clients as if his own life was in danger; so it was, in a sense, for he went to France to see the French Revolution, and came back expressing his admiration. (see p. 155)

SIR HENRY HAWKINS

It was as well his father had given him an allowance of £100 a year, or he would have starved to death. His rent for his garret cost £12 a year, and he had to buy professional books as well. (see p. 227)

F.E. SMITH IN THE HOUSE OF COMMONS

"Speaking as a lawyer – (Hear hear, and laughter) – hon. members are entitled to cheer ironically, but the opinion of a man who is not a lawyer is not worth a brass farthing." (Hear hear, and laughter). (see p. 205)

SIR RUFUS ISAACS K.C.

There is no such thing as a successful barrister who keeps short hours. He put it best. "The Bar is never a bed of roses, it is either all bed and no roses, or all roses and no bed." (see p. 264)

THE NUREMBERG TRIALS

Within fifteen minutes, however, it was clear that the unthinkable catastrophe had occurred: Goering was getting the better of him. (see p. 253)

Reproduced by permission of The Illustrated London News Picture Library

by a girl into robbery, and thence to murder and the gallows. His parents dissuaded him from that career, so he came to the Bar at the age of 24. He got plenty of briefs from his father, who was a solicitor. A typical portrait shows him in a navvy's cloth cap with two pistols stuck in his belt. All he needed was a skull and crossbones, being one of those "Yo-ho-ho and a bottle of rum" advocates who always have a place at the Bar.

He acquired a big practice in bankruptcy cases, which were lucrative if not exciting, and shone in criminal cases, where his forensic fisticuffs were seen to best effect. He became the most successful barrister with a common-law practice, and took silk in 1853. He was then 41.

His first great case was that of Walter Palmer, the poisoner, in 1856. As was usual in poisoning cases, the Attorney-General led the case for the Crown; Edwin James QC and two junior counsel made up the prosecuting team. No big case in those days was complete without four counsel on each side, because no counsel was expected to carry out two important cross-examinations in one case.

Four eminent counsel appeared for the defence, and the judicial duties were shared as well: Lord Campbell, the Lord Chief Justice, tried it with Baron Alderson and Mr. Justice Cresswell.

The prosecution case was that Palmer, being very short of money, borrowed several thousand pounds, and took out an insurance policy on one of his victims. A witness was asked if he had attested it:

The Attorney-General: Is not the other signature yours?
The witness: I will tell you, Mr. Attorney —
A-G: Don't you "Mr. Attorney" me, sir! Answer my question. Is not that your signature?
Witness: I believe it not to be.
A-G: Will you swear that it is not?
Witness: I *believe* that it is not.

Edwin James used to cross-examine in that style, but not in the Palmer case.

1856 was a general election year, and it brought him a flood of election petition cases. It was ironically, Parliamentary reform which made corrupt elections worse than ever. As long as there were pocket boroughs, the powerful aristocrats and landowners who ran them knew that their chosen candidate would be elected, and nobody was bribed in those particular seats. But the Reform Act of 1832 swept away the pocket boroughs, and widened the range of voters.

Almost overnight the voters in Bath were increased from 29 to 2900. This was an extreme example; in most boroughs the increase was merely tenfold. Many more people voted, and it was publicly reported how they voted.

Accordingly, the election agents pursued all those they thought would vote for their candidate, and plied them with food and drink. In Stafford, they even paid the voters' rates for them. Shopkeepers found it was wiser to leave town at election time than to be known to have voted one way, thus offending customers who voted the other way.

Every reform bred its own abuses. Voters had to own property worth £10; one pigsty near Leeds, made of four standing stones, somehow earned ten different people the right to vote. It was a paradise of pettifogging technicalities.

Suppose Mr. J. Jones of 10 Smith Street had a vote. If he was registered in error as Mr. K. Jones, or at 11 Smith Street, his vote was declared invalid. If he had changed his address since the register was compiled, he lost the vote which clung to the old property.

And thereby hung election petitions. The unsuccessful candidate challenged his opponent's election on such grounds, and had a fair chance of winning. Indeed, *every single seat* in Ireland was challenged by an election petition.

They do things differently there. In the Mayo election petition (when Edwin James was briefed for the losing candidate) the voters were attacked by a mob incited by a Catholic priest, shouting *in Irish*, "May the curse of God and the curse of the flock be upon any men who vote for Higgins!"

He became the leading practitioner in election cases.

"Edwin James," wrote Serjeant Ballantine, "also possessed all the qualities necessary for the work. He had great readiness,

186

handled his facts amusingly but with considerable force, and was never tedious.''

There were so many election cases at this time that members of Parliament called it a scandal. In May 1857 the Clerk of the House of Commons announced that election petitions had been presented in sixteen cases, and that there were to be no others.

The *Times* reported:

> "This was greeted with obvious relief by some hon. gentlemen who were not perfectly satisfied of the security of their seats. It was greeted with loud cheers.''

The cheers were short-lived; many more petitions were in the pipe-line. Edwin James appeared in 31 cases, and unseated the successful candidate in all but four of them.

Mr. Adderley was one of the loudest to protest bitterly about election petitions; he had been elected at the last four elections as Member for Stafford, where more than half the electorate were bribed. In truth, there were not too many election petitions, but too few.

You might find such payments at election time as "Twelve guineas to screaming women'' — they were paid to get up and scream when the opposing candidate spoke from the hustings — or "£100 to a hundred watchers.'' Watchers had to be constantly vigilant to see that likely voters for one's candidate were not kidnapped, and kept from voting. One Lord of the Manor locked his tenants inside the castle rather than let them vote the wrong way.

In many constituencies the rival candidates reached a gentleman's agreement that both sides could ply the voters with free drink; they got so drunk that they could hardly scrawl their names. In others, the losing candidate was himself so obviously guilty of corruption that he dared not bring a petition.

Sjt. Ballantine remembered a white-haired old gentleman who looked the picture of respectability, and with tears in his eyes denied any misconduct at an election; he had paid out 500 sovereigns in bribery.

It took another thirty years for elections to become honest. As the number of voters increased, it was more difficult to bribe them; once their votes were cast by secret ballot, it was not worth bribing them, because they could take anybody's money and then vote the other way.

Edwin James was not too sickened by these ulcers on the body politic to have Parliamentary ambitions of his own. In 1855 he was made Recorder of Brighton, which had returned two Radical Members to Parliament. (What else could you expect of a constituency composed, it was said, of "toffee, lemonade and jelly shops"?)

Three years after he had taken silk, the *Times* for January 1857 shows what his general practice was like.

There was a case of assault and battery. The plaintiff, a plumber and glazier, went into The Three Crowns in Fore Street, near to the Barbican.

"When we were in our third quartern of gin," he said, "I broke a glass."

The barman (represented by Edwin James) demanded 7½d for the damage, but was bargained down to fourpence. The barman's wife called the plaintiff a damn fool.

"If it was not for such fools as us," retorted the plaintiff, "you would not be wearing such fine satins and rings." At this the barman knocked him down, and threw him out into the street, where he taught him such a lesson that the plaintiff lost the sight of an eye, and won £20 in damages.

A week later, however, Edwin James obtained an order for a new trial, since medical evidence now showed that the plaintiff's eyesight had been defective for years.

Then Edwin James appeared for a Bond Street jeweller claiming £150 for jewels supplied to the third son of the Marquis of Londonderry whilst under the age of 21.

The Defence denied that the jewels had been delivered at all; even if they had been, the Defendant was under the age of 21, and being technically an infant, could not be sued for any unnecessary luxuries supplied to him. As he was an aristocrat and an officer in the Life Guards the case turned on what was necessary in his station in life.

Edwin James began by telling the jury that not a penny had been paid into Court by the Defence. This was perfectly proper in those days; indeed, counsel for the defendant rose only to protest that £60 *had* been offered, and refused by the plaintiff.

Edwin James hotly denied that such an offer had been made, and went on to explain that the jewellery included a diamond and ruby ring, and an enamelled hair-locket:

Baron Bramwell (the Judge): What is that for, Mr. James?
Edwin James: It is what you put a piece of hair in when you are attached to a young lady, my Lord.
Judge (in a devastating comment): Then all I can say is that I have been without necessaries all my life.
Edwin James (smashing the ball back over the net): Your Lordship was never an officer in the Life Guards.

There was a question about onyx cuff-links.

"You or I," Edward James said to the jury, "might wear pewter ones, worth tuppence or threepence."

But here he tugged at their heart-strings.

"Just fancy," he said, "the defendant riding with his mamma in that condition. Is not the idea perfectly absurd?"

A gold latch-key had been supplied to the defendant; all the officers in the Life-Guards, apparently, had gold latch-keys. "What", asked Edwin James in another burst of pathos, "would his mamma say if he had one of iron or steel?"

The jury must have agreed with him; they gave judgment for the plaintiff in the sum of £63.

It is startling to find that a leading QC was briefed in two such trivial cases, and that he was allowed to tell a jury how much money there was in court. The rules are quite different now; the judge would stop the case on the spot, and quite possibly report the counsel to his Benchers.

There is a legend of one counsel who told a jury that money had been paid into court; the judge exploded with anger.

"But, my Lord," protested counsel, "what I did was not illegal; it was *merely a gross breach of professional etiquette!*"

Edwin James was involved in cases of all kinds. There was a breach of promise case, and a rather mysterious claim for defamation by "a commercial traveller in butter" — rather a slippery customer, apparently. He called on a firm who complained to his employers that he had told "lie after lie" about the butter, and said he was never to darken their doorsteps again. He lightened their pockets of £25 in damages, instead.

Edwin James continued to win cases by brute force and impudence. In one of those seduction cases which gladdened the hearts of respectable Society, he called as a witness a Mr. Taylor who had invented what he called a 'clinometer'', an Indicator which showed that two people were in the bed in question. The jury laughed a good deal at this; and when the inventor admitted stealing a bottle of gin from the plaintiff's bedroom, the laughter grew even louder. They awarded the plaintiff only one farthing damages; that came as no surprise. But Edwin James' speech to them caused a national scandal:

> "My learned friend will make a good many severe observations upon Mr. Taylor's evidence; but you should bear in mind that the character of the defendant can only be established by the aid of such a person. The Journals of the House of Lords bear testimony to the fact that a Right Honourable gentleman who was once a Minister of the Crown and once attracted the wife of a noble duke, who afterwards obtained a divorce, appeared as a witness to prove her adultery."

He was referring to Mr. Gladstone's conduct in a recent divorce case!

Mr. Gladstone was stung into action. He wrote to the Editor of the *Times*:

> "Sir, I do not mean to take any steps which in former times would have been taken —" [he meant a duel] "— but I will avail myself of those weapons which are open to every man."

Edwin James apologised in a letter which made things deliberately worse, because he sent a copy to the *Times*. He gallantly suggested that Mr. Gladstone should read it aloud in the House of Commons. Mr. Gladstone declined.

In 1858 Edwin James fought one of the most dramatic cases of his career, defending Dr. Simon Bernard on a charge of being accessory to the fact of murder. Three conspirators tried to assassinate the Emperor of France as he arrived at the Opera at Paris; they threw grenades at him. He escaped injury, but eight people were killed.

The prosecution alleged that Dr. Bernard had bought the grenades in England, and taken them to the Continent for the assassination. A police sergeant gave evidence of Dr. Bernard attending political meetings in London. It was not the most crucial evidence, but Edwin James sought to discredit him by calling him a spy:

Q: What were they discussing?
A: Mr. Bernard was in the chair, and they were discussing political matters.

Q: Well, what was the subject that they were discussing?
A: It was a question showing the difference between democratic and Imperial governments.

Q: Between democracy and despotism?
A: Yes, and despotism...

Q: You went there as a spy, did not you?

The Attorney-General (for the Crown): It would be fairer to the witness, as well as to those who sent him, if you were to ask him what his instructions were.

Edwin James: Well, what were your instructions?
A: To attend that meeting and report on it.

Q: And what did you report?
A: That a number of persons were there, and that Mr. Bernard was put in the chair; also the nature of the subject discussed ... I went the next time on the following Monday.

Q: As a spy?
A: I went as directed.

Q: That is a plain English question. Did you go as a spy?

Chief Justice Campbell: You had better get the facts from him and you can draw any inference you please.

Edwin James: It is a plain English question, and I submit that I may ask it.

There was then a heated legal argument. The Chief Justice ruled that it was not for the witness to state whether he was a spy, but for the jury to decide facts. Edwin James attacked the witness again:

Q: What did you hear — something very shocking?
A: No, sir.

Q: Well, what was it?
A: I would not undertake to swear to the remarks I heard.

Q: What were they about? You made a report, you know.
A: Political subjects.

Q: What political subjects? The administration of India, or Parliamentary reform, or what?
A: I do not remember.

Despite all this, the evidence against Dr. Bernard seemed overwhelming.

It was said of Edwin James that he was no great lawyer, but his chief skill lay in appealing to the ignorant instincts of a jury. English juries are not, on the whole in favour of foreign assassins. Still, he made play of the fact that this case was tried in England at all. He said to the jury:

"The Attorney-General has never explained how it comes about that for the first time in the annals of jurisprudence such a prosecution has been brought before a jury in this country, and it is right that this should be explained to you before you give a verdict upon a charge by which — not content with the blood of Orsini and Pieri [two conspirators who had been guillotined] — it is sought to stain an English scaffold with the blood of the prisoner at the Bar ..."

He ended with a fine flourish:

"Tell the prosecutor in this case that the jury box is the sanctuary of English liberty. Tell him that on this spot your predecessors have resisted the arbitrary power of the Crown, backed by the influence of crown-serving and time-serving judges. Tell him that under every difficulty and danger your predecessors have secured the political liberties of the people. Tell him that the verdicts of English juries are founded on the eternal and immutable principles of justice. Tell him that, panoplied in that armoury, no threat of

192

arms or invasion can awe you. Tell him that, though 600,000 French bayonets gleamed before you, though the roar of French cannon thundered in your ears, you will return a verdict which your own principles and consciences will sanctify and approve, careless whether that verdict pleases or displeases a foreign despot, or secures and destroys for ever the throne which a tyrant has built upon the ruins of the liberty of a once free and mighty people.''

This speech was greeted with cheers and applause. The jury then retired for eighty minutes, and announced its verdict: Not Guilty.

There was an uproar. The cheering was so deafening that the usher, shouting for order at the top of his voice, could not be heard. Ladies of quality waved their handkerchiefs in delight; Chief Justice Campbell sat as if carved in stone. It was a great victory for Edwin James.

In 1859 he entered Parliament, having won the seat of Marylebone by a comfortable majority. The speeches he made in Parliament do him credit. He attacked the low rate of soldiers' pay, which tended to mutiny, and the large arrears of divorce cases which awaited hearing. He opposed the introduction of majority verdicts in criminal cases, and scorned the antiquated duty upon Sheriffs to provide Assize Judges with a retinue of ''javelin men'', as they were called:

> ''It is well known that the judges have the power to impose a heavy fine on Sheriffs for the non-attendance of javelin-men — a power which more than once they have exercised; and it is proposed by this Bill to take away the power. This is not a question of keeping order, but of state and pageantry; and there is no pageantry in having two decrepit old men moving before the judge and preceded by an asthmatic trumpeter. The time has arrived when javelin-men ought to be done away with. The judges do not want them; they are continually in the way, and are not of the slightest use in maintaining order.
>
> The Right Honourable Member for Oxfordshire asks, in his own emphatic language, If there is a row, where will the javelin-men be? My answer is, Everywhere but where the row is.''

He urged electoral reform, and was a member of a House of Commons Committee on Corrupt Practices. He questioned the commissioners from the Gloucester election, which had been notoriously corrupt:

> *Edwin James:* Suppose a very patriotic cabmaster volunteered to take up voters to the poll in his own cabs, at a metropolitan election, would you unseat the member in that case?
> *The Commissioner:* That would be "providing carriages". [Therefore illegal].
> *Edwin James:* I mean a perfectly *bona fide* loan of conveyances of a patriotic character?
> *The other Commissioner:* I think the Hon. Member is suggesting a case that does not very often occur.

A name which was found frequently in election cases was John Sadleir, a crooked solicitor, who was said to manufacture election petitions, and withdraw them if offered enough money. He was also involved in the case of *Scully v Ingram.*

Mr. Scully had sold a large estate of land in Cork at a handsome profit, because Sadleir had exaggerated its value. By the time the case was heard, in December 1858, Sadleir's huge frauds in banking shares had come to light. He committed suicide, and it was no good suing his estate, so Mr. Scully sued Mr. Ingram instead. Mr. Ingram could only be liable if it could be proved that he knew perfectly well that Sadleir had exaggerated the value of the land.

There was little evidence against him on that score. The case was more than six years old, and as counsel for the Defence pointed out:

> "The Plaintiff, with all the skill of a lawyer, has been brooding over the case since 1856, and has detailed conversations which occurred six years ago with a familiarity as if they had occurred yesterday."

Edwin James, who appeared for the plaintiff, cross-examined Mr. Ingram mercilessly.

"I must tell you," said a friend, "that if ever a man had a narrow escape of causing another man's suicide, you did it on that occasion."

The jury found for the plaintiff, but the trial was unsatisfactory, and Mr. Ingram obtained leave for the case to be tried again. He stood in mortal fear of another cross-examination.

"I must lend Mr. James some money," he told a friend; "I must — I am so afraid of him; I must do anything he asks, and you must lend him the money for me."

£1000 changed hands.

Ingram went on holiday to America, and was on board a steamer on the Great Lakes when a storm blew up, and the ship sank with all on board. More was to be heard of that case.

Edwin James had Republican sympathies for the Europeans struggling against archaic monarchies. His defence of Dr. Bernard showed this; so did his visit to Garibaldi's camp in the autumn of 1860.

Garibaldi enjoyed a remarkable popularity in England. Three years after he won his campaign, and proclaimed Italy to be one Kingdom rather than a collection of kingdoms, he came to England, and was given the Freedom of the City of London. He was welcomed by the Prince of Wales, Florence Nightingale, Gladstone and Tennyson; named after him were Garibaldi suits, Garibaldi perfumes, and of course, Garibaldi biscuits.

In 1860 he liberated Calabria, and moved northwards from Salerno. Edwin James was with him on the train as they approached Naples on September 7th. Garibaldi was warned that the guns of the fortress were trained on the railway station, but took courage from the crowds that welcomed him all along the route.

"What cannon?" he asked. "When people greet us like this, there will be no cannon."

He was right. The fortress surrendered without a single shot being fired, and Naples was his.

Edwin James sent despatches back to England of the campaign. Twelve days later there was a skirmish near Capua; he wrote scathingly of some cowards who deserted their regiment:

> "I followed these mischievous and cowardly fellows to Caserta, asked for the Colonel of a regiment who spoke French, gave him my name and address, pointed out the fellows as they entered the square in front of the Palace, and, although I did not request it as a personal favour, I certainly suggested that they should be marched out and shot; they were at once taken to the guardhouse

and were no more seen by me. It is only just to say that several regiments passed these dastardly renegades unnoticed, and marched on to the relief of the village."

Garibaldi succeeded in his campaign, and, back in England, Edwin James went from strength to strength. In 1861 he appeared in Canada on a case which attracted the sympathy of the world, that of The Slave Anderson.

John Anderson was a negro slave, married to a slave negress who worked on the next plantation; they could see each other regularly. But Anderson was sold to another master 30 miles away on the other side of the Missouri, so he ran away. Another plantation owner, one Seneca T.P. Diggs, chased him for the reward a caught runaway slave would bring. When cornered, Anderson drew a knife and stabbed Diggs to death. He escaped to Canada.

Mr. Justice Maclean, in the Canadian court of King's Bench, had no doubt that English law applied:

"Can, then, or must the law of slavery in Missouri be recognised by us to such an extent as to make it murder in Missouri while it is justifiable in this Province to do precisely the same act? I confess that I feel it too repugnant to every sense of religion, and every feeling of justice, to recognise a rule, designated as a law, passed by the strong for enslaving and tyrannizing over the weak — a law which would not be tolerated for a moment if those who are reduced to the condition of slaves, and deprived of all human rights, were possessed of white instead of black or dark complexions."

He was in a minority. The other judges held that Anderson should be extradited to America. Then the British and Foreign Anti-Slavery Society issued a writ on his behalf, so that he could be brought to England on a writ of *habeas corpus*. Even this plan was dangerous, as it was winter. All the Canadian ports were iced up, and Anderson could only be brought to Britain through the United States, where he might well be arrested. So he applied for a writ in Canada declaring that his detention was illegal; this being granted, he was finally set free.

The result threw great credit on Edwin James, who was very active upon Anderson's behalf. He could be said to have reached the peak of his career. So he had; a plunging precipice lay immediately beyond.

Four months after the Anderson case, he was condemned, disgraced, and ruined; in a word, disbarred.

Nobody could believe it. Henry Hawkins was astonished:

"He was a Queen's Counsel, a brilliant advocate in a certain line of business, and a popular, agreeable, intellectual, and amusing companion. In every Society paper, amongst its most fashionable intelligence, there was he; and Society hardly seemed to be able to get along without him.

One Sunday afternoon I was reading in my little room when this agreeable member of the elite called upon me. My astonishment was great, because at that time of my career not only did I not receive visitors, but *such* a visitor was beyond all expectation, and I wondered, when his name was announced, what could have brought him, he so great and I comparatively nothing ...

His manner was agreeable, and his face wore a smile of complacency at variance with the nature of his errand, which he quickly took care to make known by informing me that he was in a devil of a mess, and did not know what he should do to get out of it.

'The fact is, my dear Hawkins,' said the wily intriguer, for such he was, 'I'll tell you seriously how I stand: tomorrow morning I have bills becoming due amounting to £1250, and I want you to be good enough to lend me that sum to enable me to meet them.'

I was perfectly astounded! This greatness to have come down to £1250 on the wrong side of the ledger ...

However, I went to my bankers' and made arrangements to be provided with the amount. I met him at the place of appointment, and was quite surprised to see the change in his demeanour since the day before. He was now apparently in a state of deeper distress than ever, and, thinking to soothe him, I said, "It's all right; you can have the money.""

Edwin James had not been frank with Hawkins. He needed at least double that sum; Hawkins trustingly lent it him, and lost every penny.

The first ominous signs of trouble, as far as the general public was concerned, were his withdrawal from the House of Commons in April 1861, and his resignation from Brooks's and the Reform Club. Then creditors came down on his house in Berkeley Square for debts of £100,000. This might have been mere misfortune, or financial folly; but accusations began to accumulate against Edwin James.

On June 7th 1861 the Benchers of the Inner Temple began an investigation into allegations that he had fleeced young Lord Worsley, who had just come of age, of £35,000; that he had obtained £20,000 from a West Country solicitor upon false pretences; worst of all, that he had taken £1500 from Mr. Ingram, after the first trial of Mr. Scully's action against him, on the basis that he would go more easily on him in cross-examination during the retrial. He had certainly received the money.

The motive was in dispute; but, as the *Times* bluntly put it:

> "If any counsel on the eve of an important trial is to be allowed to borrow money of his adversary's client, and remain a member of the Bar, the sooner a new Temple is built the better."

It was an age when people seemed to have less regard for those awesome figures, the Benchers of their Inn. At this very time Mr. Digby Seymour QC was facing his Benchers because of questionable gold-mining shares sold in partnership with a Mr. Hudson, who appeared before the Benchers, and asked to see a damaging document. It was handed to him, whereupon Mr. Hudson thrust it coolly into his pocket.

This was the scene as described by that year's *Annual Register*, a sober and useful digest of public events:

> "Dire was the confusion and great the outcry. The fourteen or fifteen Benchers present sprang to their feet, uttered promiscuous expressions of wrath, and it was said that even oaths were heard. They directed their under-treasurer and porters to recover possession of the abstracted document; these aides-de-camp threw themselves upon the detainee, and a wild and irregular struggle ensued."

The document was recovered, and on the strength of one of the charges, Mr. Digby Seymour was severely reprimanded.

Edwin James' situation was far worse.

The Benchers of the Inner Temple called him to explain the shady money transactions, and his sudden withdrawal from Society.

He tried to play for time. He got a week's adjournment, to

prepare his arguments, and a further adjournment to obtain a transcript of the witnesses' evidence. Two days before the resumed hearing he wrote — from Paris, of all places:

> "My temporary absence from England caused by my unfortunate pecuniary position, has disabled me from preparing the statement to be laid before the Bench. Now that I have the whole evidence, I will with the assistance of my friends at once devote myself to the task."

Further adjournments were requested and refused; thus, on July 18th 1861, the Benchers ordered "that the Call to the Bar of Mr. Edwin John James QC be vacated, that he be disbarred, and his name struck off the books of this Society [of the Inner Temple.]"

He had admitted receiving too many of the discreditable loans for it to be otherwise.

No longer able to hold up his head in England, he went to New York, and persuaded the Bar there to admit him as one of their members, rather against their better judgement. Then he went on the New York stage.

Eleven years later, in 1872, he was back in England, and delivered a public lecture on America. It was well attended, and there were shouts of "Welcome back!"

Apart from a new moustache, he seemed his usual self, and tried to retrieve his position, but his Benchers would not rescind their decision. He was adopted again as a Liberal candidate for Marylebone.

"Except within the narrow circles of my own profession," he declared, "I believe I have not a single enemy in the world."

He was well received, but he was not elected. He became an articled clerk to a City of London solicitor, and gave legal opinions to his clients; he lectured about his friend Garibaldi, but his fortunes fell into a decline. When he was 69 years old his friends rallied round, and there was talk of them raising a public subscription for him when he died, in 1882.

He is now totally forgotten, and lives on only in the immortal pages of Charles Dickens and Anthony Trollope, a distinction indeed.

Dickens saw him in his Chambers and at the Old Bailey, and drew a pen-portrait which he felt hit him off very nicely, as Serjeant Stryver in *A Tale of Two Cities*. We learn from Dickens, but nobody else, that Edwin James was a drunkard:

> "Those were drinking days and most men drank hard... The learned profession of the law was certainly not behind any other learned profession in its Bacchanalian propensities; neither was Mr. Stryver, already fast shouldering his way to a large and lucrative practice, behind his compeers in this particular, any more than in the drier parts of the legal race ...
>
> In the Court of King's Bench, the florid countenance of Mr. Stryver might be seen, bursting out of the bed of wigs, like a great sunflower pushing its way at the sun from among a rank gardenful of flaring companions."

Dickens called him glib, unscrupulous, and bold:

> " 'And now,' said Mr. Stryver, shaking his forensic forefinger at the Temple in general, ... 'My way out of this, is, to put you all in the wrong.'
>
> It was the art of an Old Bailey tactician, in which he found great relief.
>
> 'You shall not put me in the wrong, young lady,' said Mr. Stryver; 'I'll do that for you.' "

Sjt. Stryver's appearance in *A Tale of Two Cities* is disappointingly brief; but Anthony Trollope did him proud, for Edwin James appears as "Mr. Chaffenbrass" in *The Three Clerks* (1857), *Orley Farm* (1862), and *Phineas Redux* (1874).

Trollope, whose father was a Chancery barrister, knew the legal world very well; Mr. Chaffenbrass is perhaps the most vivid picture of a barrister in the whole of literature. In *Orley Farm* he wrote:

> "Mr. Chaffenbrass was a dirty little man; and when seen without his gown and wig, might at a first glance be thought insignificant. But he knew well how to hold his own in the world, and could maintain his opinion, unshaken, against all the judges in the land."

He was, indeed, one of the few counsel who could stand up to Lord Campbell, the Lord Chief Justice.

Trollope wrote this in 1862, the year after Edwin James was

disbarred. Nobody else describes him as dirty — this may be an imaginative touch — but he was certainly a bully.

"You can frighten a witness, Mr. Chaffenbrass," says one of the characters in *Phineas Redux*.

"It's just the trick of the trade that you learn, as a girl learns the notes of her piano," replies Mr. Chaffenbrass. "There's nothing in it. You forget it all the next hour. But, when a man has been hung whom you have striven to save, you do remember that ..."

Mr. Graham, a young barrister in the same book, is horrified by Mr. Chaffenbrass. But Trollope takes a broader view, which will serve as a memorial for Edwin James and the select few who follow in his footsteps:

> "Considering the lights with which he had been lightened, there was a species of honesty about Mr. Chaffenbrass which certainly deserved praise. He was always true to the man whose money he had taken, and gave to his customer, with all the power at his command, that assistance which he had professed to sell.

> But we may give the same praise to the hired bravo who goes through with truth and courage the task which he has undertaken. I knew an assassin in Ireland who professed that during twelve years of practice in Tipperary he had never failed when he had once engaged himself. For truth and honesty to their customers — which are great virtues — I would bracket that man and Mr. Chaffenbrass together."

The saddest verdict on his career came from Henry Hawkins, who never got his money back:

> "Sometimes, in spite of *all*, I feel a moisture in my eye when I think of him. Had he been true to himself, what a brilliant life was open to him! What a practice he had! Up to the last he told me that he turned £14,000 a year. He worked hard, very hard, and his gains went to --- or to chicken hazard (a gambling game).

> Poor fellow!"

TWELVE

F.E. In Silk

*To most of us it never happens, and it is better for us
that it should not happen. But when it does, one is forced
to go beyond the common rules.*

Anthony Trollope, *Dr. Wortle's School*

"The House of Commons crowded, silent. A young man,
immaculately dressed, his black hair plastered back from his
forehead, speaking in even tones, without gesture."

"He rises slowly from his place, thrusts his head slightly forward
from his shoulders, and slips into his speech with a little stream
of pleasant words which in their soft tones exactly match his
personal appearance. And then to your surprise, it comes upon you
that these soft words are laden with bitterness. A new man grows
up before you. You see, beneath the surface suavity, intense scorn,
seething indignation."

These descriptions, taken from newspapers of the time,
perfectly describe the new Unionist Member for the constituency
of Walton (Liverpool), when he rose to deliver his maiden speech
in March 1906. He was F.E. Smith, forever to be known as
"F.E."

He joined the ranks of the Conservatives in Parliament, their
ranks much thinned after an electoral landslide which put the
Liberals into power with a massive majority. When he rose to
make his maiden speech, he was attacking a well-established
majority:

"All great political parties have skeletons in the cupboard. Some
have manacles on and some only have their hands behind their
backs. [Laughter]. The quarrel we have with hon. gentlemen
opposite [the Liberal Government] is the astonishing indelicacy
they show in attempting to drag their skeletons out into the open.
[Laughter]."

Having been amusing, he attacked Lloyd George on the question of Tariff Reform:

"It is far easier if one possesses a charming literary style, to describe Protection as a 'stinking, rotten carcase', than to discuss scientifically whether certain limited proposals were likely to be protective. [Cheers]. It is far easier to suggest to the simple rustics of Wales, as Mr. Lloyd George has done, that if they voted for his opponent the Conservative party were likely to introduce slavery into Wales." [Opposition cheers].

Mr. Lloyd George: "I did not say so." [Hear hear].

F.E. then produced the newspaper cutting which reported Lloyd George as having said that very thing. He next turned his scorn upon Winston Churchill, then a Liberal; few of the Liberals escaped his lash. He sat down after an hour's speech which held the House spellbound, and made him a household name.

Lloyd George then rose to his feet. "We have just listened to a brilliant speech," he said.

"His speech was a pudding nearly all plums," reported the *Standard*.

The *Daily Chronicle*, a Liberal paper, was rather more grudging in its praise:

"It was excessively witty, and it was impertinent beyond description. The delight of the front Opposition bench was pathetic. You could have placed an apple in Mr. Austen Chamberlain's laugh at any moment ... Sir Edward Carson was so happy as to look almost human."

F.E.'s speech was in all the papers. A reporter from *The World* went to see him at his chambers on the second floor of Elm Court, with a lovely view of the Temple. His desk was covered with briefs; proudly displayed in the room was a model of the barque *Veronica*, a ship with a terrible story of piracy and murder. F.E. had prosecuted the culprits to conviction; they were hanged.

What were his first impressions of Parliament? the reporter asked him.

"Its strenuous energy and apparently inexhaustible capacity

for work," he replied. He paid a special and perhaps unexpected tribute to the attitude and bearing of the Labour members, whose example in some respects could profitably have been followed by some of their Liberal allies. This, however, did not save them from his merciless sarcasm in his second speech.

It was eagerly awaited. The *Liverpool Courier* wrote:

"When it came, the majority of members were taken by surprise. He made a dull, almost commonplace speech ... Only the old Parliamentary hands guessed what was in the wind. Having made a reputation for brilliancy and wit, he had wisely made up his mind to create a new one on a sounder basis of solid party work."

Most speakers would give their right arms to be no duller than F.E. on that occasion, speaking about the Trades Disputes Bill and the right of strikers to picket their colleagues. He said:

"The views I have always held are not those of the hon. members below the gangway [the Labour Party]. But I, with no false pretences, represent a working-class constituency ... I do not merely represent, as hon. members below the gangway do, with immense ability, the interests of organised labour and trade unions; I represent large numbers of men who are not members of trade unions, and never from these men have I heard expressions of a desire to be subject to "peaceful persuasion." [Hear hear].

What is the House required to do by this Trade Unions and Trade Disputes Bill? To permit 100 men to go round the house of a man who wishes to exercise his common law right to sell his labour where and when he chooses, and to allow these 100 men to advise him and peacefully persuade him not to work?" [Hear hear].

I know no member of the House more respected, more peaceful, than the hon. member for Merthyr [Mr. Keir Hardie], and I am sure the Attorney-General agrees no man can be more persuasive [laughter].

If I were a man wishful to dispose of my labour as I chose, then although the Member for Merthyr might not persuade me, yet if he came with 50 other peacefully persuasive men to my house where my wife lives and is equally nervous as myself, then I might be more ready to yield to peaceful persuasion than if the hon. member came alone [laughter]."

Most politicians make politics seem trivial and dull. F.E. found them fascinating, and even after eighty years his speeches are as bold as ever. He frequently scored off his opponents; they seldom scored off him. He went on:

"Is it more convenient to impart information by 50 men than by one? Even in the House of Commons — with occasional exceptions — it has been recognised as a general principle that it is convenient that the House shall be addressed by one member at a time" [laughter].

... - Speaking as a lawyer [Hear hear, and laughter] - hon. members are entitled to cheer ironically, but the opinion of a man who is not a lawyer is not worth a brass farthing." [Hear hear, and laughter].

Mr. Crooks, Labour member for Woolwich: "Good trade unionism, this."

F.E.: "Yes, members of my profession are trade unionists, but they do not ask to be allowed to exercise their powers of persuasion in large numbers upon their competitors!"

He had won another victory before the greatest audience of all — the House of Commons. A man in the spotlight there was seen by all the world.

From this time onwards he stayed in London. He left his busy practice at the Bar in Liverpool, and was seldom seen there in Court again. In that year of 1906 he made his name in Parliament, but appeared in no cases of undying fame. He continued the almost endless litigation on bahalf of Ogdens, the tobacco firm, brought by shopkeepers who were promised special discounts they did not receive. There were hundreds of claims to defend.

He had a breach of promise case, a claim that excessive water-pumping had led to the subsidence of a house, and an Admiralty case about two ships which collided.

It was in a London County Court that he appeared for an insurance company, when an injured plaintiff claimed that the accident had crippled his right arm.

"How high could you raise your arm *before* the accident?" asked F.E., innocently.

The Plaintiff obligingly demonstrated, thus proving his own fraud.

These cases do not stir the blood; despite his dazzling talents at the Bar, F.E. shone more in politics than he did in Court. His performances in the House of Commons showed him at his most forensic; some of his cases in Court showed him at his most statesman-like.

He would never have been allowed to treat witnesses in the way he handled his political opponents. He usually masked his deadliest thrusts with a cloak of humour. Only once did he go too far. It was in 1908, when the Education Bill threatened to deprive schools of their religious instruction. F.E. was the most ardent defender of that practice.

"Mr. McKenna," he said, speaking of the Liberal politician who was introducing the Bill, "appeals from his embarrassed political side to his corrupt judicial side" [Ministerial cries of "Withdraw"] "to his *partial* judicial side." [More cries of "Withdraw"].

The Deputy Speaker rebuked him. "The hon. and learned member has no right to make a charge of corruption."

"In deference to the ruling from the Chair," said F.E., "I will substitute for the charge of corruption a charge of partiality."

"There are just two perils to this promising young man," wrote T.P. O'Connor in a very fair assessment:

"One danger is that his mordant wit may betray him into too unmitigated rancour of speech, and rancour is not a temper which is ever acceptable to the House of Commons. Mr. Smith is, I am sure, not in the least a rancorous man; he was my opponent for two years in Liverpool, and I ought to know; but his bitter wit gives the false impression. Let him cultivate the same geniality in public that he reveals in private life, and he will be more acceptable in the House."

F.E. could never do it. Some barristers have a swashbuckling style of advocacy, sometimes referred to as the "Yo-ho-ho and a bottle of rum" technique. F.E. never used it at the Bar, or abandoned it in his political speeches.

In 1907 he violently attacked the Liberals' proposals to reform the House of Lords:

"A most offensive habit which the Liberal party has in dealing with this question is to talk of England as if it were a permanent Radical pocket borough, much on the same principle as if a valet were to wear his master's clothes in the servant's hall." [Cries of "Oh! Oh!" and laughter].

In another speech he said:

"During the first year in which it was in office, the present Government created sixteen new peers — one new peer every three weeks. I can see the mouths of hon. members opposite watering." [Laughter]. The Prime Minister [Asquith] at a banquet of the National Liberal Club, said 'the question I want to put to you is this — is this state of things to continue? We say it must be brought to an end, and I invite the Liberal party tonight to treat the veto of the House of Lords as the dominating issue.' As indicating the stern principle of the strenuous men assembled on that occasion, the *Times* reporter called attention to the fact that the company at that point stood up and waved their dinner napkins." [Laughter]. It is a somewhat inauspicious omen that, even at that early stage of the campaign, they should have marched under the white flag." [Renewed laughter].

F.E. was often progressive in his thinking. His Campaign leaflet for the 1910 election set out different views on the House of Lords.

"I am in favour of a Reformed Second Chamber, but only because it will thereby be made stronger. Half the House of Lords should be elected; and disputes between the two Chambers should be adjusted in joint session. Matters of high Constitutional and political importance should be decided in a referendum by the people."

It was not only his mordant humour, but also his burning seriousness of purpose, which made him such a devastating opponent. His knowledge of political history, and his great clarity of thought, enabled him to show up the fallacies of his opponents' arguments with merciless accuracy.

Many of his speeches were tinged with deep humanity. In 1907, when he was supporting the establishment of a Court of Appeal for criminal cases, he quoted case after case in which the wrong man had been hanged for murder, and was later proved to have been innocent. He said:

"It is simply horrible that such things could be possible, and that there could be no chance of the interposition of the Court of Appeal. [Cheers]. "If it is necessary that in civil matters an opportunity should be given of revision of the most trivial points, it is intolerable that on issues of life and death the same safeguards should not be provided." [Cheers.]

His proposals became law.

At the Bar F.E.'s practice grew by leaps and bounds. One of his regular clients was Horatio Bottomley, who frequently appeared in the Courts as plaintiff or defendant, according to which tack he was on as he sailed closer and closer to the wind. F.E. regretted very much that his practice sometimes kept him from the House of Commons during an important part of the proceedings. But it must surely have been his status in Parliament which ensured that he took silk in 1905 at the age of 35, younger than any other man had ever achieved that promotion. He was also made a Bencher of Gray's Inn.

He was seen everywhere in the best society.

Christmas, spent with the Duke of Marlborough at Blenheim, was a favourite social occasion. They ate off gold plates, and were served by tall footmen with powdered hair. There were torchlight processions in the park, and oxen roasted whole. For the hunting season he took four hunters to ride on, and three grooms. A less dangerous sport was shooting rabbits. Blenheim established a world record when 6943 of them were shot in one day.

T.P. O'Connor saw the risk of his head being turned by success.

"And so the usual attempts have been made to spoil F.E. Smith," he wrote. "But he smiles and goes back to his briefs and his horses, and looks ahead, patiently, but with his eyes on high lodestars."

He continued to increase his practice at the Bar. In the case of *Capron v Scott* he appeared for the Plaintiff, who was claiming that a will which left more than one million pounds to Lady Sackville was invalid. It was a tactical error on F.E.'s part to take the case, because he knew Lady Sackville socially, and she took advantage of it.

Even during the trial she kept writing him personal letters.

"Surely you must be aware," he replied, "that I should deserve to be disbarred if my professional conduct were influenced by any circumstances of private acquaintance."

But she embarrassed him even in open Court.

"Her methods as a witness", wrote her daughter Vera Sackville-West, "I need hardly say were completely irregular. The ingenuity she displayed in evading any question she didn't

want to answer was a triumph of femininity at its best and worst.
she was disconcerting, maddening, witty. At moments she had
the whole Court in roars of laughter, when even the judge
permitted himself a smile. For one thing she insisted on treating
the opposing counsel (F.E. Smith) as a person she knew socially,
as indeed she did.

"You would have said just the same thing yourself, Mr.
Smith. We meet at dinners, so I know you would."

"We will not argue about that, Lady Sackville."

Sometimes she appealed direct to the judge.

"My Lord, may I ask you something? My Lord, you may
remember, and the gentlemen of the jury —"

F.E. (wearily): I will sit down.

He was seldom outmatched, either in Court or in the
Commons.

He continued to increase his practice at the Bar and his
standing in the Commons. He never lost an opportunity of
pouring scorn on his best friend, Winston Churchill, who was
then a Liberal, and Under-Secretary for the Colonies. He was
also his firm friend; he named his son "Frederick WINSTON
Smith"; Churchill was the boy's godfather:

"The right hon. gentleman has observed that there are more ways
of killing cats than choking them with cream. I may be allowed
to add that there are more ways of addling a political egg than by
giving it to the Under-Secretary to sit upon." [Laughter].

Again, at a public meeting at Huddersfield:

"I think the Socialists had better not cheer the name of Mr.
Churchill, for he will most likely in the end steal their clothes when
they go bathing — if they do bathe — which I doubt." [Laughter].

He was even more offensive about Lloyd George, whom he
called a "pot-house demagogue."

"Mr. Lloyd George," he said at Derby, "is a perfect
gentleman except when he becomes angry, and then he reverts
to type and becomes Mr. Lloyd George." [Laughter].

Not to be outdone, Churchill said that "whereas Mr. Lloyd
George is invariably witty, Mr. F.E. Smith is invariably vulgar."

What fun it all was! In those days a political meeting could fill a large hall to overflowing, and F.E. drew the biggest crowds of all. But his gibes did not cloud his own vision. There was a distinct chance in 1910 of a coalition government, and F.E. wrote privately "I am absolutely satisfied of Lloyd George's honesty and sincerity. He has been taught much by office."

F.E. had learnt a lot too. In 1911 the *Standard* assessed his position after he made a devastating attack on the Parliament Bill's sweeping proposals for Ulster:

"Mr. F.E. Smith moves from cleverness to statesmanship, and his speech tonight advanced him another stride as a power in Parliament. It was the most analytical and deadly critical contribution he has made to debate. Though at one point his voice faltered, and it was difficult to hear him, there was a sustained strain of clear argument which not only interested, but enthralled, the House. His manner has softened, the pace of his diction has become more dignified, and, altogether, he has strengthened.

His long, lithe, dark figure was slightly bent as he attacked the Parliament Bill. It was no bludgeoning process; rather it was the quiet, skilful death-by-the-hundred cuts method that he adopted."

In 1911, after an exhausting election campaign when he spoke up and down the country, F.E. was the guest of honour at the Constitutional Club. Mr. Balfour praised him to the skies:

"He was here, he was there, he was everywhere — and was courageous, and was witty, and was a master of his audience." [Cheers].

F.E., replying to the toast, observed that a weekly paper had stated that there were four people who ought to be drummed out of English politics: Lord George, Churchill, Sir Edward Carson, and himself.

"I am therefore thankful to say," he added, "that I have not altogether laboured in vain." [Laughter].

He had earned his reward. That year, only five years after entering Parliament, he was made a Privy Councillor, and sat on the Conservative Front Bench.

He gave a splendid fancy dress ball at Claridges, where the dominant colour scheme was blue and white. There was a large display of blue hydrangeas and Madonna lilies, with a background of palms and other tropical greenery. F.E. was dazzling in a white 18th-century Court suit. Not to be outdone, Winston Churchill turned up in a scarlet domino.

In this frenzy of activity, it is a wonder that he found time to practice at the Bar. But he appeared in many cases which are still leading authorities. There was *Wise v Dunning* in 1909, where George Wise, the Protestant preacher, made provocative remarks about the Catholics in Liverpool, and refused to be bound over to keep the peace.

There was *Chaplin v Hicks* in 1911, concerning a newspaper stunt in the *Daily Express*. The popular actor, Mr. Seymour Hicks, offered twelve out of twenty-four young ladies whose photographs appeared in the paper, a three-year contract to appear on the stage. Miss Chaplin was one of the lucky ones. Mr. Hicks wrote to her offering an audition, but sent it too late for her to attend. F.E. persuaded the judge that his negligence had lost her the chance of a stage contract. It was the first time that damages had been awarded for loss of a chance.

He appeared in many striking libel cases. In one of the a business partnership had introduced a new system for running trams, not by overhead wires, but by "live" studs in the road. Sir John Benn, of the Progressive Party, wrote a withering attack on it:

> "You know the terrible story of the Mile-End Road from June 25th to July 12th last. 50 live studs a day; injured people, roasted horses, fireworks at night, and the danger of a fatal accident to any person who chanced to strike a stud."

The tramway partners sued him for defamation, and F.E. won £12,000 on their behalves. The Court of Appeal, however, ruled that the criticism, though unfair, did not reflect on their personal character, and therefore damages for defamation were not appropriate.

He appeared for the Times Book Company, which sold copies of two biographies of the composer Gounod. Georgina Weldon, the composer's mistress, complained that she was compared in the books to one of the Sirens, and the Avenging Furies. The judge, however, suggested that she was presuming too much upon her old campaigns, and the jury gave her no damages.

F.E. also appeared for the *Daily Express* when it was sued by a "Captain" Tupper. He made inflammatory speeches in South Wales, telling the miners that he was convinced that if a coal strike took place, monarchical rule in Britain would cease to exist, and there would be five or six million workers wandering over the face of the country. He claimed he had been at Harrow and Sandhurst, and had served as an officer in the Boer War. F.E. proved that he had once been a private for a short time before going on the music-hall stage, and ran a patent-medicine business until he went bankrupt.

F.E. certainly had the style and ability to hold a libel jury enthralled, and was a master of abuse. Mr. Acland, a Liberal Minister, expressed the view that, while Lord Roberts was a very great soldier, he was not necessarily a very great statesman. It is often true of soldier-politicians, but at a public meeting F.E. counter-attacked Mr. Acland furiously:

> "A priggish underling, a man not of the slightest account anywhere, has the insolence to come forward and lift his tiny little tongue and squirt his feeble little venom on a man old enough to be his grandfather, and great enough to make people forget that Mr. Acland was ever born." [Laughter and cheers.]

Mr. Acland, who in modern times would certainly have sued for defamation, wrote good-humouredly to the *Times* to say that he used to listen to F.E.'s efforts in abuse at the Oxford Union twenty years before; "they did not matter then, and they do not matter now."

F.E. wrote an even more insulting answer to the *Times*, in which it became clear what his real grievance was: Mr. Acland held the view that for England to build up her forces to be prepared to meet Germany was "a wicked proposal."

It was 1912: F.E. had warned the public for years about Germany's plans for aggression. In 1909 he said:

> "We waste our lungs in talking about free food and we forget, many of us, that any food at all depends upon the maintenance of an unchallengeable Navy. [Cheers]. Looking on the naval preparations of Europe in the last few years, can we doubt that there is an increasing determination on the part of Germany to challenge our supremacy?"

Another key issue at that time was Votes for Women. F.E.

was wholly against it. The emotional qualities of women, he wrote to the *Times*, "especially in moments of public excitement, might prove a source of instability and disaster in the State."

On the subject of Home Rule for Ireland, F.E. was equally determined. It is not easy to understand why he espoused the Ulster cause so passionately, except that he was born on Orange Day! He was not Irish by birth. Nevertheless, he made hardly a single speech on the subject in which he did not preach the right of Ulstermen to rise in open rebellion, should the British Government seek to impose Home Rule on them.

"If they try it," he said at Warrington, "a day will dawn in English history which will recall the most tragic events of our civil disturbances in the past." [Cheers].

F.E. went to Ulster in the summer of 1913, and made a speech described by an admiring listener as "like the flight of a strong bird."

"It becomes you," he told an audience of thousands in Belfast, "from now henceforward to prepare silently, steadfastly, and constantly for the gravest crisis which has tested the men of your race for more than two centuries."

The air rang with cheers, and he was presented with an orange sash. He returned to Liverpool, where he and Carson rallied a torchlight procession of 100,000 men, and there was talk of rifles going off one day. The day did not seem to be far distant.

For years, in Parliament and out of it, he fought the Home Rule proposals until, in January 1913, the Bill was carried in the House of Commons by a majority of more than 100, and passed in the House of Lords. All that had to be done — all! — was to carry it out. But there the trouble lay.

He went off to Ulster again with Carson, who outshone even F.E. on a political platform; but F.E.'s speeches were still of high quality.

"I have always refused to believe," he said in East Antrim, fearlessly or treasonably according to one's point of view:

"that the occasion would ever arise that even the Government, corrupt and guilty as it is, would dare to attempt to mobilise the English Army to march on Ulster. If that unhappy moment in the history of the country arises I, on behalf of the Unionist Party in

213

Great Britain, say that from that moment on we will hold ourselves absolved from all allegiance to that Government ... from that moment we will stand by the side of Ulster, refusing to recognise any law and prepared with them to risk the collapse of the whole body politic to prevent this monstrous crime." [Cheers.]

Two events in 1914 saved him from this confrontation. The Army mutinied at the Curragh, thus postponing indefinitely any British attempt to impose Home Rule by force; and World War 1 broke out. At once an unofficial truce was declared over the affairs of Ulster, and F.E. was able to throw himself wholeheartedly behind the Government in the fight against Germany.

Within three days of the outbreak of war he was appointed, through no choice of his own, to take charge of the Official News Bureau, and handle official censorship of the news. As Lord Beaverbrook said:

"It was a dangerous and thankless task; every time news was wisely witheld, it was a secret victory for which he could never claim credit; every time his decision was questionable, it brought a storm of protest."

Whereupon, with his usual heat and energy, he would appear in Parliament to reject the criticism. He also found time to make, in September 1914, a great speech supporting Mr. Churchill's call to the nation.

It began jokingly:

"I have known Mr. Churchill many years, and for a great part of those years it has been considered by many of my greatest friends that this association was unworthy of me. [Laughter]. I have never paid the slightest attention to lectures on this point. I have frequently not agreed with what Mr. Churchill has done, and have very seldom under the conditions under which our party politics are conducted agreed with what he has said. But I have never had the slightest doubt that a great and patriotic Englishman was devoting the best of his powers to his country. That is a sufficient justification for any friendship which exists between us." [Cheers].

He went on to denounce the Germans for invading Belgium despite the "scrap of paper" in which they promised to respect Belgium's neutrality. He included one of his finest phrases, which has entered the English language almost as a proverb:

"The question is sometimes asked where is this war to end? I heard a pessimist say, when the news appeared for the moment to be gloomy a week ago, 'This is the beginning of the end.' [Laughter]. He was wrong. It is only the end of the beginning. [Cheers]. This war is going to end either when we break this barbarous system or when this barbarous system breaks us. [Cheers]. There is no other end. It is a fight to the finish. [Cheers]. The terms of peace will be arranged either in London or Berlin. We think, on the whole, that it may be Berlin." [Laughter].

Soon after this F.E. was able to leave the Official News Bureau, and would have liked to join his regiment, the Queen's Own Oxfordshire Hussars. Instead he was appointed to the Indian Corps as Intelligence and Recording Officer. It seemed positively eccentric.

Many sneering comments were later made that he had an easy sort of war whilst others suffered and died, but these were unfair. F.E. always faced up to danger — his position on Ulster showed that. Furthermore, in October 1914 he was with the Indians in and near the front line in France, ready to suffer every hardship save one. He wrote to his wife:

"Also, my angel, do send me from the Stores every 20 (or perhaps 18) days a box of my cigars. I can live, as I am doing, on bully beef. I can drink, as I am doing, cocoa and tea. But I cannot, and I will not, as long as my bank will honour my cheques, wash them down, so to speak, with nothing but a pipe."

With a typical touch of wit he arranged for her to send him his precious cigars under the label of:

"ARMY TEMPERANCE SOCIETY
PUBLICATIONS SERIES 9."

His other letters were more serious:

November 1st 1914: "All this talk about the men coming singing out of the trenches is damned nonsense — they come out dead to the world and some of them gibbering idiots."

November 2nd: "Our line, about 15 miles, is held by Indians alone without any reserve (none can be spared), and we are told on the Staff to have our motors or horses prepared in case the line is broken ...
I am sure the main fight tonight will be at Ypres, 15 miles away,

where, with the French, we are making a very strong counter-attack which may (how I hope so) reproduce the victory of the Marne. The artillery is sounding even here while I write, and we are just going out at 11.0 at night to observe the fortune and development of what may possibly be the decisive moment of the greatest battle in the greatest war human beings have ever waged.

You cannot imagine how horrible war is — how vile and foul! One must laugh and joke always, or else one would weep.''

He came home on leave in March 1915, and two months later was made Solicitor-General. He never again returned to the Front, but the war still came close to him. There was a Zeppelin raid in September 1915, when two bombs were dropped on Gray's Inn; they did little damage. There was another raid in October, and a bomb went through the roof of the Benchers' robing-room.

"A few seconds sufficed to make this room a furnace,'' it was recorded; "the open door showed nothing but one white sheet of rolling flame.''

Fortunately, nobody was injured. A number of his comtemporaries were less fortunate and many young men went from the Bar to the Front, never to return.

F.E. wrote the preface to *The War Book of Gray's Inn*, which told something of their heroic stories.

There was Captain H. Finegan, whose early career might have been a carbon copy of F.E.'s. He was a brilliant athlete, and won every prize in History and Law at Liverpool University. In 1913 he won a scholarship to Gray's Inn in 1913. Two years later he was in France. He said jokingly that he would either come back with the Victoria Cross, or stay there with a wooden cross. He led an attack on trenches occupied by the Prussian Guards, saying "Come on, Irish! Let's show what we can do.''

He was killed immediately.

Cosmo J. Romilly, the great-grandson of Sir Samuel Romilly, was in Gallipoli. His Commanding Officer wrote, "Fear was unknown to him, he was always calm and practical in emergency, and a very lovable comrade.''

He was killed by a sniper's bullet.

Lt.-Commander Dawbarn Young volunteered for the Navy as soon as the war began, and served in mine-sweeping and the dangerous Dover Patrol.

216

He spent the last night of his leave in 1918 dining at Gray's Inn, a haven of wit and fellowship. The next day was his last day, at Zeebrugge.

Now he was active in politics again, and at the Bar, but doing a very different type of case, with the statesman in him uppermost. Few of his official cases called for jury advocacy. Instead there were cases on income tax, and important questions about ships captured at sea. This "Prize" jurisdiction needed careful investigation, for large sums of money were at stake. Some Scandinavian ships were stopped in mid-ocean laden with cargoes of food, lard and rubber from America. Which of them were genuinely intended for the Danish Government, and therefore legitimate, and which of them were really for Germany, and therefore to be confiscated? Only a detailed comparison with peacetime tonnage of these commodities could show. After fourteen hearings, some proved to be contraband, and some legitimate trade with a neutral country.

Then there was the Defence of the Realm Act, which gave the Government wide powers of action; not too wide to be tested in the courts, though. Could the Government take over land for an aerodrome without compensation? What were the rights to requisition shipping? What claims had the Inland Revenue on mineral rights?

All these questions had to be patiently considered and argued. As Solictor General he also advised the Government on legal measures, and steered legislation through Parliament. A moment of light relief arose in October 1915 over the question of Night Clubs, which had to be licensed under stringent terms. This time it was another Member of Parliament who was flippant, and F.E. serious:

Mr. Ellis Griffiths: I do not understand the alarm that, if the bill were passed, clubs like the Carlton and the Athenaeum would be tarred with the same brush as the night clubs. I have no fears of that kind. I think it would be a good thing if all bishops ought to be in bed by half past 12 o'clock. [Laughter].

The Solicitor-General: The extent of the inconvenience to which reputable clubs will be exposed by the Bill is extremely small. Having regard to the fact that we are at war and of the further fact of the grave injury inflicted by disreputable clubs on young officers, often resulting in their ruin, reputable clubs would have little to complain of if it were said that all clubs should be closed at 12.30.

In November 1915 Sir Edward Carson resigned as Attorney-General, and F.E. was appointed to his place. His work was much the same as when he was Solicitor-General, only at a more intense level. He proved that the German ship *Ophelia* was rather too well equipped for sending secret messages, and rather too ill-equipped for picking up survivors at sea, to be a genuine hospital ship.

He supported the Crown's right to requisition 41 tons of Blairgowrie raspberries to be made into jam for the troops.

In the field of criminal law, he successfully argued that when a man was charged with indecent offences against two boys, it was admissable in evidence to show that in his pockets he carried two powder-puffs, and photographs of naked men. As the Lord Chief Justice put it, "Ordinary men do not walk about carrying powder-puffs in their pockets."

In the House of Commons, he had to deal with various complaints. It was said that a woman had been unfairly interned; she had, he replied, stayed several days in a Swiss hotel with a notorious German spy.

Then a Labour MP declared that the *Bystander* magazine should never have been prosecuted under the Defence of the Realm Act for publishing a cartoon of a soldier lying dead drunk with a bottle of rum beside him. The caption was "Found Missing"

F.E. replied, "It was a vile picture, and I am glad the magistrate who tried the case took the same view." [Hear hear].

Under the same Act a prosecution was brought against eight members of the Amalgamated Society of Engineers, who had been on strike. At the last moment, they agreed to go back to work, and the prosecution was withdrawn. F.E. stated in open court how serious the situation might have been:

"The certain result of persistence in this strike would have been, within a month, - it might have been in two months, but within some definite period of time - a shortage in shells, in aeroplanes, and in heavy guns at the front. The certain result of that shortage would have been this, that men who could not strike, our soldiers, would be killed who otherwise would not be killed.

The responsibilities of his office were not light. They were perhaps heaviest in June 1916, in the most famous and controversial of all his cases - the trial of Sir Roger Casement.

Casement was a distinguished diplomat who had served and been honoured by the British Government; he was also an Irishman, and his conflict of loyalties brought him into the realms of treason. As Attorney-General it was F.E.'s duty to conduct the prosecution. This was unfortunate, in view of his strong attitudes in Ulster. Nevertheless, this case showed him at his most statesman-like.

Two allegations were made against Casement. During the winter of 1914-15 he circulated freely among Irish prisoners-of-war in Germany, encouraging them to form an Irish Brigade "to fight solely for the THE CAUSE OF IRELAND, and under NO CIRCUMSTANCES shall it be directed to any GERMAN end".

But was this the full truth? Sir Roger never gave evidence; he preferred to make a statement from the dock, and could not be cross-examined. F.E. invited the jury to use their common-sense:

> "I will ask again, a question which has never yet been answered. - Why did Sir Roger Casement go to Germany at all? How did he get to Germany, and what was the nature of the assurances and arrangement given to him before he went to Germany? How was it, when his country was at war with Germany, that we find him a free man moving about Germany without restraint? No answer has been given to these questions, because none can be given consistent with the integrity of the accused."

The jury were therefore entitled to infer that Casement intended to help Germany.

The evidence also suggested that Casement landed on the coast of Ireland with two companions, a map, revolvers and ammunition, together with a code for such phrases as "further ammunition is needed" and "the railway has been cut." The jury were entitled to infer that he was anxious to stir up a rising which would distract the British Government, divert troops needed desperately elsewhere, and thus help the Germans.

It has been said that F.E.'s conduct of the prosecution was vindictive.

His most telling phrase came at the end of his opening speech:

"In my submission the prisoner, blinded by hatred to this country, as malignant in quality as it was sudden in origin, has played a desperate hazard. He has played it, and he has lost it. Now the forfeit is claimed."

And it was paid. Casement was convicted. An appeal to the House of Lords was only possible if F.E. gave his consent to it as Attorney-General. He considered the matter carefully. The only grounds for appeal were legal arguments which had been rejected at the trial, and which had been rejected in similar cases in the past. F.E. therefore refused his consent, and Casement was executed.

There will always be those who passionately believe that he should never have been prosecuted, let alone convicted.

1917 came, and the war went on and on. One of the greatest errors of political judgment F.E. ever made came in a speech he made in Blackpool, on the subject of Russia's part in the war:

"We are hoping that the Russian giant will yet shake his limbs and give effective hope to M. Kerensky, who still holds aloft the torch of Russian hope. The history of this amazing people shows that apparently the darkest moment is the time of most brilliant recuperation."

The October Revolution came one month later.

Despite the demands which were made on him, F.E.'s powers were undimmed, though the *Times* criticised one of the Prize cases about enemy shipping as being bungled by F.E.'s "extravagant and almost grotesque claims for the Royal Prerogative."

F.E. never accepted criticism silently. He wrote back suggesting that those who administer public rebuke should surely take the trouble to acquire some elementary knowledge of the matter dealt with in their homilies. He had never raised any claim on the Royal Prerogative, he said.

The *Times* quoted its own law reports to show that he had, and suggested that his advice on the conduct of the case must have been bad. F.E. reported that the *Times* had adopted a "very characteristic position," which in the context meant "cowardice" - the *Times* knew he could never reveal what his advice had been.

Quite so, replied the *Times;* but then F.E. must either have given bad advice, or been content to follow it. There was no answer to this; F.E. found himself for once out of countenance.

Late in 1917 he set out on a mission of incalculable importance to this country. It may have made a decisive difference to the success of the war. Things had almost reached stalemate on the Western Front; some people were saying that peace should be patched up on some terms or other. The Government was short of funds, and launched an appeal for War Loan bonds at £95 apiece, which would be redeemed for £100 in the year 1947!

There is no knowing what would have happened if America had not entered the war. Equally, America would have joined in with far less enthusiasm if F.E. had not made a whirlwind tour of the States. Never was his audience appeal put to better use. As the Mayor of Cleveland, Ohio, cabled to England:

> "The visit of Sir F. Smith, the Attorney-General, is a great success. It is most important that explanation of England's determination and part be fully expounded here. He does it admirably."

There was immense applause for him in New York; in Chicago, the audience stood on their chairs and cheered him for many minutes. At Columbia, Missouri the farming community pledged their sons in the trenches, and food for the Allies; at Kansas City, Topeka, and Lincoln, Nebraska it was the same. Thousands of people gathered for every meeting, and sometimes he had five such meetings per day. It must have taken tremendous effort, but it brought tremendous results. Once America entered the war, the final result was not long in doubt.

F.E.'s last great case in 1918 came at the end of July; it concerned the ownership of large areas of land in Southern Rhodesia. It has been said that, before he rose to his feet to address the Privy Council on behalf of the Crown, the case was as good as lost; but that when he sat down, it was decisively won. That is the sort of legend which grows up readily around great advocates. Nevertheless, he succeeded in a case of the utmost importance.

Then, by a happy chance, the annual banquet at the Guildhall in 1918 coincided with Armistice Day. F.E. made one of the speeches. Long gone were the days when he had mocked Lloyd George; throughout the war he had paid tribute to his great qualities with unswerving loyalty, and on this night he repeated his tribute.

"If at this moment," he said, "we did not possess a Lloyd George, it would be necessary to find one to fill his office." [Cheers]

Peacetime had come. Three days later it was announced that the petrol allowance could soon be increased; insurance policies against aircraft and bombing would be renewed without further premiums; and the Director-General of National Salvage no longer required collections of fruit-stones and nutshells for use as a filtering agent in gas-masks.

F.E. announced his wish to help any members of the Forces who wished to come to the Bar; he had had many letters to that effect, and welcomed more.

It was time for a new election. F.E.'s rival candidate in his Liverpool constituency of Walton taunted him about his "princely salary" and his "funk-hole in the Press Bureau"; F.E., in return, referred to him as a "frock-coated revolutionary", and "this Lenin in a top-hat." What fun it all was again!

F.E. was returned to Parliament - his defeat was unthinkable - but his time in office was short-lived. Lloyd George had a Cabinet reshuffle, and to everyone's utter astonishment appointed F.E., who was then only 47, to be Lord Chancellor.

Before the appointment was made, firm doubts had reached Lloyd George from Buckingham Palace:

"His Majesty does not feel sure that Sir Frederick has established such a reputation in men's minds as to ensure that the country will welcome him to the second highest position which can be occupied by a subject of the Crown.

His Majesty, however, only hopes he may be wrong in this forecast."

Public opinion shared the doubts of George V. One newspaper said the appointment was "carrying a joke too far," and the *Times* went as near to calling the appointment a disaster as the *Times* ever does. It referred to his career as a succession of "remarkable and promiscuous experiences," and described him as "impetuous and intrepid in several causes"; it criticised his "fatal fluency of thought and speech." In contrast, it praised the retiring Lord Chancellor as sound in his scholarship, sound in his law, and sound in the manner and tradition of the English Bar.

It was like a Headmaster's report on a wayward pupil.

But the thing was done. On January 1919 F.E., wearing the Lord Chancellor's black and gold robes of office, stood in a crowded Law Court reading the traditional oaths of allegiance to the King and of impartiality to the administration of justice. He took the title of Lord Birkenhead, and was now entitled to combine his duties as the highest judge in the land with his political career, making speeches in the House of Lords. Here, from the very first, he took an active part.

Before settling down to these new duties, he paid a flying visit to Paris. A shocked diplomat wrote home about his behaviour there:

> "I was told of him only yesterday dining in a restaurant with a big cigar in his mouth. Quite harmless things in themselves, but still just the thing that a Lord Chancellor ought not to do."

Yet F.E. had pursued his whole career with, so to speak, a big cigar in his mouth. Why should he stop now?

THIRTEEN

Courage, Courage, Courage!

Your own resolution to succeed, is more important than any other one thing.

Abraham Lincoln

The world continues to offer glittering prizes to those who have stout hearts and sharp swords.

F.E. Smith

If one asks a barrister the most important quality one needs at the Bar, he will probably say "hard work", especially if he has been working too hard.

Judge Parry, in his book *The Seven Lamps of Advocacy*, listed these seven virtues: honesty, courage, industry, wit, eloquence, judgment and fellowship.

Wit is a useful tool, but to be sparingly used. Fellowship certainly oils the wheels of litigation, but there is no special difficulty in fighting a case against a total stranger. One could include "presence", without which a barrister makes no impact. Nor should "memory" be forgotten, but courage is properly placed high in the list, and is perhaps the most interesting quality to describe.

Demosthenes, the famous orator of ancient Greece, was once asked what are the three greatest qualities in an Advocate. "Action, action, and action!" he replied.

"Impact, impact, and impact" might be a better translation, for it is not on animated gestures that an advocate relies. Demosthenes started his career with courage; he had to cure a bad stammer by speaking with a mouth full of pebbles, and developed the power of his voice by standing on the sea-shore, and making himself heard over the noise of the waves.

There is hardly a great advocate who did not suffer terribly from nerves when he first stood before a court. The great Irish advocate J.P. Curran was so terrified in his first case that he could not utter a single word, while Roger North, who became

224

Lord Chancellor, described the experience as being like the loss of a maidenhead. On this statement lady barristers refuse to be drawn, but everybody knows what Roger North meant.

Courage was certainly shown by Edmund Saunders, who rose to be Lord Chief Justice in 1683, but started life as a beggar-boy. He took shelter in Clement's Inn, where he "lived by obsequiousness, and courting the attornies' clerks for scraps." He could neither read nor write, but ran errands for them, and sat at the top of a staircase in a set of chambers learning to write, not only the ordinary running-hand which children learn, but the more specialist art of court-hand, that archaic script introduced by the Normans, with strange curlicues for abbreviated Latin words which only intensified the mysteries of the law.

There he sat in winter, his shoulders covered in a blanket, and hay-bands tied round his legs for added warmth, rubbing his fingers to keep them from freezing as he wrote. He copied deeds and law papers with such diligence that he picked up the extraordinary language in which legal documents were then expressed.

"Equity relieves en plusors cases l'ou les printed livres deny it" is a fair sample of that linguistic cocktail of English, Latin, and Law French. It meant "Equity relieves in many cases where the printed books deny that a relief exists."

Saunders acquired so much legal knowledge by these practical means that he was called to the Bar after only four years, not the usual period of seven years.

Serjeant Ballantine, who enjoyed a brilliant career in Victorian times, knew what it was like to start on the verge of starvation.

> "My father had undertaken to furnish my chambers, and one of the principal articles he sent me was a horsehair arm-chair with only three legs, upon which I got so accustomed to balance myself that I scarcely felt safe on one furnished with the proper complement."

In his pupillage he was hardly inspired by a blazing beacon of inspired advocacy. He was pupil to William Henry Watson, who later became a Baron of the Exchequer. No doubt his erudition was greatly to be admired; but it was singularly tedious to emulate. Ballantine wrote:

225

"He received some ten or a dozen pupils, whom he permitted to learn what they could, and by judging by myself, this was very little... I have little to record of the two years I passed in these chambers amongst a mass of papers, copying precedents of pleading which were a disgrace to common sense, and in gossip with my brother students, most of them as idle as myself."

It took courage to survive those years of hardship and despair.

Still, the day came when he was called to the Bar, and was entitled to make a fortune from his efforts. In theory, at least. Cheap though his chambers were, his money dwindled away to nothing. Less than nothing; he had to obtain goods on tick from Mr. Gill, a tradesman in Essex Court, till the day came when Mr. Gill would stand it no longer. No butter; no more blacking for his shoes. No penny roll for his breakfast; nothing for his dinner.

But a miracle occurred: a solicitor's clerk arrived with three of the humblest briefs - they were called "half-guinea motions", and they were a gift from heaven. Dazzled with wealth in his pockets he went off to a modest restaurant with a charming waitress:

"The glorious repast still remains imbedded in my memory. Twice of saddle of mutton; I am afraid to say how many helps of jam tart. After a handsome honorarium of threepence to Mary, who had never looked coldly upon me in my worst hours of impecuniosity, I had still twenty-five shillings left."

He could have spun it out thriftily for several weeks, but - fool that he was! - went into a gambling house. It was a shame to end his brief career like that. Still, he gambled the money, and he won. He won! He won the colossal sum of £35:

"I was a millionaire. Gill once again smiled upon me, and the penny roll and pat of butter upon my breakfast table next morning testified to his restored confidence."

In his first six months at the Bar he earned merely four and a half guineas. In his next year, thirty; the year after that, seventy-five. He never looked back.

But the first brief had to be done; it was a simple application for the renewal of a theatre licence for the Garrick Theatre in Leman Street, Whitechapel:

"I rose," he wrote, "but could see nothing; the court seemed to turn round, and the floor to be sinking. I cannot tell what I asked, but it was graciously granted by the bench. For this performance I received half a guinea, the sweetest that ever found its way into my pocket!"

At the same time the future Mr. Justice Hawkins set himself up on the fifth floor of No. 3 Elm Court, in the Temple. He stayed there from ten in the morning till ten at night, waiting for fortune to smile upon him. He wrote:

"Hundreds of times had I listened with vain expectations to the footsteps on the stairs below - footsteps of attorneys and clerks, messengers and office-boys. I knew them all, and that was all I knew of them. Down below at the bottom flight they tramped, and there they mostly stopped. The ground-floor was evidently the best for business; but some came higher, to the first-floor. That was a good position; there were plenty of footsteps, and I could tell they were the footsteps of clients. A few came a little higher still, and then my hopes rose with the footsteps.

Now someone had come up to the third-floor; he stopped! Alas! there was the knock, one single hard knock; it was a junior clerk. The sound came all too soon for me, and I turned from my own door to my little den and looked out of the window up into the sky, from whence it seemed I might just as well expect a brief as from the regions below."

At last, at long last, his first half-guinea motion arrived. It was as well his father had given him an allowance of £100 a year, or he would have starved to death. His rent for his garret cost £12 a year; his kindly old laundress, almost as much; and he had to buy professional books as well.

In his second year at the Bar he earned but £50, but doubled it in the following year.

Most English barristers could tell a similar story; but they are not alone. In 1837 there was a business panic in Springfield, Illinois. Banks failed, loans were called in, and money was tight. The young Abraham Lincoln, who had been called to the American Bar only the year before, rode into town and asked at Joshua Speed's store, what the price was of bedclothes for a single bedstead. It was 17 dollars. Lincoln replied:

"Cheap as it is, I have not the money to pay. But if you will credit me until Christmas, and my experiment here as a lawyer is a success, I will pay you then. If I fail in that I will probably never pay you at all.''

Seldom had such dismal prospects been voiced. But Speed trusted him. Lincoln set up in practice in a little room above the courtroom furnished with few loose boards for bookshelves, an old wood stove, a table, a chair, a bench, a buffalo robe and a small bed.

Lincoln wrote to Mary Owens, the woman he hoped to marry:

> ''There is a great deal of flourishing about in carriages here, which it would be your doom to see without sharing in it. You would have to be poor without the means of hiding your poverty. Do you believe you could bear that patiently?''

She did not come. But many women have married barristers at such a stage in their lives.

Each Barrister has to announce at the Circuit mess that he is getting married.

''It was passed over with a simple admonition,'' wrote Ballantine, ''on the ground that it carried its own punishment with it.''

Barristers' wives could say the same. And yet the early days of hope and courage have their own distinct quality. Robert Henley, who became Lord Chancellor Northington, used to recall with a special pleasure the frugal early days of married life. At first he lived in Cursitor Street, near Chancery Lane. ''This was my first perch,'' he recalled. ''Many a time have I run down from Cursitor Street to Fleet Market to buy sixpenn'orth of sprats for our supper.''

John Scott, the future Lord Eldon, began his married life at the humble address of Great James Street, Bedford Row, ''where a leg of mutton lasted them three days; the first day hot, - the second day cold, - and the third day hashed.''

Once he begins at the Bar, the barrister may lose his initial jitters, but must always be ready for total catastrophe. Things happen which are so awful that he wishes the floor of the court would open up and swallow him forever.

Eric Crowther, now a Metropolitan Magistrate, had as bad an experience as can be imagined.

His client was a girl who complained that a certain man was

the father of her illegitimate child. Before the case started he found out that she was, so to speak, the Good Time that had been Had by All. He decided, quite rightly, that the best way to minimise the harm was for the girl to announce right at the start that she had had many liaisons with young men. The lady magistrate listened to all this with a somewhat frosty air:

> *Lady Magistrate:* Tell me, my gal, have you ever been intimate with any other young men, apart from those just mentioned?
> *The girl:* Nah, I don't fink so.
> *Lady Magistrate:* You don't THINK so. Are you not sure?
> *The girl:* Well, there's always Spud Baker.
> *Lady Magistrate:* Spud Baker! Then why did you not mention this, er, Mr. Baker when your counsel was going through what I can only call this CATALOGUE?
> *The girl:* Oh well, old Spud - 'e don't count. ALL the girls round 'ere have been 'ad by Spud Baker.
> *Lady Magistrate: I* have never been "had", as you put it, by Spud Baker.
> *The girl:* Nah, I don't suppose you 'ave. It's only the young and pretty ones 'e goes for.

Eric Crowther stood his ground, and lost the case manfully. He could have been forgiven for crawling away on all fours.

Perhaps the worst ordeal for any barrister is waiting, whether for the first brief, or for a brief to be heard. It used to be the rule in the King's Bench, before Lord Mansfield become Chief Justice in 1756, that juniors clutching their precious half-guinea motions had to wait until their elders and betters had been heard, such as the Solicitor-General and the Attorney-General. Days went by without the juniors being heard at all; by the last day of term they still might not have been heard.

Promising young men were forced to sit and wait for all eternity, or so it must have seemed to them. The solicitors, on the other hand, observed that there was no hope of their cases being reached unless they were entrusted to the senior counsel. So the seniors had more work than they could cope with, and the juniors fretted at the back of the court.

Lord Mansfield, to his undying glory, swept this rule aside. He insisted that nobody should be heard twice until everybody had been heard once. Even if the case of young Mr. X was not reached at the end of one day, he would be first in the queue on the morning after.

Sometimes waiting for a case to begin could be too exciting:

Q. What should a lawyer do if he is defending a negro charged with rape in the Southern states of America, and an angry lynch-mob surrounds the gaol, firing revolvers?
A: Hope that the National Guard arrives. On no account apply for an adjournment; it is more than the lives of yourself and your client are worth.

This situation arose on several occasions.

In *Moore* v *Dempsey* (1923), some negroes were charged with murder arising out of an incident in which whites killed many other negroes. Counsel who was assigned for the Defence did not see the defendants before the case began, and called no witnesses on their behalf. The trial lasted 3/4 hour, and the defendants were convicted in five minutes. It was said that no juryman could have acquitted them, and lived, in Phillips County.

In *Downer* v *Dunaway* (1931), where a number of negroes were accused of raping a white woman, a mob of perhaps 1500 people surrounded the gaol. The warders drove the defendants away to another city; the mob pursued them, firing revolvers, and then attempted to storm the new gaol in which they were housed, firing shots and throwing dynamite at it. They were dispersed by machine-guns. Counsel was only able to meet the defendant an hour before the trial began; the trial began promptly at 10 a.m., and lasted twelve hours. The jury were only out for five minutes.

In Alabama in 1949 a negro shot a police officer five times with a pistol. The defence was that he had drunk a pint of whisky and a gallon of home-brewed liquor, and did not know what he was doing.

His counsel, fearing for his client's life, applied to the judge in chambers for an adjournment.

"Judge," he said "If this case is continued there never will be another Negro that kills a white man that will go to trial in Calhoun County."

"Roderick," said the Judge, "if I pass [adjourn] this case the people of the county will storm the gaol."

It is not fair to judge the American legal system as a whole by these extraordinary cases; but they are certainly worthy of note.

As the author of a book called *The Right to Counsel in an American Court* dryly puts it, "A substantial number of "speedy" proceedings in serious cases have taken place in Kentucky. Negroes are the defendants in many of these cases."

He analyses the behaviour of counsel to an extent not to be found in English law.

In an Arkansas case a boy of 14 was accused of clubbing a man to death. His explanations were not satisfactory, but the only definite evidence against him was that a few drops of blood were found upon him, and six half-dollars in his shoe.

The boy went to stay with his Defence counsel, Mr. Roberts, for two months before the case began; it is not clear why. After the jury had retired the lad made a statement admitting the murder, and Mr. Roberts did nothing to stop him. Indeed, he said he was glad that at last the truth had come out; he had tried to get at the truth, without success. Then he turned to the jury and said that he never expected to have anything more to do with the lad, no matter what happened, and, in the presence of the jury, *"he bade the lad a tragic-goodbye"*.

Even after that the jury retired all night, and did not bring in a verdict of guilty till noon. The lad was granted a new trial, and Mr. Roberts' conduct was strongly criticised. Whatever made him do it? Losing his nerve perhaps, in the face of a difficult case.

It is easier to warm to Mr. Jennings, defending in a Minnesota case, who remained drunk throughout the proceedings. For several days he remained in a stupor, and, like the dormouse in *Alice in Wonderland*, had to be pummelled and pinched to wake him up. Sometimes, however, he would clap his handkerchief to his mouth and make a dash for the exit, or stand in the hallway abusing the trial judge in a loud voice. At the end of a three-week case most of his final speech, which lasted five minutes, was devoted to the personal merits of counsel for the prosecution.

The defendant was granted *habeas corpus* because of Mr. Jennings' obvious shortcomings.

There have, of course, been English advocates who were too

fond of the bottle; even the great Erskine used to carry a flask of madeira in his pocket, and a speech which he made in the House of Commons on the subject of the East India Company was a drunken disgrace.

It is unfair to describe some of the weaker American advocates without also including Abraham Lincoln, that giant among men, whose every word had a simple appeal.

A judge once reminded him that he was putting forward an argument which was directly against what he had been saying in a different case that morning.

"I thought I was right this morning," said Lincoln coolly, "but, your Honour, I *know* I am right this afternoon."

Barristers are often asked why they should defend someone whom they "know" to be guilty. There is one simple answer: their clients might have been the Trailor brothers.

Archibald, William and Henry Trailor were three rough men; their victim was Archibald Fisher, who was known to carry large sums of money. He was last seen in their company; there were signs of a struggle in a thicket, and cart tracks leading towards the millpond. William and Archibald were later seen spending more gold pieces than they had ever had before.

Before the trial, their brother Henry gave evidence that they had killed Fisher, and brought back his body to where he stood watching. Although the body had not been found, the circumstantial evidence was overwhelming. Any advocate would need courage to fight the case, but Abraham Lincoln, defending the case in Springfield Illinois, was undaunted.

In due course he called a doctor from the next county who said that Fisher was still alive and living in his house. He had not brought him to the court, he said, because of his poor health; besides, he was subject to frequent fits of mental derangement.

The jury acquitted Archibald and William Trailor. It was just as well, because on the following day, Fisher, the murdered man, was brought back alive into the town.

The full truth of this strange story will never be known. Perhaps the brothers indeed attacked him, robbed him, and left him for dead. Henry Trailor would be a devastating witness for the prosecution, if he fully believed what he thought he saw.

Members of the public cannot guess how much effort it takes for a barrister to put forward a ridiculous case. Bernard Levin quotes a case about a boundary dispute, where a post stood on the edge of the two properties. The post did not extend beyond the boundary, but a piece of string did which was tied round the post.

Thus the defendant trespassed upon the plaintiff's property *by the thickness of a piece of string.* Neither the judge nor the outside world could know how much the plaintiff's advisers must have warned him against taking such a ludicrous claim to court; but he insisted, and his counsel had no alternative but to put forward an argument he would blush deeply even to have contemplated.

Many and awful are the experiences of counsel facing bad judges, the taming of whom is a public service which almost calls for the erection of a public statue in their honour. It used to be a ground for disqualification of an advocate - possibly dating back to Roman times - that he had "fought toothed beasts in the arena."

I cannot think why.

When Lord Chancellor Shaftesbury first took office in 1672, Roger North tells us, "he slighted the Bar, and declared their reign was at an end. He would make all his own orders his own way, and in his discourse trampled on all the forms of the Court."

The Bar did their best to reason with him courteously:

> "yet he would not accept of their civility, but cut and slashed after his own fancy; and nothing would down with him that any of them suggested, though all were agreed upon the matter."

So they gave him his head. For some time they let him make whatever orders he liked, however outrageous. But gradually the seeds that he had sown ripened into a harvest. They showed him all his extraordinary decisions, and he realised what he had done. North wrote:

> "And from a trade of perpetually making and unmaking his own orders, he fell to be the tamest Judge, and, as to all forms and modes of proceeding, the most resigned to the disposition of the Bar that ever sat on the bench."

Perhaps there is no judge quite as bad as a bad Lord Chancellor. Lord Eldon was never discourteous to the counsel who appeared before him, but he drove them to distraction by reserving judgment on the simplest cases. It was often years before he could bring himself to make a decision.

Sir Samuel Romilly was once addressing Lord Eldon, who agreed with everything he said. It was a simple case; he could have given judgment there and then.

"However," he said, "I will take home the papers and read them carefully, and will tell the parties on a future day what my judgment will be."

It was more than Sir Samuel could stand. He rose to his feet, and turned round to the junior members of the Bar:

"Now, is not this extraordinary? I never heard a more satisfactory judgment; yet the Chancellor professes that he cannot make up his mind. It is wonderful; and the more so, because however long he takes to consider a cause, I scarcely ever knew him differ from his first impression."

It was easier to whip treacle into a foam than to make Lord Eldon reach a decision.

This was not the problem with Lord Brougham, who either leapt into the arena and questioned all the witnesses himself, or lapsed into boredom. He sat on the Bench working out algebra, calculating cube roots, writing letters, or even reading the newspaper. Sometimes he uttered a sarcastic remark; but he seldom bestowed his undivided attention upon the court.

In 1834 Bickersteth was addressing him, in an important dispute between London and Cambridge University, on the legal nature of degrees. The Chancellor said rudely:

"What is to prevent this *joint-stock company*, or call it what you will, from not merely giving certificates of proficiency, but assuming to confer degrees, except an Act of Parliament, which there might be some little difficulty in passing at present?"

"In the first place," retorted Bickersteth, *"the utter scorn and contempt of the world."*

This silenced Brougham, who deeply resented it as "extremely offensive to me personally," but it taught him a lesson.

Lord Chief Justice Tenterden was also known to be fiery: "You've told us that three times, Mr. Maule."

"Only twice, my Lord," said Mr. Maule.

Young Frederick Thesiger, the future Lord Chancellor Chelmsford, stood up to Lord Tenterden. "I don't understand being addressed by your lordship in such a tone," he said, "and it is highly improper for a judge to use to any gentleman of the Bar, and I will not submit to it."

Lord Campbell regarded impudence as an important quality in an advocate; it certainly had to be used against himself, because he behaved intolerably on the bench, marching up and down, and casting furious glances at a counsel who incurred his displeasure.

It can be done indirectly. Jenkin Jones was constantly being interrupted by Mr. Justice Hallett, a notoriously talkative judge, at Swansea Assizes, so he suddenly turned his back on the bench. "There is too much talking in this court!", he thundered at inoffending members of the public.

It is not easy to map out the frontiers of courage, impudence, and foolhardiness; their realms are adjacent, in mountainous terrains. Lockhart, the leader of the Scottish Bar, was certainly impudent when he addressed young Alexander Wedderburn as "a presumptuous boy."

Wedderburn then displayed courage, or perhaps revenge; he and some young colleagues had vowed to get even with the arrogant Lockhart when opportunity allowed.

"I care little, my Lords," said Wedderburn to the Bench, "for what may be said or done by a man who has been *disgraced in his person and dishonoured in his bed.*"

The Lord President rebuked Wedderburn for language unbecoming an advocate and a gentleman; he should retract his words, on pain of deprivation [being disbarred]. Wedderburn said:

> "My Lords, I neither retract nor apologise, but I will save you the trouble of deprivation; there is my gown, and I will never wear it more. *Virtute me involvo.*" [I wrap myself in my own integrity].

He laid down his gown upon the bar, and never entered a Scottish court again. Had he not come to the English bar and risen to be Lord Chancellor Loughborough, the world might have heard no more of him.

It was in another Scottish case that a barrister earned a Victoria Cross for exceptional courage in the face of the enemy.

John Clerk was one of the defence counsel in the trial of Deacon Brodie, in 1788. Deacon was the Christian name of a highly skilled and respected cabinet-maker in Edinburgh. He was also a burglar and robber; his strange double life inspired Robert Louis Stevenson to write *Dr. Jekyll and Mr. Hyde*.

The trial took place before a full bench of judges, the senior judge of whom was Lord Braxfield, the only judge who is regularly mentioned in the same breath as Judge Jeffreys for judicial ferocity. He was, to be sure, a profound lawyer; but his wrath was like the eruption of Vesuvius. Stevenson's *Weir of Hermiston* is based upon him.

Henry Erskine, the brother of Thomas Lord Erskine, was the leading advocate for the defence; some people thought him equally great as an advocate. Earlier that year Thomas Erskine had defended the Dean of St. Asaph for seditious libel, and insisted that a jury should be allowed to take its entirely unfettered view of a case; even on matters of law. It was a dangerous path for an advocate to follow.

In Deacon Brodie's case, the Crown called two accomplices, despite defence objections. Henry Erskine was then the leader of the Scottish Bar, and could withstand criticism. John Clerk, however, was very inexperienced. He rose to address the jury at an hour familiar to advocates in those days: two o'clock in the morning.

Lord Braxfield warned him to be brief, so John Clerk stated flatly that the Court should not have let the accomplices give evidence. It was a bad point, and met with a broadside from all the five judges on the Bench:

Lord Braxfield: Do you say that, sir, after the judgement which the court has pronounced? That, sir, is a most improper observation to address at the outset to the jury.

Lord Stonefield: It is a positive reflection on the court.

Lord Hailes: It is a flat accusation that we have admitted improper evidence.

Lord Eskgrove: I never heard the like of this from any young counsel at the beginning of his career at this bar.

Lord Braxfield: With these admonitions, go on, sir: proceed, sir.

John Clerk then referred to the accomplices as "infernal scoundrels", "infamous characters," and "vagabonds", and repeated that their evidence should not have been admitted. He received another devastating rebuke, to which he replied:

"No, my Lords, I am not attacking the court; I am attacking that villain of a witness who, I tell your Lordships, is not worth his value in hemp."

Henry Erskine was not prepared to follow Clerk into this battle, but Clerk persisted:

Lord Braxfield: Sir, I tell you that the jury have nothing to do with the law, but to take it *simpliciter* from me.
Clerk: That I deny.

This was when the floor of the court should have opened and swallowed him up.

Lord Braxfield: You are talking nonsense, sir.
Clerk: My Lord, you had better not snub me in this way. I never mean to speak nonsense.

There is an awful fascination in this young man baiting Lord Braxfield, who asked the Lord Advocate whether he wished Clerk's words to be written down, a first step towards his deprivation.

The Lord Advocate replied, "Oh no, my Lord, not exactly yet. My young friend will soon cool in his effervescence for his client."

He was wrong. Clerk continued:

"Gentlemen of the jury, I was just saying to you, *when this outbreak on the bench occurred*, that you were the judges of the law and of the facts in this case."

Lord Braxfield told him that he was behaving intolerably; Clerk replied that if he could not address the jury on this subject, he would sit down. So he sat down.

Lord Braxfield insisted, "Go on, sir; go on to the length of your tether."

Mr. Clerk stood up, and repeated his defiant submission.

Lord Braxfield warned, "Beware of what you are about, sir."

Mr. Clerk sat down again. But he made it clear that he had not finished.

Lord Braxfield invited him to continue his speech:

Clerk: "I have met with no politeness from the court. You have interrupted me, you have snubbed me rather too often, my Lord, in the line of my defence"

He was not finished even then. During Lord Braxfield's summing-up, he leapt to his feet and shook his fist at him. His client was duly hanged; John Clerk later became a judge.

He seems to have led a charmed life. But, however much a counsel may validly challenge a judge, it is not part of his duty to make personal remarks. Serjeant Wilkins was appearing before Baron Gurney, who was certainly not as bad as Lord Braxfield.

"There exist those upon the Bench," Sjt. Wilkins told the jury, "who have the character of convicting judges. I do not envy their reputation in this world *or their fate thereafter.*"

The judge was old, and in bad health; his death was not then far off. Such a personal attack on him could never be justified.

But those who make biting attacks must be prepared to withstand them. It was said of Sjt. Wilkins that a successful repartee threw him upon his back, and ridicule drove him frantic. He had just finished one pompous speech when his opponent, Sjt. Thomas, fixed his gaze upon him and said solemnly,

"And now the Hurly-Burly's done —"

Sjt. Wilkins gathered up his gown and fled the court.

An advocate should know what is going on behind him, as is illustrated by the case in which Kermit the Frog perverted the Course of Justice.

Mr. Fotheringay, let us call him, rose to his feet in the Crown Court at the beginning of a shop-lifting case.

"Members of the Jury," he began, "in this case the Defendant went into Woolworths and there stole a toy which I am informed is called Kevin the Frog."

238

"Kermit the Frog", said the Circuit Judge, whose family loved watching that puppet on television.

Mr. Fotheringay continued:

"I am much obliged, your Honour. Anyway Members of the Jury, the Defendant went into Woolworths where they sold, this, er, Curtis the Frog, and he picked it up and hid it under his jacket. He left the shop without paying for it, and was then stopped by the Store Detective. The police arrested him, and subsequently charged him with the theft of this, er, Kenneth Toad thing."

During this speech a clerk appeared at the back of the court carrying a three-foot high effigy of Kermit the Frog, which was the stolen item. It was placed immediately behind Mr. Fotheringay.

The jury fidgeted uneasily, not being sure if they were allowed to laugh. But some temptations are too much even for a Circuit Judge, who leaned forward in his chair.

"I think, Mr. Fotheringay," he said, *"your learned junior* has some instructions for you."

Mr. Fotheringay, who had no junior in the case, turned round in some surprise. He came face to face with Kermit the Frog, and laughed so much that the case came to a halt.

And that is how Kermit the Frog perverted the Course of Justice.

Many Lord Chancellors came from the humblest beginnings, and faced the greatest hardships.

No barrister ever came nearer to death than Hardinge Stanley Giffard, later Lord Chancellor Halsbury. He prosecuted a case at Cardiff in 1854 involving a demented clergyman, who caused a disturbance.

A few weeks later Giffard was in the Old Bailey, waiting for a case to begin, when the clergyman appeared again.

"Do you remember Cardiff?" he said, and fired a pistol point-blank into Giffard's face. He had loaded it himself, and forgotten to put a wad into the barrel; the bullet rolled out as he jerked it upwards. Even so, the flash from the powder burnt and scarred Giffard's cheek.

He began his case as if nothing had happened.

An even greater outrage occurred to another Lord Chancellor, who bore it with a fortitude which passes all understanding.

Robert Finlay was an outstandingly successful barrister in cases of international importance. He was called to the Bar in 1867, and was already an old man when during the First World War Lloyd George asked him to become Lord Chancellor. He made it plain that when Finlay retired he would not be allowed a Lord Chancellor's pension, because there were already four ex-Chancellors alive and drawing their pensions, and he said the country could not afford a fifth. Few great men have been treated so meanly.

Two years later, when the war came to an end, Lloyd George decided that he would appoint his great friend, F.E. Smith to the Woolsack. He wrote Finlay a brief letter saying that he was being replaced in office. F.E.'s appointment was generally regarded as most unwise, and Finlay could have caused a tremendous political rumpus.

But he behaved with the greatest restraint, and the greatest courage. His biographer states:

> "As he read the letter, his face darkened as if he had been personally insulted, and he slowly tore it across and threw it in the waste-paper basket. Otherwise he did not show his chagrin before his friends or subordinates."

Indeed, he continued to show the greatest good will towards F.E.

At every stage in a barrister's career there are moments of hardship and vexation. He have take them all in his stride.

I can never forget seeing Mick Maguire Q.C., the Leader of the Northern Circuit, about to go into court. During the Second World War he earned his Military Cross on the fiercest battleground of the Italian Campaign.

"Well," he said, squaring his shoulders resolutely, "it can't be worse than Monte Cassino."

So he went into court to face Mr. Justice X, on a bad day.

FOURTEEN

The Nuremberg Trials

You could not live among such people; you are stifled
for want of an outlet towards something beautiful, great
or noble.

George Eliot, *The Mill on the Floss*

Nuremberg. An English traveller in Tudor times wrote:

"Although it do lie in sandy ground, yet very delightful, placed round about with pleasant woods, and hath a very wholesome air ... They have no dung-hills in all their streets but in certain odd by-corners. Neither is it the custom to make water in the streets, or to throw out any urine before 10 of the clock at night. I think there is not a city in the world where the people are more civil."

Nuremberg was the city of the Mastersingers, and the birthplace of Albrecht Durer. When plague struck the city in 1505, Durer portrayed King Death riding through the streets. It was a city of light and shade; its charming mediaeval streets survived unscathed the First World War, at the end of which Adolf Hitler was a Lance-Corporal.

It escaped a Communist uprising which broke out in Munich; troops were appointed "Instruction Commandos" to preach different politics, and Hitler discovered his almost hypnotic powers of oratory.

All Germany suffered from the reparations her conquerors demanded. France occupied the Ruhr, throwing the German economy into chaos. The currency rocketed through the floor, so to speak; in ten months £30 became worth one penny. People lived off raw cabbage leaves then, and Hitler tried to seize power in Munich. He was thrown into prison for nine months; it gave him time to write *Mein Kampf*.

Then he began to hold the annual rallies of the Nazional Sozialists (Nazis) in Nuremberg, and switched his attacks from the owners of private property to the Jews. After the Wall Street crash in October 1929, Germany had a new financial crisis. All of a sudden the Nazis held 107 seats in the Reichstag; their policies seemed to offer some shadow of hope in those desperate days of mass unemployment. Hitler came finally to power in 1933, forming his own government, and there was no looking back.

When the Reichstag (the German Parliament building) burnt down that year, by accident or design, Hitler threw his opponents into "protective custody" of concentration camps, with "possible re-education;" he made the Nuremberg rallies a showpiece of Nazi glory.

The Doric columns of the stadium were draped with swastika flags and golden ribbons; the beams of 130 searchlights converged 20,000 feet up in the night sky. As a British diplomat said, it was "like being in a cathedral of ice," and Hitler's sermons roused the congregation to fever pitch.

Here, in 1935, he proclaimed the Nuremburg Laws which banned Jews from calling themselves Germans, or marrying them; in a gesture of tragic farce he even forbade them to play the "Aryan" music of Bach, Beethoven and Wagner.

Here, in 1938, was the "Crystal Night" when the mob smashed the windows of every Jewish shop in the city, and burnt down their Synagogue. It seemed as if Hitler's demonic reign would never end; and yet, twelve years after he came to power, it was all over. In 1945 his kingdom was destroyed, and Nuremberg, the "Holy City" of Nazism, was reduced to rubble by RAF bombing. All its mediaeval buildings had been destroyed save, by a ghastly irony, the Hangman's Bridge.

Nuremberg was chosen as the place for the trials of the Nazi war criminals because its prison was still intact. Mr. Justice Jackson, the American judge who was appointed to be one of the leading prosecutors, visited the city before the trials began. He wrote:

"On each side of the main roads, there were banks of rubble containing — so General Clay informed me — so many corpses that he feared for his water supply. The old walled town was a heap of ruins. Machine-gun cartridges littered the streets where a couple of SS divisions had made a stand. There were even some in the precincts of the court house and adjacent prison. People peeped at us from bunkers under partly shattered houses, apathetic and wretched. The only sign of civilisation was a succession of shabby, noisy and crowded trams, which were still running.''

A month later, in August 1945, he signed the agreement between the Allies under which the trials were held. "WHEREAS," it began, "The United Nations have from time to time made declarations of their intention that war criminals shall be brought to justice ... NOW THEREFORE —" the International Military Tribunal was set up.

Two judges each were appointed from Britain, France, Russia and the United States. Presiding over them was the English Lord Justice Geoffrey Lawrence, who stamped his personality upon the proceedings from the very first.

THE PRESIDENT: I will now call upon the Defendants to plead Guilty or Not Guilty to the charges against them. They will proceed in turn to a point in the dock opposite to the microphone. Hermann Wilhelm Goering?
GOERING: Before I answer the questions of the Tribunal whether or not I am guilty —
PRESIDENT: I informed the Court that Defendants were not entitled to make a statement. You must plead Guilty or Not Guilty.
GOERING: I declare myself in the sense of the indictment Not Guilty.
PRESIDENT: Rudolf Hess?
HESS: No.
THE PRESIDENT: That will be entered as a plea of Not Guilty. [Laughter. The President, sternly:] If there is any disturbance in Court, those who make it will have to leave the Court.

When the defendants had all entered their pleas, the case was opened by Mr. Justice Jackson:

"May it please your honours. The privilege of opening the first trial in history for crimes against the peace of the world imposes a grave responsibility. The wrongs which we seek to condemn and punish have been so calculated, so malignant, and so devastating that civilisation cannot tolerate their being ignored, because it cannot survive their being repeated. That four nations, flushed with victory and strung with injury stay the hand of vengeance and voluntarily submit their defeated enemies to the judgment of the law is one of the most significant tributes that Power has ever paid to Reason ...

In the prisoners' dock sit twenty-odd broken men —"

The most important of them was Goering, Hitler's second in command; as Jackson put it, "the podgy finger of Goering was in every pie."

There was Ribbentrop the Nazi diplomat, Streicher the Jew-Baiter, Funk the banker, and many others. The most likeable of them was Albert Speer, the architect; the most questionably sane, Rudolf Hess.

Dr. Gilbert, an American psychiatrist, kept the defendants under constant survey, and reported that Hess was suffering from nothing more than amnesia. He could remember nothing that had happened more than two weeks previously. A man with no memory may perfectly well have committed crimes; Sir David Maxwell-Fyfe, presenting the British prosecution case, might almost have been arguing the case at a Quarter Sessions:

"It is always presumed that a person is sane until the contrary is proved. Now, if I may refer the Court to one case which I suspect, if I may so use my mind, has not been absent from the Court's mind, because of the wording of the notice which we are discussing today, it is the case of *Regina v Pritchard* in 7 Carrington & Payne 303 [a law report from 1836], which is referred to in Archbold's *Criminal Pleading* in the 1943 Edition, at page 147. In Pritchard's case —"

But Hess himself brought the argument to a close.

"Henceforth, my memory will again respond to the outside world. The reasons for simulating loss of memory were of a tactical nature. Only my ability to concentrate is in fact somewhat reduced. But my capacity to follow the trial, to defend myself, to put questions to witnesses, or to answer questions myself is not affected thereby."

It is hardly surprising that the Court then ruled him sane, but by the end of the trial his memory was reduced to a few hours. Rebecca West, the distinguished writer who sat through the whole trial, thought him "plainly mad. His skin ashen, and like other lunatics he falls into odd positions, and stays like that for hours."

By the end of the trial he was not so much a man as a gaping chasm, to be shunned and feared.

"It was," she wrote, "as if the gate of Hell had fallen ajar."

The charges against the accused covered a period of many years. They included the secret rearmament and fortification of the Rhine in the mid-1930s; the invasion of Austria in 1938; the "Night and Fog" decree of 1941, when Nazi prisoners vanished out of sight, and the millions who died at Auschwitz and other death camps.

It was too much for each of the four prosecuting countries to handle, so some of the work was shared out. The British, for instance, dealt with war crimes at sea; the Americans, with the general Nazi conspiracy; the Russians, with the atrocities in Eastern Europe, and the French with those in Western Europe.

Hartley Shawcross made the opening and closing speeches of the British case; Maxwell-Fyfe was the chief prosecutor. Griffith-Jones dealt with crimes in Poland; Elwyn-Jones, with Norway and Denmark; Phillimore with Greece and Yugoslavia.

The Russians were the least familiar with cross-examination, but much of the evidence spoke for itself. General Pokrovsky cross-examined Ohlendorf, head of one of the Special Action groups which followed the German army into Russia and exterminated civilians on a massive scale. It was said that in one year ninety thousand people died at their hands.

POKROVSKY: I wanted to know whether you received reports that members of the execution squads were unwilling to use the vans and preferred other means of execution?
OHLENDORF: That they would rather kill by means of the gas vans than by shooting?

Q: On the contrary, that they preferred execution by shooting to killing by means of the gas vans.
A: Yes, I have already said that the gas vans —

Q: And why did they prefer execution by shooting to killing in the gas vans?
A: Because, as I have already said, in the opinion of the leader of the Special Action Commandos, the unloading of the corpses was an unnecessary mental strain.

245

Q: What do you mean by "unnecessary mental strain"?
A: As far as I can remember, the conditions at that time - the picture presented by the corpses, and probably because certain functions of the body had taken place leaving the corpses lying in filth.

Q: You mean to say that the sufferings endured prior to death were clearly visible on the victims? Did I understand you correctly?
A: I can only repeat what the Doctor told me, that the victims were not conscious of their death in the van.

Q: In that case your reply to my previous question, that the unloading of the bodies made a very terrible impression on the members of the execution squad, becomes entirely incomprehensible.

Another of the Russian team led evidence of the fake station which the Nazis built at Treblinka for Jews from the Warsaw Ghetto:

MR. COUNCILLOR SMIRNOV: Please tell us, what was the subsequent aspect of the station at Treblinka?
SAMUEL RAJZMAN: At first there were no signboards whatsoever at the station, but a few months later the commander of the camp, one Kurt Franz, built a first-class railroad station with signboards. The barracks where the clothing was stored had signs reading "restaurant", "ticket office", "telegraph", "telephone", and so on. There were even train schedules for the departure and arrival of trains to and from Grodno, Suwalki, Vienna and Berlin.

Q: Did I rightly understand you, witness, that a kind of make-believe station was built with signboards and train schedules, with indications of platforms for train departures to Suwalki, and so forth?
A: When the prisoners descended from the trains, they really had the impression that they were at a very good station, from where they could go to Suwalki, Vienna, Grodno or other cities ... Between July and December 1942 an average of three transports of sixty cars arrived each day. In 1943 the transports arrived more rarely.

Q: Tell us, witness, how many persons were exterminated in the camp, on an average, daily?
A: On an average, I believe they killed in Treblinka from ten to twelve thousand prisoners daily.

None of the defence counsel had any questions to ask of this witness.

The general opinion was that the British advocacy was quite outstanding. Francis Biddle, one of the two American judges, thought that Elwyn-Jones was always relevant and lucid, with the best presentation of any advocate. He was less flattering about the American counsel who began by saying "The voice you hear is the knocking of my knees. They haven't knocked so hard since I asked my wonderful little wife to marry me." Goering laughed till he was crimson in the face.

"Jesus!" was Biddle's comment in his diary.

The contrast in national styles appears strikingly in the cross-examination of one of Ribbentrop's witnesses. Harry Phillimore was on brilliant form:

Q: And then, you see, the Führer goes on to describe [the Jews] as "tuberculous bacilli." Now, in the face of that document, do you still say that the Defendant Ribbentrop was against the policy of persecution and extermination of the Jews?
A: I said yesterday already that Herr von Ribbentrop, when he was with Hitler —

Q: Never mind what you said yesterday. I am putting it to you now, today. You have now seen that document. Do you still say that Ribbentrop was against the policy of persecution and extermination of the Jews?
A: ... He followed completely the orders given by Hitler.

Q: Yes, and to the extent of conniving at any and every atrocity, is not that right?
A: Since he had no executive powers he personally did not commit these cruelties.

Phillimore sat down; he had made his point. Colonel Amen, an American, rose to cross-examine.

"Do you consider Goering to be a typical Nazi?" he asked.

That vague question was met with a series of vague answers which did Goering no harm at all: "He is a unique person and one cannot compare his manner of living with other National Socialists."

When Colonel Amen invited the witness to state which of the defendants he considered to be a "typical Nazi," there was so

247

much laughter in Court that the President had to intervene very sharply.

Among the judges, Mr. Justice Birkett fretted and fumed. He had been one of the greatest advocates at the Bar — Sir Patrick Hastings reckoned that if ever he was foolish enough to cut up a lady in small pieces and put her in an unwanted suitcase, Norman Birkett would have persuaded the jury (a) that he was not there; (b) that he had not cut up the lady; and (c) that if he had, she thoroughly deserved it anyway.

Birkett was never as successful a judge as he had been an advocate; he would sooner have been in the arena, asking his own devastating questions. He was driven to distraction by the French counsel spending hours in describing the looting of art treasures from France in "a maddening, toneless, insipid, flat, depressing voice."

As a master of the English language he was tortured by the jargon dinned into his ears by the interpreters: "clarify, concept, ideology, subjective ..."

Above all, he loathed the mountain of documents which threatened to submerge the trial. Goering's counsel, for instance, said:

"We cannot find document 672. We have 673. We have nothing but loose sheets ... It is very difficult for us to follow a citation, because it takes us so much time to find the numbers even if they have been mentioned correctly."

Even as the trial proceeded, Nazi documents were found hidden in salt mines or walled up in a Bavarian castle. Each one had to be examined, translated, copied, and compared. Maxwell-Fyfe and the British team weeded out every document which might be irrelevant or open to question; they confronted the defendants with guilt which stared them in the face.

The slow pace was almost more than Birkett could stand. He noted in his diary:

"When I consider the utter uselessness of acres of paper and thousands of words, and that life is slipping away, I moan for this shocking waste of time."

The outside world was not aware of this. Fritzsche, the Nazi radio-commentator who was acquitted at the trial, looked back on it eight years later:

"Curiously enough, it was to Lawrence's colleague, Birkett, that the hopes of many of my companions turned. His long, lean red face and bristly reddish hair, his angular gestures and owlishly blinking eyes, aroused kindly feelings among us, though I doubt whether he would have set any store by our sympathy, even had he known of it. His rule was primarily that of assistant to his fellow Englishman, and the two frequently took counsel together."

When Birkett was invited by the Lord Chancellor, Jowitt, to be one of the judges of Nuremberg, he was told that they wanted a trained lawyer who would be a model of fairness. He was very disappointed when he found that the Foreign Office had insisted that Lord Justice Lawrence, a more senior judge, should preside.

But Lawrence was the right choice. In appearance he was short, round, rubicund and healthy, like John Bull. Fritzsche felt that he was a giant:

"His powerful and bald head seemed to call for a conventional full-bottomed wig as his cold judicial glance swept back and forth across the hall. Lawrence never wasted words, but settled hundreds of controversial points with classical brevity, sometimes deciding in favour of the prosecution, sometimes of the defence. In almost every instance he would consult his colleagues, no matter how briefly, but following such consultation his authority was absolute."

At one point he cut through a long argument by saying "the document speaks for itself."

Goering turned to Fritzsche. "D'you hear the wings of the Angel of Death?" he whispered.

Each day in court began at nine-thirty. Everyone was sat in their plush tip-up seats. With the word "Attention!" the assembly rose, and the judges entered. There were no wigs and gowns; the prosecutors wore uniforms; only the French judges wore legal robes.

There were no windows in the court, no outside views to distract the attention. The hall was of brown panelling, with silver-grey carpet and immensely long pale green curtains. It may sound monotonous, but it was a riot of colour to the prisoners emerging from the greyness of their cells. The lights dazzled them; except for the times when the photographers took pictures, they were allowed to wear dark glasses. Sometimes the lights in the courtroom were lowered so that a film could be shown. One was Leni Riefenstahl's famous *Triumph of the Will*, in which Hitler's rise to power was shown, and the Nuremberg Rallies with thousands of people in uniform drilled to perfection, for the glory of Hitler.

But it had vanished. "Is this the tin god we all worshipped?" asked Hans Frank, who was dubbed "The Butcher of Poland". He had once said "We must not be squeamish when we hear of the figure of 17,000 shot," but when the films of the Belsen concentration camp were shown, the defendants were markedly subdued. The lights came up again, and the eight judges left the court without a single word.

Sometimes spectators packed the gallery — Rita Hayworth was there one day — but for the most part the trial was sparsely attended. The strongest emotion felt there was boredom, "boredom on a huge historic scale," according to Rebecca West; the guards' faces were puffy with boredom. She wrote:

> "every person was in the grip of extreme tedium. This is not to say that the work in hand was being performed languidly. An iron discipline met that tedium head on, and did not yield an inch to it."

The High Priest of Boredom was Dr. Kubuschok, who represented Van Papen. Birkett refused to describe him as a "windbag", because that implied some powers of rhetoric and possibly eloquence:

> "Clouds of verbiage, mountains of irrelevance, and oceans of arid pomposity distinguish his every moment in the Court, and it is difficult to avoid the extremest forms of irritation with him. I have not avoided it, I regret to say!"

All bad things ought to come to an end, but:

> "when Fleischer [representing Speer] succeeded Kubuschok at the microphone, it became clear that there were lower depths of advocacy to be reached, unbelievable as it sounds. Whilst Kubuschok sleeps in the Court room, his fell work accomplished, Fleischer carries on the evil tradition with unashamed and unabated zeal."

Von Papen, however, was acquitted.

The advocates of each nation had a different stance in court. The Russians let their hands hang by their sides; the French put their fingers into their coat pockets. The Americans thrust theirs into their trouser pockets. But the English gripped their lapels in the best Old Bailey style as seen on stage and screen.

Griffith Jones may go down to posterity as the prosecuting counsel in the "Lady Chatterley" trial of 1956 who asked the somewhat archaic question "Would you have allowed your servant to read this book?", but he was formidable in cross-examination.

Fritzsche thought the technique almost unfair, but could not deny that it showed people in their true colours. He wrote:

> "The way in which this shrewd Englishman ensnared his quarry was almost diabolically clever, and fascinating to watch. Most of the time one of the prosecutor's slender hands would grip the lapel of his coat; then, with a seemingly friendly gesture it would seem to invite the boorish man in the dock to what was almost a friendly chat and all of a sudden, Streicher would find that he had walked into another trap."

Julius Streicher was the squat, bald Jew-baiter known as "the Beast of Nuremberg." From 1923 onwards his paper, *The Storm-Trooper*, had spewed out obsessive articles about Jews having sex with German girls. He was in the eyes of Rebecca West a dirty old man.

His intelligence was lower than any of the other defendants, who shunned him. What he said to Doctor Gilbert explained why.

"Three of the judges are Jews," he claimed.

"How can you tell?" asked Dr. Gilbert.

> "I can recognise blood; I have been studying race for twenty years. Himmler had negro blood himself."
>
> "Really?"
>
> "Oh yes, I could tell by his head-shape and hair. I can recognise blood."

Griffith Jones had no difficulty with him:

> "I want to make myself quite clear to you in what I am suggesting. I am suggesting that from 1939 onwards you set out to incite the

251

German people to murder and to accept the fact of the murder of the Jewish race. Do you understand?"

"That is not true."

"No doubt you will say it is not true. I just wanted you to be quite clear of what my suggestion is going to be."

He invited Streicher to read paragraph after paragraph from *The Storm-Trooper*.

"They must be utterly exterminated," he read out, "then the world will see that the end of the Jews is also the end of Bolshevism."

"Who wrote that article?" asked Streicher.

Griffith Jones replied:

"It is published in your *Storm-Trooper*, and you have told the tribunal that you accept responsibility for everything that was written in that newspaper."

"All right, I accept responsibility ... This is a theoretic and very strong-worded expression of opinion of that Anti-Semitic person."

"All I ask you about that is, if that is not advocating the murder of Jews, that article? If not, what is it advocating?"

While Streicher squirmed in the witness-box, Goering hid his face in his hands.

Goering's evidence was the most important part of the trial. He was no longer the bloated bladder of a man who had strutted his way through the years of Nazi success; the months of captivity had deprived him of drugs and luxury. He was a mere shadow of his earlier bulk, but still alert. Rebecca West noted "the coarse bright skin of an actor who has used grease paint for decades, and the preternaturally deep head of a ventriloquist's dummy."

On March 13th 1946 Goering entered the witness box. He gave his age as 52, and described his career. He had been an air ace in Von Richthofen's Flying Circus during World War I, and had been with Hitler from the first, as his second-in-command. He founded the Gestapo; "every bullet that leaves a policeman's pistol is my bullet," he stated; "if this is murder then I have murdered."

He set up the concentration camps for the "protective custody" and "possible re-education" of Nazi victims. He commanded the Storm Troopers when Hitler came to power in 1933.

For three days in his rasping voice, he explained and excused everything he had done. "In the struggle of life and death there is no legality", he insisted.

Mr. Justice Jackson rose to cross-examine him at 12.15 on the morning of March 18th 1946. It was a great moment; Goering had displayed the greatest presence among the defendants.

There were plenty of critics who had said that the Nazi leaders should have been executed without trial. If Goering was exposed in all his evil, well and good; but if he should talk his way to an acquittal by plausible excuses, the damage could never be repaired. Still, Jackson's opening speech had been a masterpiece, and there was no reason to expect less of him now. Fritzsche wrote:

> "His opening questions were delivered almost in a spirit of *bonhomie*. Was this, we wondered, a danger signal? Or simply the result of the lawyer's misunderstanding all the change brought about by the Defence? The general view was that such benevolent politeness implied that the prosecutor was sure of his prey."

Within fifteen minutes, however, it was clear that the unthinkable catastrophe had occurred; Goering was getting the better of him. Nobody had been prepared for the fact that Goering was a master of the details of the case. He knew all the documents backwards, and had an answer for everything.

Jackson phrased his questions far too widely. "You are the only one who can explain this Nazi Philosophy for us," he said. Goering did precisely that, taking the heaven-sent opportunity to make long speeches. Jackson began to bluster. He protested:

> "This man is adopting in the dock and the witness-stand an arrogant and contemptuous attitude towards a Tribunal which is giving him a trial which he never gave a living soul."

The President of the Tribunal suggested discreetly that they should adjourn, but Jackson floundered deeper and deeper. He asked whether Germany's preparations for mobilisation had not been kept secret.

"I don't recall ever having read of the US Government publishing *their* preparations for mobilisation," retorted Goering.

253

Jackson protested that he was making "unseemly remarks," and when he referred to his answers as "Nazi propaganda" earned a rebuke from the President.

Birkett was appalled; he thought that Goering should have been stopped from making long speeches. In this he was wrong, because the Tribunal would have ceased to seem impartial. Besides, as he recognised, one could not say that the answers to the questions were irrelevant.

Goering had triumphed. His eyes glittered, and he swelled visibly in confidence. The French prosecutors were to ask him no questions at all, and the Russians were even less successful than Jackson.

> "Did you conspire to wage an aggressive war against the peace-loving democracies? Answer Yes or No."
> "No."
> "I accept your answer."

Only Maxwell-Fyfe could save the day. He was much feared by all the Nazis. Some of his most lethal questions began with the words "I want to be completely fair", and wiped the complacent smiles off the faces of those who had to answer them. Maxwell-Fyfe recalled:

> "When I took over from the discomfited Jackson, Goering's confidence was overweening; 'I have destroyed Jackson,' his eyes seemed to say as I approached him; 'I am going to enjoy dealing with you.' "

He did not make Jackson's mistake of couching his questions too widely. One of his main points was very precise. 76 RAF officers escaped from a prisoner-of-war camp in what has been known ever since as "The Great Escape." Most of them were recaptured, and Hitler ordered 55 of them to be shot. If he had known of the order and had passed it on, he would share the guilt for it.

Goering claimed that he knew nothing of the matter, because he had been on leave until March 29th 1944; but Maxwell-Fyfe pointed out that the shootings had lasted until a fortnight later, and that his Luftwaffe staff had told him.

MAXWELL-FYFE: You understand what I am suggesting to you is that here was a matter known to your own Director of Operations,

General Foerster, who informed Field Marshall Milch. I am suggesting to you that it is absolutely impossible and untrue that in those circumstances you know nothing about it.
GOERING: Field Marshall Milch was here as a witness and regrettably was not asked about these points.

Q: Oh, yes, he was, and Milch took the same line as you, that he knew nothing about it. What I am suggesting is that both you and Milch were saying you know nothing about it when you did, and are now trying to shift the responsibility on to the shoulders of your junior officers.
A: That is untrue. I consider this matter the worst business of the whole war. I never contradicted Hitler so strongly or so sharply as I did over the RAF fliers. I told him my view. Because of that the Fuehrer and I did not speak to each other for months.

MAXWELL-FYFE: Well, that may be your view, but I am suggesting that when every one of these officers of yours knew about it you knew about it too, and that you did nothing to prevent these men from being shot. You cooperated in this foul series of murders.

There was no scoring points off Maxwell-Fyfe. Goering clenched his fists, and his face was red with anger. He seemed almost happy when, after ten days in the witness box, he resumed his place in the dock; he had at least been able to say everything he wanted. For the rest of the trial he sat with his chin on his clasped hands. It may have seemed arrogant, but Fritzsche knew better; Goering realised that his fate was sealed.

When all the evidence had been given and the final speeches had been made, the defendants had a last opportunity to speak on their own behalf. Goering pledged his allegiance to Hitler:

"I identify my fate with yours for better or worse. I dedicated myself to you in good times and in bad, even unto death. I really meant it, and I still do."

The tribunal adjourned for a month to consider the verdicts. When the sentences were passed, on October 1st 1946, each defendant entered the dock separately to hear his own.

Goering came in undaunted, put on his headphones, and heard the words "Death by the rope." The headphones clattered as he set them down again on the table, and he left the dock abruptly.

Down in the cells below, he spoke but one word to Dr. Gilbert — "Death!"

Field-Marshall Keitel, who would have faced a firing squad unflinchingly, said

"Death — *by hanging!*" "Death! Death!" said Ribbentrop, the Nazi diplomat. "Now I won't be able to write my beautiful memoirs. Tut! Tut! So much hatred! Tut! Tut!"

Many of the other defendants were sentenced to death. Hess received life imprisonment; Speer, 20 years imprisonment. Fritzsche and Von Papen were among the few to be acquitted.

Dr. Gilbert had administered the ink-blot test to each of the defendants, and reminded Goering of his reaction:

"Do you remember the card with a red spot? Morbid neurotics often hesitate over that card, and then say there is blood on it. You hesitated, but you did not call it blood. *You tried to flick it off with your finger,* as though you thought you could wipe away the blood with a little gesture. You have been doing the same thing all through the trial — taking off your earphones in the courtroom, whenever the evidence of your guilt became too unbearable. And you did the same thing during the war, too, drugging the atrocities out of your mind. You did not have the courage to face it. That is your guilt. I agree with Speer: you are a moral coward."

But he met a death of his own choosing. Two hours before he was due to be hanged, he was found dead in his cell; he had taken a cyanide capsule.

The hanging took place under glaring lights in the prison gymnasium, a grubby room smelling of cigarette smoke. The bodies were cremated at Munich, and the ashes washed away by the river. There are no tombs at which admirers may gather.

Many people have forgotten the Nuremberg trials now. It was hoped that they would light such a beacon that similar crimes could never be repeated, but the world has tyranny and atrocity still.

Twenty years after the trials Hartley Shawcross, who had made the opening and closing speeches, wrote sadly that "Our Nuremberg hope that we had made some contribution to a transition to a peaceful world under the rule of law has not been fulfilled."

Was it all, then, in vain? I think not. The mountains of paper

256

which drove Mr. Justice Birkett to despair are still there for all to read. They set out in volume after volume the facts of the worst crimes ever to be tried in a court of law.

FIFTEEN

All Things Must Change

*With all its possible defects, English justice is the best
thing that is left to us. If I could give one word of advice
to the great minds who will be chosen to control our
destinies, I would suggest to them that, with all the
changes they will be called to make, they should leave
our Law alone.*

Sir Patrick Hastings, *Cases in Court*

If a man wishes to be a great painter, he must sit in front
of great paintings in a gallery, minutely studying the brush-
strokes. If he is taught by a great painter, he may one day be
allowed to paint some of the background for a Madonna and
Child.

The pupillage system at the Bar has been much like that, ever
since Cicero's day. In the Fourteenth century the apprentices
at the Bar sat in court watching the cases closely, and making
notes.

Sir James Dyer, one of the earliest authors of law reports,
used to attend court every morning with a notebook, taking
down the arguments and judgments in shorthand. He wrote
them up every evening. His industry and learning made him
a most respected Chief Justice. But the serjeants had to be
recruited from somewhere; and it must have been from the more
experienced apprentices whom they got to know.

As Sir John Metingham had the duty of monitoring candidates
appropriate to be approved as advocates, the practice may have
grown up even then of keeping notes about promising members
of the profession who deserved advancement, as is done for
prospective Queen's Counsel and appointments to the Bench.

One can guess how this happened from the career of Lord
Chief Justice Saunders, who was appointed to that position in
1683. Roger North wrote:

"I have seen him for hours and half hours together before the court sat, stand at the bar, with an audience of students over against him, putting of cases, and debating so as suited their capacities and encouraged their industry. And so in the Temple, he seldom moved without a parcel of youths hanging about him, and he merry and jesting with them."

This must have been how the young men got to know their elders, who would soon spot the most promising students. We can see what the serjeants did, from the Year Books. But there were many tasks which must have been given to apprentices of the law — going to distant courts to apply for adjournments, devilling the pleadings for busy serjeants, and handling the smaller cases themselves.

Perhaps the serjeants' clerks would send out the young men on these cases just as if they were going to a modern magistrates court or County Court.

It is sad to think that no busy modern practitioner could possibly spare as much time for the students as Saunders did. But time is what you make it.

Chaloner Chute, who was the Speaker to one of Cromwell's Parliaments, would sometimes say to his clerk, "Tell the people I will not practise this term."

When he returned, his practice had not diminished at all.

"I guess", wrote Roger North, "that no eminent chancery practiser ever did or will do the like; and it shows a transcendant genius superior to the slavery of a gainful profession."

In 1300, the long vacation lasted for three months, but was reduced by two commissions of Assize which lasted for three weeks in July, and a further three weeks from mid-September. This remained the pattern for hundreds of years.

Some counsel went on long holidays; others stayed with their noses to the grindstone.

Ballantine tells the story of the two experienced silks, in Victorian times, who met each other after the long vacation. One was bronzed and healthy, from a trip on the Continent.

"I have not stirred from town," said the other, "and have been doing lots of work."

"What's the use of it?" asked the first. "You can't take your money with you when you die — and if *you* could, it would soon melt!"

259

Perhaps the pupillage system has always been the same, with many applications made to the most successful practitioners. The future Lord Atkin decided at one glance who was the man for him. He recalled:

> "I went into the courts one afternoon and saw a tall, bearded junior waving his arms at a judge who was listening benevolently to an address in which it was obvious the speaker was complete master of the facts and the law. I found out who he was and induced him to let me read with him."

It was Scrutton, one of the keenest minds in the law, but not the most explicit pupil-master. He would meet his pupils for tea, but did not discuss his papers at all:

> "He, silently absorbed in thinking about his work, would stride about the room until, almost daily, the top of his head crashed into the knob of the chandelier that hung from the ceiling."

One quality now taken for granted in the legal profession, is integrity. English barristers and judges do not take bribes, which is one reason why, despite all the criticisms made of it, the English legal profession is probably the best in the world. Yet only three centuries ago Bacon, one of the finest minds of his age, and occupying the highest judicial office of Lord Chancellor, was fined heavily for corruption.

The poet Martial recognised this hazard:

> The judge is on the take, and counsel too.
> I'd *pay* my creditors, if I were you.

Corruption was part of the legal scene. Some counsel took fees from both sides, and some judges, until Cromwell's Parliaments banned them, accepted gifts.

Lord Chancellor Nottingham, who was appointed in 1673, used to receive about £3000 a year from the customary New Year's gifts of money from those who appeared in his court. However, he so hated himself for having to accept the money that he would cry out in his lisping voice '*OH, TYRANT CUTHTOM!*', as he pocketed the money.

Lord Chancellor Cowper discontinued this practice in 1705.

Martial had another important warning to give about the law, in relation to its delays:

Twenty icy cold winters have come and have gone
Since you sued in three courts, but you still carry on.
If you think after twenty years' suing you'll find
Anybody's a winner, you're out of your mind!

Dickens would certainly agree. A case today may take unduly
long to come to court, and there is room for improvement; but
our ancestors would regard the present process as dizzyingly fast.

The law is less pernickety now over tiny details. Long gone
are the days when a prosecution collapsed because some cut-
throat was described in the indictment as "Jack Smith" instead
of "James Smith."

The intricate details of "special pleading" have likewise passed
away, and their special brand of pleaders. Sjt. Ballantine wrote:

> "Joseph Brown will go down to posterity as the admired author
> of the longest set of pleadings ever known. At the bar his arguments
> have been most exhaustive, and *never weakened by any approach
> to levity.*"

It would be wrong to sneer too much at special pleaders. Good
causes have sometimes been defeated by tiny technicalities, but
so have bad ones.

Chitty, one of the most famous special pleaders in Victorian
times, was brought into a murder case. He rose to move in arrest
of judgment after the defendants had been convicted, and when
Mr. Justice Park was just about to put on the black cap and
pronounce sentence of death. His objection was that the trial
had begun on January 6th, the Feast of the Epiphany, which
was not a day appointed for business in the courts, so the whole
proceedings were void.

"Why, Mr. Chitty," said the judge, "the court frequently
tries cases on Good Friday."

So the technical point failed. But if it had succeeded, three
men would have been saved from the gallows.

Tidd was another famous special pleader; many of his pupils
went on to become great lawyers. Young Copley, for instance,
had a clear head and a remarkable memory. But he had no
practice to speak of, and was on the point of quitting the circuit
when the Luddite riots broke out in Nottingham and Derby.
His client was charged with hostile activities towards the
"proprietors of a silk and lace cotton manufactory", and it would

have gone hard with him if he had been convicted. But Copley took the point that one of the two factories involved made cotton lace, and the other silk lace; neither of them made "silk *and* cotton lace", so that the indictment was bad.

On this technical point the defendant was acquitted. Copley was carried shoulder-high in triumph by the defendant's friends. Work came flooding in to him so fast that by the next year he was made a serjeant, and ultimately became Lord Lyndhurst, one of the best Lord Chancellors.

It is one of the natural processes of mankind that the laws should first issue unchallenged from a king, or a group of priests; next, that they should be written down on tablets of stone; finally, that they should become more informal, and open to flexible application.

This has reached its furthest development in the work of legal tribunals, where most of the long-standing rules about hearsay evidence and other formalities are relaxed. It is the most rapidly growing field of law, and its whole approach is new.

There is a body of law on the subject of sexual discrimination; this is the summary of one such case, which appeared in Current Law:

"*Wylie* v *Dee & Co (Menswear)* (1978) IRLR 103. D & Co., men's clothiers, who already employed 7 male sales assistants, refused to consider W, a woman, to fill a vacancy for a sales assistant on the ground that the job involved taking inside leg measurements. *Held*, that D & Co. had unlawfully discriminated against W. on grounds of sex. There was insufficient evidence that the requirements to take inside leg measurements arose often and one of the male assistants could take the measurement when necessary."

There was certainly sexual discrimination against women as far as the Bar was concerned. In his famous and influential book *Speculum Juris* ("The Mirror of Law"), Guillaume Durand listed who was not allowed to be an advocate in the 13th century. He could not, for instance, be someone who was then insane, or a woman, or blind. To quote some rhyming Latin verses:

An advocate cannot be blind,
Or a woman, or *one of the feminine kind.*

In 1903 Miss Bertha Cave applied to the Inns of Court for

admission, but was refused. She appealed to a committee of judges, who refused her appeal.

F.E. Smith would share their view. In a discussion in the House of Commons in 1908, he was more in favour of Barmaids than of maidens at the Bar:

> *F.E.:* I do not pretend to so close an acquaintance with the habits of barmaids as some hon. members who have spoken, but they are as well conducted and as moral in their habits and as deserving of protection from the House as any other women in any class of employment. (Cheers).
>
> ... I could give the committee case after case in which respectable women are earning their living in public-houses for whom no other method of employment could be suggested, and who are supporting relatives. The philanthropists have never suggested any other employment for these women.
>
> *Dr. Rutherford:* Admit them to the legal profession. (Labour cheers).
>
> *F.E.:* I do not regard the remark of the hon. member as a serious or worthy interruption. (Opposition cheers).

But the Sex Disqualification Act of 1919 opened the gates to women, and on June 13th 1923 Miss Edith Hesling was called to the Bar by Gray's Inn. It is pleasing to know that her own daughter was called to the Bar in 1951. After the Second World War women began to come to the Bar in considerable numbers, and their success is now beyond dispute.

But for many years the public had some rather overheated ideas about woman barristers; it was feared that a Harsh Oath in open court would give them a fit of the vapours. It has never been known to happen.

I used to be plagued with friends who approached me with silly grins, and then asked "What do you call a lady barrister who has lost her briefs?"

(I could never think of the answer, which must be "Bar-bra Nicholas.")

They receive more than their fair share of vexation from Male Chauvinist Pigs. One lady barrister I know was carrying out a devastating cross-examination until her opponent passed her a note saying "There is a ladder in your stocking."

She blushed to the roots of her hair, and took a cautious look at her legs. There was no ladder there at all, but her opponent had done his worst. Her cross-examination was ruined.

She deserved revenge. I suggested that, on a later occasion, she should wait till her opponent was on his feet, then pass him a note saying "Your flies are open, but you have very little to be embarrassed about."

She was too lady-like to do it.

I have seen a lady barrister enraged because her opponent referred to her in open court as "My learned and attractive friend." She regarded it as a sexist remark. But nobody has ever described her opponent as attractive, and never will.

Then there was the New York judge who greeted a lady advocate who entered his Courtroom with the words "What knockers!"

But, whatever the failings of male barristers, a remarkably high proportion of lady barristers marry them, even from the same Chambers.

If one thing has remained permanent over the years, it is that there is no such thing as a successful barrister who keeps short hours. Rufus Isaacs put it best: "The Bar is never a bed of roses. It is either all bed and no roses, or all roses and no bed."

In 1861 *The Times* wrote a leader about the hours that a barrister with a large practice had to keep:

> "He must be called at 4 o'clock and sit reading his papers by candlelight when less prosperous Christians are asleep. He must be holding consultations at hours when the most humble bank clerk is only just getting his breakfast. He must be in court with half a day's work done for the most part at nine-o'clock. Then he has his weary hours of wrangling, reading, verifying authorities and spinning out hours of talk, less to convince the court than to satisfy his clients. In the afternoon, when the burden of the day is thrown off by all ordinary labourers, the prosperous barrister is needed at Chambers."

It is difficult to know which member of the Bar worked the hardest.

Lord Keeper Williams ranks high amongst the contenders. He used to study the law almost non-stop from 6.0 a.m. to 3.0 a.m. Lord Campbell wrote:

> "He surrendered up his whole time to dive into the immense well of knowledge that hath no bottom. He read the best, he heard the best, he conferred with the best, exscribed, committed to memory, disputed; he had some work continually upon the loom."

He came into Chancery between six and seven a.m. in the winter, by candle-light, and heard cases. From eight in the morning till after one in the afternoon he sat on the Woolsack in the House of Lords, and then returned to the Chancery court to hear further cases. From eight o'clock at night until one in the morning he was simply at home, looking at further papers.

Roundell Palmer, later Lord Selborne, once worked from two a.m. on a Monday morning until late on the Saturday night without going to bed at all, but he spent the whole of Sunday in bed.

One of the problems which faces junior members of the Bar is that of promotion. Until the reign of Queen Elizabeth, when Francis Bacon was appointed the first Queen's Counsel, nobody could be made a judge unless he was first a Serjeant. One might have expected great enthusiasm from members of the Bar to apply for that position.

It was quite the reverse; the king had to serve writs on those he wished to raise to this exalted station:

"The king to his well beloved John of Preston, greeting: For as much as we, with the advice of our justices of either bench, and other learned men of our council, have nominated and listed you (together with other notable persons sufficiently trained in the law and customs of our realm) to receive the estate and degree of serjeant of law on the 25th of April 1412—"

Up to this point the formal Latin phrases seem friendly enough. But the "well beloved" John of Preston was about to be shown the steel fist in the velvet glove:

"— We strictly enjoin and command you to be ready and prepared at that day ... If at the aforesaid day you should be careless or remiss in receiving this estate and degree, we shall cause you to be utterly barred and thereafter discharged from all pleading in all our courts and places whatever."

There were complaints at that time of a shortage of serjeants to deal with the most serious cases. Their promotion stopped them from being Members of Parliament, and required them to go on circuit as Judges of Assize; that might have been one of their objections. But though serjeants certainly earned more than the other advocates, the ceremonies of their appointment cost a large fortune. They had to give gold rings to the judges, and provide a banquet which the King attended, almost as expensive as the feast at a coronation.

Whatever the reason, nobody wanted to become a serjeant.

Thus, in 1412, when nine persons were required to become serjeants, three of them flatly refused. Henry IV committed them to the Tower of London. A few months later, in March 1413, the King died. Henry V served those three, and two more, with fresh orders to become serjeants.

All five of them refused. The penalty for refusing now included a fine of 500 marks; in 1415, the year of Agincourt, it was increased to 1000 marks. They still refused, though they gave way later, under further pressure.

As time went on, the Crown selected barristers to become serjeants, instead of forcing them. They were independent-minded individuals. By the 17th century they had a monopoly of special pleading in the Court of Common Pleas, and threatened to strike when attorneys sought to share this work.

Chief Justice North called their bluff; he said that if they would not do the work themselves, he would let the attorneys do it for them.

This was "like thunder to the serjeants ... for none of them imagined it would have such a turn as this was ... one of them broke the silence of the court, more like one crying than speaking."

In the 19th century, the work of the Court of Common Pleas declined a great deal, and the serjeants were very unpopular in the profession because of their restrictive practices. Even if the pleadings were drawn by a first-class pleader, and a first-rate QC was briefed, the interlocutory matters ® preliminary steps before the trial itself⅜ could be conducted only by a Serjeant.

In an age when the courts regularly sat late at night, the Court of Common Pleas often rose at noon because one of the Serjeants had a cold. Critics attacked the

"indolent gossiping colloquial habits of a domestic tribunal where one learned brother nods to another and then telegraphs a communication with the Bench that they intend giving themselves a half-holiday."

Time was running out for the serjeants. Serjeant Wilde hastened their exit by arrogant words to Lord Chancellor

Brougham at a dinner, who brought in a measure to end their monopoly. A court case proved it to be invalid, so the serjeants, who revelled in their Latin motto *Honos nomenque manebunt* ("their glory and their title shall remain forever") refurbished Serjeants' Inn at tremendous cost.

In 1874, however, Lord Chancellor Cairns created Serjeant Robinson, and let it be known that no more serjeants would ever be appointed. Serjeants Inn was disbanded in 1877; the premises were sold for £57,000, and when Lord Lindley died in 1921, the order of serjeants came to an end.

The importance of serjeants had been overtaken by that of Queens Counsel. It became the best road forward to success at the Bar.

One of the most striking changes in the history of the Bar was that of travel. In the earliest days, when practitioners were members of the clergy, they rode with their servants around the country, probably staying at the nearest monastery.

As time went on, they came to use carriages, and stopped at whatever accommodation they could find in the circuit towns.

In Boswell's time ordinary barristers were expected to stay at lodgings; the Judges, and the most senior members of the circuit, stayed at hotels. There was often a terrible scramble for the existing accommodation.

Barristers had to be very careful how they travelled on circuit. On the way to the circuit they were allowed to travel by stage-coach, if they chose; the slow-coach, as it was called, was far cheaper than the fast one.

Experienced members of the circuit whiled away the journey by reading their briefs. The briefless youngsters, however, fixed a plank from one window to the other, as a makeshift table, and played whist on it. Once they approached a circuit town, however, the stage-coach was totally forbidden to the Bar.

"We were not allowed to use public conveyances or live at hotels," wrote Serjeant Ballantine, who was a member of the Home Circuit in the days when London to Chelmsford was a long journey. "The leaders generally travelled, accompanied by their clerks, in their own carriages, the juniors two or three together, in dilapidated post-chaises."

To arrive by stage-coach would be vulgar and ungentlemanly,

which was bad enough; but far worse was the risk that a barrister might *meet an Attorney!*

The plague was not more strictly shunned, for the worst crime a barrister could commit was to go seeking work from those in a position to bestow it. When attorneys walked the streets in Assize towns in search of a counsel to brief, the barristers watched like starving dogs hoping to be tossed a bone.

When the railways came, the rule was changed; barristers might arrive upon the circuit by train — provided they travelled first class.

One barrister, who shall be nameless, brought shame upon the entire profession when he arrived *by tram*. Still, the effect of travel warped the whole fabric of society.

"I have lived," wrote Serjeant Ballantine, "to see an archbishop arriving in a hansom cab!"

For ordinary members of the Bar, the lodgings were frugal almost to a fault. James Parke was delighted when his wife sent him a consignment of marmalade and rhubarb, to eke out his diet.

Mr. Clinton, at Lincoln, was outraged when his landlady charged him sixpence an egg. He demanded the bill, and added another sixpence to it. She asked him why.

"You have charged *nothing for the salt*," he snorted.

All this was opulence compared with the circuit accommodation Abraham Lincoln found in 1842 in America:

> "The tavern bedrooms had usually only a bed, a spittoon, two split-bottom chairs, a washstand with a bowl and a pitcher of water, the guest in colder weather breaking the ice to wash his face. Some taverns had big rooms where a dozen or more lawyers slept of a night. In most of the sleepy little towns 'court day' whetted excitement over trials to decide who would have to pay damages or go to jail."

The excitement of "court day"! It is long since forgotten, now that the Crown Court, like an ever-rolling stream, seems to continue almost without interruption from one year's end to the next. The Long Vacation used to start in August, and end in October. There were barristers who would lock up their chambers, head for the Continent, and not be seen for two months. But now the Crown Court sits into the second week of August, and may soon erode the remaining period.

Lawyers on circuit need text books and law reports. In the 13th century a lawyer's complete library was little more than those works known as Glanville, Bracton, and Fleta.

In Victorian times each circuit had a pantechnicon to carry the baggage, especially the book-boxes, from one circuit town to the next. It was quite a sight to see the Western Circuit's van standing in Brick Court in the Temple for several days before the Assizes began, to give the circuiteers time to load it up. Once railway travel made the van unnecessary, it was sold to a travelling menagerie.

Once in court, the Victorian barristers set out to enthral their audiences by any device they could think of. Not perhaps by producing a blood-stained sword, as in ancient Rome, but by bringing little children into court, to rend the hearts of a gullible jury.

Everyone knows the story about F.E. Smith in a London County Court, who suggested that a little child, who had been brought into court for sentimental effect, should be passed round the jury-box.

Henry Hawkins, some thirty years earlier, found that children were not quite as appealing as he thought. He defended a man who suddenly killed his wife for no apparent reason. The local Vicar gave evidence that the man had been a faithful churchgoer for 35 years, and the defendant's two little children duly sobbed their hearts out in court, and played no small part in their father's acquittal.

That night Hawkins dined with someone from the same village, who had seen the children only a few days before the trial. They were playing on an ash-heap, swinging a dead cat about with a string round its neck, and singing:

> This is the way poor Daddy will go!
> This is the way poor Daddy will go!

"Such, Mr. Hawkins," said the villager, "was their excessive grief!"

In an age when the Assizes was the most dramatic event of the year, every case, no matter how trifling, was reported in the local paper. Jurors liked advocacy to be bold and striking.

At the Guildhall the great Erskine once told a jury,

"The reputation of a cheesemonger in the City of London

269

is like the bloom upon a peach. Breathe on it, and it is gone for ever."

Thomas Platt, who specialised in a "wife-and-twelve-children" brand of pathos, won huge damages for his client, a young girl, when he told a jury that "This serpent in human shape stole the virgin heart of my unfortunate client *whilst she was returning from confirmation."*

Sjt. Vaughan poured scorn upon a witness by saying "And then we come to Brown. Ah, there the impudent and deceitful fellow stands, just like a crocodile, with tears in his eyes and his hands in his breeches pockets!"

Juries loved that style, though it was usually ill-suited to technical cases. Digby Seymour QC was briefed in a compensation claim in relation to some grass-fields near Neasden, where a large number of carriage-horses were allowed to graze. He made a flamboyant speech about "Arab steeds, with flowing manes and panting flanks, careering over these fields as though they had been in the desert."

His opponent, however, was a great expert in these compensation cases. He reminded the jury that they had to consider:

(a) the value of the land
(b) the number of years' purchase that should be given on it
(c) special principles of discount which applied, and so forth.

Digby Seymour listened with horror; he was completely out of his depth. "What am I to say?" he asked the junior counsel he was leading.

"Don't worry about all that rot," said his junior, "just give the jury some more of those Arab steeds with their panting flanks."

So he did, and won the highest compensation that had ever been awarded for land in that neighbourhood.

While the legal terms lasted, the courts sat very long hours. Indeed, on the very last day of term, the Courts might well sit until midnight, if that was necessary to clear the list of cases.

It was not so much the lateness of the hour which affected the nature of justice, so much as the fluid which oiled the wheels after a break for dinner. The famous utterances of Sjt. Arabin, who sat as a Judge at the Old Bailey from 1830 to 1839, have a distinct flavour of alcohol. For instance,

"No man is fit to be a cheesemonger who cannot guess the length of a street."

Or this:

"If ever there was a case of clearer evidence than this of persons acting together, this is that case."

In those days the Hon. Charles Ewan Law, the Recorder at the Old Bailey, was described as "dignified in manner *before dinner* always". He used to have a tray of coffee with him upon the bench. Once, after dinner, he succeeded in upsetting it over the Clerk of Arraigns, who sat below him in the Court. The Recorder said not a word.

On the following morning he had another tray of coffee on the bench, and by a further unhappy accident the Clerk of Arraigns was once again dunked like a doughnut. The Recorder said to the jury:

> "Gentlemen, I have constantly begged that the desk should be made broader. I met with the same accident on another occasion."

The Bar is much more serious now, and less thriving. Fifty years ago, there were three shops in the Temple which sold wigs and gowns; now there is only one. Ten years ago, the robing rooms at the Royal Courts of Justice were a seething mass of barristers; now, they are more like a ghost town.

Many types of work have been lost to the Bar. A great deal of time used to be spent fighting divorce cases, and drafting the so-called "discretion statements", in which clients were required to set out for the court the details of their matrimonial indiscretions.

Brawny sailors would have to set out the occasions on which they docked at San Francisco, Shanghai, and Singapore, and committed adultery with girls known to them only as "Dolores" and "Tiger Lily." Barristers, having reduced these exploits to a few paragraphs of cool prose on their clients' behalf, sometimes inadvertently signed them, which led divorce judges to congratulate them upon their personal stamina.

But all this work has gone now. The courts are saved a great deal of bickering between the parties, and it is now almost absurdly easy for a husband and wife to end a marriage which has run into difficulties. It is highly debatable whether society has gained from that change in the law.

Up to twenty-five years ago, most barristers worked in Chambers on Saturday mornings. The future Lord Goddard was rewarded for such assiduity. A firm of solicitors came to him because nobody else was available. He had just read a recent Law Report on a banking case, which answered the very point on which they consulted him. It was the foundation of a big practice in banking cases.

Nowadays, Chambers are shut for ordinary business on Saturdays. A dedicated few go there to work uninterrupted by the usual telephone calls. The pattern of work has changed, but its basic nature remains the same. Youngsters still despair of making a successful career; established barristers have to work overtime upon overtime, to keep abreast of their work.

Sometimes success comes soon; sometimes it departs, seemingly for ever. It is hard to imagine that even Sir Edward Marshall Hall, one of the giants of the English Bar, once found failure staring him in the face.

He had not been long in silk when, in 1902, he appeared for an actress named Hetty Chattell. She was enjoying a successful career at the age of 28 when the *Daily Mail* said that a Gaiety Girl called Rosie Boote was her daughter. It was not true; Miss Chattell had never been married. Thus, at a stroke, the *Daily Mail* implied that she had had an illegitimate daughter and must be a lot older than she gave herself out to be.

The *Daily Mail* never apologised; Marshall Hall won £2500 damages for her. The case went to the Court of Appeal where Lord Justice Mathew, who disliked him intensely, delivered a stinging criticism of Marshall Hall which all the papers printed gleefully. He had won large libel damages for his clients against too many of them.

His own reputation was now attacked. His confidence was completely shattered; his regular clients deserted him. Only by selling his extensive collection of silver did he manage to tide himself over the period of notoriety, till he was once more a public favourite.

And so the Bar will always be a profession where reputations can be made or broken overnight.

It will always have different styles of advocacy — melodramatic, sober, or the light and conversational type, which is especially popular with juries.

272

I warm to Crassus, who fought a case about the wording of a will against Cicero's pupil-master, Quintus Scaevola. Scaevola made his points methodically and carefully. Cicero tells us:

"How full and precise he was on testamentary law, on ancient formulas, on the manner in which the will should have been drawn if Curius were to be recognised as heir even if no son were born; what a snare was set for plain people if the exact wording of the will were ignored, and if intentions were to be determined by guesswork, and if the written words of simple-minded people were to be perverted by the interpretation of clever lawyers.

... In saying all this with mastery and knowledge, and again with his characteristic brevity and compactness, not without ornament and with perfect finish, what man of the people would have expected or thought that anything better could be said?"

But Crassus started with a story:

"There was once a boy who was walking along the shore, when he found a thole-pin. From that chance he was infatuated with the idea of building himself a boat to fit it."

He suggested that Scaevola had built up a whole boat to match his little thole-pin of fact and tortured reasoning.

"From this beginning," wrote Cicero;

"and following it up with other suggestions of like character, he captivated the ears of all present and diverted their minds from earnest consideration of the case to a mood of pleasantry — one of the three things which I have said it was the function of the orator to effect."

Crassus' home-spun style comes closest to that of Abraham Lincoln, who charmed the ears of every jury that heard him. Lincoln would sit up half the night broadening his mind and deepening his studies. Crassus used to spend his noon day siesta not in idleness, or sleep, but in deep thought about the case in hand, from which his friends knew better than to disturb him.

It takes a profound mind to achieve such simplicity; but fortune sometimes favours the clumsy, as in "Codd's Duck Puzzle."

Codd was an elderly barrister, whose client was accused of stealing a duck. The defendant was not entitled, in those Victorian days, to give evidence on his own behalf; so Codd put forward a number of alternatives on his behalf:

(a) The defendant bought the duck and paid for it.

(b) He found it.

(c) It was given to him.

(d) It flew into his garden.

(e) He was asleep, and someone put it into his pocket.

At this point an evil-minded colleague whispered to Codd that perhaps (f) there had never been a duck *at all*. The jury, totally baffled, acquitted the Defendant.

Codd was not always so lucky. He once defended a man for stealing from a post-office, and cross-examined one of the prosecution witnesses.

"What is your occupation?"

"A supervisor of the Post Office," said Anthony Trollope.

"And have you also written a book called *Barchester Towers?*" The witness agreed.

"Was there a word of truth in that book from beginning to end?"

"It was a work of fiction", said Trollope.

"Fiction or not," said Codd relentlessly, "was there a word of truth in it from beginning to end?"

"Well, if you put it that way," said Trollope, "there was not."

Codd sat down in triumph. He invited the jury in due course to consider whether they could possibly convict on the evidence of a man like that.

They could and did. But you can never tell with juries.

Whether the advocates have worn togas, clerical robes, or wigs and gowns; they are merely the outward trappings of the same calling.

Norman Birkett defended a financier called Clarence Hatry, who had swindled people out of huge sums of money. He was convicted, and sentenced to 14 years imprisonment. His appeal against sentence failed.

Then Birkett went to see him in the cells. "It's a terrible sentence," said Hatry, "but I'll do it. And one of the thoughts that will help me through is the rememberance of the great fight you put up for me."

It is also one of the great justifications of the advocate's calling.

All things must change. The Bar must change too. But its tradition of fearlessly defending unpopular causes remains unbroken from the day when Cicero appeared before Caesar, the most powerful man in the world, to argue the case of Ligarius.

The result was a foregone conclusion. Still, as Caesar said, "We might as well hear another speech from Cicero."

When Cicero began to speak, Caesar was moved to an amazing degree. It was obvious that he was in the grip of violently conflicting emotions. Eventually he was so affected that his body trembled, and some of the papers he was holding fell from his hands.

Cicero's words contained such a variety of pathos, and such a delightful choice of language, that Caesar could not help but listen. And as he listened, the colour came and went from his cheeks.

Sources, Further Reading, & Notes

Chapter One: IN ANCIENT ROME

One of the best ways of enjoying Latin literature is through the Penguin Classics series, each one excellently translated. A great deal of Cicero appears in it. For a good picture of Roman Life see Cicero's *Letters to Atticus*, his *Letters to his Friends*, and the *Letters of Pliny the Younger*.

For the most part I have gratefully used their translations, but the translations of Martial are my own.

The quotations from Quintilian come from the Loeb edition, translated by H.E. Butler (1920).

Other very helpful books include:

Jerome Carcopino's *Daily Life in Ancient Rome* (1941)

F.R. Cowell, *Cicero and the Roman Republic* (1948)

J.A. Crook, *Law and Life of Rome* (1967)

W. Warde Fowler, *Social Life at Rome in the Time of Cicero* (1908)

Elizabeth Rawson's *Cicero* (1975)

Charles W. Stedler's *Guide to Cicero*

David Taylor, *Cicero and Rome* (1973)

p.1: Scipio appoints an advocate. Cicero's *De Oratore* (LXIX)

p.2: The Twelve Tables, and Slapping someone for threepence: Aulus Gellius, *Noctes Atticae* XX i.

"A browser upon leeks". Henry Maine, *Early Institutions* c. ix.

The Horns, and The Constant Liar. Aulus Gellius, *Noctes Atticae* XVI ii (trans. W. Below, 1795)

The Crocodile problem. Quintilian I.x.3.

p.3: Martial's hours of the day. *Epigrams* IV. 8.

Young Crassus and Caesar. Cicero's *Brutus* and *Orator* XLVIII.177, LXXII. 252 (Loeb edition pp. 151, 217)

The lay-out of the Forum. Siedler's *Guide to Cicero* p.13
The Centumviral court. Pliny's *Letters* IV.16 (Penguin
Classics p.124)

p.4: Arguing yourself hoarse. Juvenal *Satire VII.*
Catullus' poem on Cicero. *Catullus*, XLIX. My own
translation.
Domitius Afer's ungrateful client. Quintilian VI.
iii. 93
Diodorus has gout. Martial's *Epigrams* I. XCVIII.
Cicero defends Tuccius. Cicero's *Letters to his friends*
VIII.8. (Penguin Classics p.175).
Fishing for fortunes. Horace's *Satires* II.5.21 (Penguin
Classics p.99)

p.5: Cicero acts for Roscius the actor. *(Pro Quinctio).*
Roscius of Ameria. *(Pro. Sex. Roscio).*

p.6: Cicero's sabbatical. Cicero's *Brutus* and *Orator* XC.313.
(Loeb edition, p.271)
Pleading justifiable homicide. Quintilian VII.i.7.

p.7: Does a new-born baby need a ticket? Justinian's *Digest*
19.2.19.7
The bed-wetting slave. Justinian's *Digest* 21.1.14.4
Adjournment for a nightmare. Pliny's *Letters* I.18
(Penguin Classics p.50)

p.8: Cicero's jokes. Jokes coined by other people were often
attributed to him. His own books of jokes have been lost.
Some were quoted in the mediaeval best-seller *Gesta
Romanorum.*
Bulbus and Gutta. *Pro Cluentio*, c.26.71. (My own
translation.)

p.9: The opening words of Cicero's First Catiline speech (My
own translation).

p.10: Churchill's speech, 13th May 1940. Quoted by Cecil W.
Wooten's *Cicero's Philippics* (1983), p.172.
Pliny's lengthy speech. His *Letters*, II.ii. (Penguin Classics
p.67 *et seq*)
Water-clocks. W.I. Milham's *Time and Time-Keepers*
(1923).
Aeneas Tacticus, *Fragments.*
Pliny's *Letters* II.ii. (Penguin Classics p.67) Martial on
water-clocks. *Epigrams* VIII. vii.

Chapter Two: THE FIRST BARRISTERS

A key work to this early period is Herman Cohen's *A History of the Bar to 1450*. It is a mine of information which I have gratefully used, but it is not easy reading for the ordinary reader.
Useful works on the general background to this chapter

include W.C. Bolland, *The Year Books* (1921).

Robert C. Palmer's books such as *the County Courts of Mediaeval England 1130-1350*, (Princeton 1982) make it clear that the County Courts are an amazingly rich area for exploration.

p.18: The Gallic Bar. Robert Jones, *History of the French Bar* (1855)

Worshipping Hercules. Paul Lacroix, *Science and Literature in the Middle Ages* (London, 1877)

Juvenal on British advocates. *Satire XV*, 110-2.

Claudius' debating competition. Lacroix, *Science and Literature in the Middle Ages*.

The laws of Burgundy. Cohen, *History of the Bar* p.547.

Clothair's laws. L. Gaudry, *Histoire du Barreau de Paris* (1864)

p.19: The Laws of Ethelbert: *English Historical Documents*, Vol. 1. This book is to be found in most public libraries, and the early laws make fascinating reading.

The *forespeca*. Herman Cohen, *A History of the Bar* p. 3.

Roman versus Lombard Law. Cohen, *History of the Bar* p.33.

p.20: Bishop Odo's career is described in Lord Campbell's *Lives of the Chief Justices* (3rd Ed., 1874), Vol. 1.

Lanfranc's career: *Dictionary of National Biography*.

The trial at Pinnenden Heath: *English Historical Documents* I.449.

Sake and Soke in 1321: *YB 14 Edward II (1321)*, Selden Society Vol. 85 p. 296.

p.21: The laws of William I. *English Historical Documents* II. No. 10.

Lanfranc's dream of St. Dunstan. Cohen, *History of the Bar* p.52.

Sacol and Godric. The *Abingdon Chronicle*, cit. Cohen's *History of the Bar* p.46.

p.22: Ranulf Flambard's career. Lord Campbell, *Lives of the Chancellors* (5th Ed., 1868) p.44.

William of Malmesbury's view. *Gesta Regum Angilorum* IV.314.

Special services of serjeants. A.L. Poole's *Domesday Book to Magna Carta* (2nd Ed.) p.18.

p.23: The trial of Richard de Anesty: *English Historical Documents* I. 456.

p.24: Glanville and Walter Mapes. Cohen's *History of the Bar* p.84.

p.25: Trial by battle at Meaux. *Chronicle of Melsa* II.97-100 (Rolls Series)

The Abbott of Fountains Abbey. YB, Selden Soc. Vol. 43 p.134.

The Bishop of Salisbury's champion. J.J. Jusserand, *English Wayfaring Life in the Middle Ages* (London 1889) p. 117.

Abbot Samson's career. *Chronicle of Jocelin de Brakelond* (Camden Soc. Vol. 73 pp.24 et seq. But the *Dictionary of National Biography* gives a less enthusiastic picture of him.)

p.26: Selecting the best advocates and attorneys. 20 Edw.I. (1292) 1 Rot. Parl. 84, quoted by W.C. Bolland, *Two Problems in Legal History* (1908) LQR XXIV, 392-402.

Westminister Hall to be built. John Stow's *London Under Elizabeth* p.420.

Henry III bans law schools. *Middle Temple Records* Vol.I, Introduction.

p.27: A countor assaults a Justice of the Jews. Pollock & Maitland, *History of Eng. Law* Vol. I p.194.

Suing promptly for fees. Cohen's *History of the Bar* p.107.

Symon Wyberd's conduct. Robert C. Palmer, *the County Courts of Mediaeval England 1150-1350* p.93.

Counsel's fees at St. Ives. (Ditto)

p.28: A retainer fee from Shap Abbey. (Ditto)

Suing the Bishop of Rochester. Robert C. Palmer, *The Origins of the Legal Profession in England*. Irish Jurist (1976) Vol. 11 pp.126-146.

p.29: Robert of Warwick's career. Palmer, *County Courts of Mediaeval England*, p.97.

A Prior "gratifying" the judges. *The Barnwell Priory Book* ed. Willis Clark (1907), quoted by Cohen, *History of the Bar* p. 152.

The Statute of Westminster I. Coke's *Statutes*, p.212-225.

p.30: Malpractice in 1280. *Liber Custumarum* p.280.

The duties of a countor. *Liber Albus* (1419) pp.449,480.

The Husting Court. John Carpenter and Richard Whitington, *Liber Albus* (1419). F.M. Stenton's *Norman London.*

p.31: Lampreys from Nantes. H.T. Riley, *Memorials of London* p.83.

Meat not to be sold by candle-light. *Liber Albus*, p.621.

Tprhurt, Tprhurt. H.T. Riley, *Memorials of London* p. 27.

Robert of Sutton insulted, and re-listed as a practitioner. H.T. Riley, *Memorials of London*, p.53,58.

Chapter Three: ALL JANGLE AND RIOT

Most of the material in this chapter comes from the Year Books (YB) published either by the Rolls Series or the Selden Society, to whom every student of legal history owes an immense debt of gratitude. Its published works are full of interest, and very reasonably priced for what they represent. I joined that Society far too late during the writing of this book ...

The Year Books contain much invaluable material, but the general reader will not find them all of equal interest. A good one to start with is *Eyre of Kent, 6 & 7 Edward II, 1313-4*, Selden Society Vol.24, p.118.

p.32: The purpose of the Year Books. W.C. Bolland, *The Year Books* (1921)

All jangle and riot: See F.W. Maitland's introduction to the *YB of Edward II (1307-9)*, Selden Society Vol. 17.

Making notes in court. *YB 8 Edward II (1314-5)*, Selden Society Vol. 41 p.87.

p.33: A lawyer's library. Cohen, *History of the Bar* p.506.

The compiler's opinion. *YB 6 Edward II (1313)*, Selden Society Vol. 43 p. 154

p.34: A dig at Stonor J. See F.W. Maitland's introduction to the *YB of Edward II (1307-9)*, Selden Society Vol. 17.

The man in the brothel. *(Ditto.)*

The Three Gallows. *YB 2 & 3 Edward II (1313)*, Selden Society.

The Sealed tallies. *YB 3 Edward II*, Selden Society Vol. 20 p. 47.

p.35: More sealed tallies. *YB 8 Edward II (1314-5)*, Selden Society Vol. 41 p. xxxvii (But it was a rule of the City of London that sealed tallies were not to be queried. *Liber Albus* p. 189).

p.36: A Query. *YB 5 Edward II*, 1312 Selden Society Vol. 33 p. 132.

Narrators and countors. This is discussed in the introduction to *YB 3 & 4 Edward II*, Selden Society. Also by Cohen, *History of the Bar*.

Matthew Paris. *Gesta Abbatum* I. 316 (Rolls Series), quoted by Cohen, *History of the Bar*, p. 171.

Matilda's privy. *17 YB Edward III*, p. 148.

"Agnys" for "Agnes". *YB 21 & 22 Edward I*, (Rolls Series) p. 224.

"Hogheland" for "Hogeland". *YB 12-13 Edward III*, p. 54

"Joiosa" for "Jocosa". *12 & 13 YB Edward III*, p. 344.

"Tudeworthe" for "Todeworthe". *YB 13 & 14 Edward III*.

Sacramental words. Pollock & Maitland, *History of English Law* II. 603.

p.37: Dilution with swords etc. *YB Edward II (1315-6)*, Selden Society Vol. 45 p. 140.

The church of Toft Newton. *17 & 18 Edward III*, 2, p.606.

p.38: Burgesses of New Castle. *YB 17 & 18 Edward II* p. 70.

Bullocks. *YB 5 Edward II 1311-2*, Selden Soc. Vol. 31 p. 18.

Delayed by floods. *YB 33-35 Edward I*, p. 120. (Rolls Series).

p.39: Attorney in gaol. *Broke* v. *Taylard*, a case of about 1310 A.D., *YB 3 & 4 Edward II* (1309-11), Selden Society, ed. 1907.

p.40: Acting for a man with palsy. *YB 14 Edward II (1321)*, Selden Society Vol. 85 p. 225.

Chief Justice's Hengham's fine. See W.C. Bolland's Introduction to *YB 8 Edward II (1315)*, Selden Society Vol. 37.

Petty Treason by girl. *YB 11-12 Edward III* p. 626.

p.41: Dowry of a widow aged 9. *YB 3 Edward II*, Selden Society Vol. 20 p. 189. Coke thought that provided the widow was 9, the husband could be as young as 4. Pollock & Maitland, *History of English Law* II. 372.

p.42: Greedy Churchmen. *YB 3 & 4 Edward II*, Selden Society, p. 69.

Prior of Coventry, *YB 2 & 3 Edward II*, p. 71. Selden Society.

Dean of St. Paul's. *YB 14 Edward II (1321)*, Selden Society Vol. 85 p. 101.

Privileges of scholars at Rome, Oxford and elsewhere. Pearl Kibre, *Schorlarly Privileges in the Middle Ages* (London 1961). See also Hastings Rashdall, *The Universities of Europe in the Middle Ages.*

p.43: A clerk improperly dressed. *Eyre of Kent, 6 & 7 Edward II, 1313-4*, Selden Sociiety Vol. 24 p. 118.

p.44: The sleeping Ordinary. *YB 14 Edward II (1321)*, Selden Society Vol. 85 p. 82.

Snatched from the gallows. *19 YB Edward III.* p. 176.

p.16: The fatal Goodbye. *YB 14 Edward II (1321)*, Selden Society Vol. 85 p. 103.

p.17: Forgetting one's pardon. *Archbishop of Canterbury v. Dyer, YB 3. Edward II*, Selden Society Vol. 20, p. 153.

p.45: Death by drowning. *YB 30 & 31 Edward I*, xxxvii. (Rolls Society).

p.46: Joan cannot be pregnant by rape. See *Eyre of Kent, 6 & 7 Edward II, 1313-4*, Selden Society Vol. 24, p. 111. *YB 30 & 31 Edward I*, p. 520. (Rolls Society), is an almost identical case.

p.47: Justifiable homicide no defence. *YB 14 Edward II (1321)*, Selden Society Vol. 85 p. 73. (Even an accidental act had to be paid for. See Holdsworth's *History of English Law* II. 51).

p.48: Hugh's trial for rape. *YB 30 & 31 Edward I*, p. 529. (Rolls Society).

p.50: Penalty for rape. The notes to the same volume, p. xlii, show that the woman's option to marry her ravisher dates back to Roman Law. The more drastic alternatives are set out in the *Eyre of Kent, 6 & 7 Edward II, 1313-4,* Selden Society Vol. 24, p. 134.

Wat Tyler's rebellion. Thomas of Walsingham, *1 Historia Anglicana 455,* II. 2.

Court hours in Chaucer's time. Cohen, *History of the Bar* p. 504.

p.51: Chaucer's Man of Law. For an authentic confirmation of Chaucer's accuracy, see J.H. Baker's *The Order of Serjeants at Law* (1984), published by the Selden Society.

Chapter Four: EXCESSIVE EXPENSES OF CHEESE

The Black Books of Lincoln's Inn, which start in 1422, make fascinating reading. They are most likely to be found in University or Law Libraries. Edith Rickert's *Chaucer's World* (1948) is very readable.

p.52: Gentlemen of perfect descents. John Ferne, *The Glory of Generosity* (1586), quoted in Dugdale's History and Antiquities of the Four Inns of Court.

Grammar schools: Derek Brewer's *Chaucer and his World* (1978) pp. 54-60.

William of Tonge: Rickert, *Chaucer's World* p. 111.

p.53: Mr. Noy's answer: John Aubrey, *Brief Lives* (about Mr. Noy).

Clifford's Inn, Lincoln's Inn, Hereflete Inn, and others are described in various histories of the Inns of Court, from Dugdale onwards.

Studying at the Inns of Chancery: *Spelman's Reports,* Vol. II (Selden Society Vol. 94, ed. J.H. Baker, 1977).

p.54: The pleasant Temple: Sir John Fortesque, *De Laudibus Legum Angliae* (c.1468-70) c. 49.

Fitzstephen's *Description of London* (reprinted 1934).

The polluted Thames: Rickert, *Chaucer's World* p 11.

The murder of John Glemham: ibid., p. 132.

p.55: Chaucer, The Friar and the Inner Temple: ibid., p. 132.
Edward Paston: *The Paston Letters* ed. James Gairdner (1872) Vol. 1. p. 58.

p.56: Irish Barristers: *Black Books* 1437, 1451; *Middle Temple Records*, 25th November 1584.
University education: Edward Chamberlayn's *Angliae Notitia* (1672).

p.57: A Reading on Abduction of Nuns: *Spelman's Reports*, ed. J.H. Baker.
A Reading lasting 7 hours: Wilfrid R. Prest, *The Inns of Court under Elizabeth I and the Early Stuarts* (1972).

p.58: Plague in the Temple: there are many similar entries in the *Black Books of Lincoln's Inn*.
Knives, forks and spoons: Charles Cooper, *The English Table* (1929).
The Curfew in London: H.T. Riley's *Memorials of London Life* p. 93.

p.59: Passwords: E. Williams, *Early Holborn and the Legal Quarter of London*, quoted by D.S. Bland, *Early Records of Furnival's Inn* (1957).
Night-walkers: *Liber Albus* (1419).
Thomas Veer: *Black Books* May 8th, 1509.
William Elys: *Black Books* 1476, 1477, 1478, 1481, 1502.

p.60: The ban on gaudy clothing: *Middle Temple Records*, 25th June 1557. Similar bans extended to all the Inns of Court in Tudor and Stuart times.
Christopher Tropnell's crime *Black Books* 1484.

p.61: The French Pox: *Black Books* Oct. 20th 1515.
The fines for fornication: *Black Books* Nov. 20th 1489.
Richard Dewes' bastard: *Middle Temple Records*, 17th June 1642.
Middleton's bastard: *Black Books*, 1st June 1674.(Few foundlings are recorded after this, except for "George Lincoln", who was curiously bitten by a mad cat. One guinea was spent on powders for his cure. *Black Books* Vol. IV, 18 Nov. 1782.).
Stealing from the larder: eels and a quince pie, *Black Books* 1495; a doe, 1523, the swan, 1527;

the cellar, 1530, and the larks, 1551.

p.62: A swan at a banquet, and Rabbits in Gravy: T. Wright, *A History of Domestic Manners* (1682) p. 150.

Bastard gravy: Elizabeth Burton, *The Early Tudors at Home* (1976).

Cheese galore: *Black Books* 1502, 1515, 1518.

p.63: Stingy Reader's Supper: *Black Books* 21 November 1542.

Grand Christmas fare. See *Dugdale's History and Antiquities of the 4 Inns of Court*.

A carol: John Stevens, *Music and Poetry in the Early Tudor Court* (1961).

p.64: The Pillory. See *Henry Machyn's Diary,* published by the Camden Society, and to be found in University and other large libraries. It is a great pity that this vivid picture of Tudor Life is not available to general readers.

James Ellis hanged; people burnt at the stake; and the Coronation of Queen Elizabeth. Also in *Henry Machyn's Diary*.

p.65: Skipwith's crime: *Black Books,* June 4th 1627.

Laundresses: Dugdale's *History* p. 204, and many entries in the *Black Books*.

The Plague in 1626. *Black Books* 26th Jan. 1626.

p.66: The Porter's wife called a whore. *Middle Temple Records,* 29th April 1631.

The wash-pot's wife. *Black Books,* Feb. 3rd 1625.

Pumping the Pannierman: *Black Books* 1635.

The King's Messenger: 4th August 1629.

Murdering the pump: *Lives of the Chancellors* (5th Ed., 1868) V. p. 63.

Lord of Misrule's court: *Middle Temple Records,* 5th and 11th February 1591.

Lord of Misrule kills somebody: *Spelman's Reports,* Vol. II (Selden Society Vol. 94, ed. J.H. Baker, 1977).

p.67: Gambling an estate away: John Aubrey's *Brief Lives.*

Christmas 1637. *Middle Temple Records,* 25th Jan. 1638.

p.68: The Rugger scrum: Roger North's *Lives of the Norths* Vol. I p. 106.

Darwin and his dog. *Black Books,* 11th May 1719.

p.69: Easter Term menu. *Black Books,* Vol. III, p. 341.

The exceedings at table: *Lives of the Chancellors,* Vol.

VIII, p. 166.
Foundlings: *Middle Temple Records* Vol. II, for 17th June 1642. Disraeli's name taken off the books: *Black Books* 25th Nov. 1831.
Jews admitted to the Inns: *Black Books* Jan. 25th 1833.
Dickens eating dinners: *The Uncommercial Traveller*.
Wilkie Collins called to the Bar: Dickens' *The Lazy Tour of Two Idle Apprentices*, included (somewhat surprisingly) in *Christmas Stories*.
p.71: Nigel Lawson eats dinners: *The Observer*, March 10th 1985.

Chapter Five: COKE AGAINST RALEGH.

Robert Lacey's *Sir Walter Ralegh* (1973) is an admirable work on the subject.

Likewise John Winton's *Sir Walter Ralegh* (1975).

Hakluyt's *Voyages* Vols. XII-XV enable the reader to travel with Ralegh on his journies of discovery - an unforgettable experience.

Dipping into Ralegh's *Works*, especially his poetry, provides much unexpected pleasure.

Lord Campbell's *Lives of the Chief Justices* (3rd Edition 1874) Vol. I. pp.282-408 gives a very fair picture of Coke.

Catherine Drinker Bowen's *The Lion and the Throne* (1957) is the only modern biography of Coke.

Lawyers should certainly look at Coke's *Institutes* to complete their view of him.

Aubrey's *Brief Lives* gives shrewd pictures both of Coke and Ralegh.

Because these sources give so much information about their subjects, it is not necessary to provide further details of the items in this chapter.

Chapter Six: EXCOMMUNICATION AND COSTS.

The best books on Ecclesiastical Law are Phillimore's text-book, and Burn's.

The best books on *Doctors Commons* are by William Senior (1922) and G.D. Squibb (1977).

Charles Crawley's *Trinity Hall* (Cambridge 1976) also covers much of the same ground.

Brian P. Levack's *The Civil Lawyers in England 1603-1641* (Oxford 1973) describes the critical Stuart period.

For a general account of the struggle between Parliament and the Church Courts, see Cobbett's *Parliamentary History*.

p.92: The Laws of King Canute: see *English Historical Documents*, Vol. I., to be found in almost every public library.

p.93: Accursius. William Senior, *Doctors Commons* (1922) p. 3 et seq. See also *Calender of Patent Rolls of Edward I*, for the period 1275-1281.

John Lydford's notebooks: ed. Dorothy M. Owen (1974.) The general reader should certainly enjoy them; they will be found in University libraries.

Lincoln in 1236, Ely in 1364: G.G. Coulton's *Life in the Middle Ages* (Cambridge, 1928). Vol. IV p. 127.

p.94: Disorder in Exeter Cathedral. *Life in the Middle Ages.* Vol. I. p. 98.

New College, Oxford. *John Lydford's Book*, No. 5. *Wykeham's Register* Nos. 5, 6.

Winchester College. Lydford was a witness to the foundation deed.

Lydford on Heresy. *John Lydford's Book*, Nos. 206, 209, 210.

The horse-thief. *Wykeham's Register* No. 113.

p.95: The inhabitants of Hook. *Lydford's notebooks* Nos. 112-118. Also *Wykeham's Register* Vol. II p. 281. (ed. T.F. Kirby, 1896), Hampshire Record Society. As enjoyable as *Lydford's Notebooks*.

John Bentley. *Wykeham's Register* Vol. I. pp. 113, 429.

John Bentley takes sanctuary. *Wykeham's Register* Vol. II No. 429, and *John Lydford's Book* No. 241.

p.96: Penance for castration. *Wykeham's Register* Vol. II p. 379.
Stealing shrouds. *Haynes' Case*, 12. Co. p. 113, 77 English
Reports 1839.
Lydford's orders to try cases. 7th January 1376-7. (see
Lydford's Book).
Spiritual incest and incontinence. *John Lydford's Book*
No. 26.
Stealing swans. *John Lydford's Book* No. 261.

p.97: Like a sewer. William Senior, *Doctors Commons (1922).*
Breakfast-time. G.D. Squibb, *Doctors Commons* (1977).
Doctor without teeth. Dr. Steward, in 1630. See G.D.
Squibb's *Doctors Commons.*

p.98: John London's career. *Dictionary of National Biography.*
John Story's career. *Dictionary of National Biography.*
Henry Cole's career. *Dictionary of National Biography.*

p.99: Tithes of ewes' milk. *Winchester Consistory Court
Depositions (1561-1602)* ed. Arthur J. Willis, p. 11 *et seq.*
See also Burn's *Ecclesiastical Law* Vol. III.

p.100: Dr. Cowell's book. Senior's *Doctors Commons.*
Marseilles in Marylebone. *Brownlow's Reports* Vol. II pp.
110-1, quoted by Levack, *Civil Lawyers in England.*

p.101: Mr. Harris' excommunication. *Kenton* v. *Wallinger* (1601)
Cro. Eliz. 838, 78 ER 1064.
Beelzebub. *Anon*, Ld. Raym. 397, 2 Salk. 692. 91 English
Reports 1164.
Bastard-getting old rogue. *Legate* v. *Wright.*
Brandy-nosed whore. *Auberry* v. *Barton*, Ld. Raym. 1136,
91 ER 586.

p.102: The rich heiresses. Thomas G. Barnes, *Star Chamber
Litigants and Their Counsel 1596-1641.*
Delaying tactics. Barnes, *Star Chamber Litigants.*
Thomas Parry's actions.
Coloured hens. Barnes, *Star Chamber Litigants.*
Hatred of Laud.
Early divorce petitions. *Calender of State Papers (Domestic)*
1635, 1638, 1639 passim.

p.103: Persecution for piffling offences. See also Carson I.A.
Ritchie, *The Ecclesiastical Courts of York* (1956), and the
Calender of State Papers (Domestic) 1638, October 22.
Dirty ruff in church. Christopher Hill, *Society and*

Puritanism in Pre-Revolutionary England (1964).

Caterpillars in the market place, and the rude noise. F.E.G. Emmison, *Elizabethan Life - Morals and the Church Courts.* (1973) p. 312-3.

Summoners. See also Carson I.A. Ritchie's *The Ecclesiastical Courts of York* (1956). The Summoners were universally hated, from Chaucer's time onwards.

Sir John Bennet's fine. See *Bennet* v. *Easedale* (1626) Cro. Car. 55, 79 ER 651. See also *Dictionary of National Biography*, and the *Calender of State Papers (Domestic).* for 1624.

p. 104: Noncomformist with hat on. See *Haw* v. *Planner* (1666) 2 Keb. 124, 84 ER 79.

Sir Leoline Jenkins. *Dictionary of National Biography.*

Baldwin's coffee-shop. *Dictionary of National Biography.*

Drunk Dr. William King. *Dictionary of National Biography.*

Burn's advice on rebels. Phillimore's *Ecclesiastical Law* (2nd. Ed.) p. 668.

p. 105: Miss Jones' runaway marriage. *Scrimshire* v. *Scrimshire* (1752) 2 Hag. Con. 395, 161 ER 782.

Marriage for sale in Fleet Street. M. Dorothy George's *London Life in the 18th Century* (1925) p. 313.

p. 106: *The Earl of Portsmouth's Case* (1828) 1 Hagg. Eccl. 339, 162 ER 611.

Hoile v. *Scales* (1829) 2 Hagg. Eccl. 566, 162 ER 1958.

p. 107: Dickens in Doctors Commons, Sir W.S. Holdsworth, *Charles Dickens as a Legal Historian* (1929). See also William J. Carlton, *Mr. Blackmore engages an Office Boy* (The Dickensian, Vol. XLVIII p. 162). *Sketches by Boz* Chapter VIII.

p. 108: *David Copperfield.* Chapters XXIII, XXXIII.

Dr. Jenner, *Dictionary of National Biography.*

Dr. Lushington's Career. *Dictionary of National Biography* Sir John Nicholl's and Lushington's views. *Minutes of Evidence before the Select Committee on Supreme Courts of Judicature* (1840) pp. 18, 352.

p. 109: Frederick Temple. Phillimore's Ecclesiastical Law (2nd. Ed., 1895) p. 42.

p. 111: Candles burning North Sea Gas. *Re St. Andrews Dearnley*

(1981) 2 W.L.R. 37.
A disputed tombstone. *Re St. Mark's Haydock* (No2)
(1981) 1 W.L.R. 1167.
Cosey, dosey. Dickens, *David Copperfield* Chapter XXIII.

Chapter Seven: MASQUES AND ANTI-MASQUES.

Allardyce Nicoll's *The Development of the Theatre* (1927) shows
that the Italian theatre had already begun to use elaborate stage
effects, and perspective in the scenery. But Inigo Jones took
it further.

Richard Southern's *Changeable Scenery* (London 1952)
describes the stage effects more fully.

M.T. Jones-Davies' *Inigo Jones, Ben Johnson et le Masque* gives
a lot of detail, and some excellent illustrations.

William Prynne's works include *A New Discovery of the
Prelate's Tyranny* (1641), which gives much detail of his trials.

William A. Lamont's *Marginal Prynne* (1963) is a full-length
biography of him.

For centuries of Christmas revelry, see C.A. Miles' *Christmas
in Ritual and Tradition* (1913).

p.112:Masques in the 14th century. John Stow's *London under
Elizabeth*.
King Henry VIII. Elizabeth Burton, *The Early Tudors
at Home* (1976).
p.113:Le Roi Soleil, the Virgin Queen. Roy Strong's *Splendour
at Court* (1973), which gives an excellent account of the
detail and scope of masques.
Cynthia's Revels. See *The Works of Thomas Campion* ed.
Walter R. Davis 1969.
Shooting James' dog: Agnes Strickland, *Lives of the
Queens of England* Vol. IV p. 116.
Masque of the Fairies. Agnes Strickland, *Lives of the
Queens of England* Vol IV p. 69.
Masque of Blackness Ditto, p. 87.

p.115: Francis Bacon's view. Leslie Hotson, *MR. W.H.* (1964).

p.116: The Masque of 1613. A very full description is given in Nichol's *Progresses of James I*, Vol. II.567, and reprinted in the *Black Books of Lincoln's Inn* Vol. II, Appendix. Also in *The Beaumont and Fletcher Canon* Vol. I. (1966), ed. Fredson Bowers.

Farthingales. *State Papers (Domestic) James I*, Vol. 72 No. 30, reprinted in the *Black Books* Vol. II.

p.117: The bills. *Black Books of Lincoln's Inn* Vol. II. p. 154.

p.119: William Prynne's appearance. John Aubrey's *Brief Lives*. *The Quakers unmasked*. See *Documents Relating to William Prynne* (1877) ed. J. Bruce, Camden Soc. 2nd series, Vol. 18.

Lincoln's Inn was a centre of Puritanism - see Wilfrid R. Prest's *The Inns of Court under Elizabeth I and the Early Stuarts* (1972).

Mr. Wingate coaches Henrietta Maria. Agnes Strickland, *Lives of the Queens of England* (1865) Vol. IV pp. 193-4.

p.120: Prynne's *Histriomastix:* See *Black Books of Lincoln's Inn* for the 24th and 29th April 1634.

The Triumph of Peace. James Shirley's *Works* Vol. VI. William Lawes wrote some of the music for it. "Bad as the music of Lawes appears to us," writes Dr. Charles Burney in *A General History of Music* (1935), "it seems to have been sincerely admired by his contemporaries in general." There is now an increasing interest in it.

p.121: Prynne's books in Lincoln's Inn: *Black Books*, 10th June 1634.

p.122: Prynne's position restored. *Black Books*, 25th May 1641. Tripping over his sword: John Aubrey's *Brief Lives*. Masques after the Restoration. *Black Books*, Vol. III Appendix p. 440.

Prynne keeps the Records in the Tower. See the *Dictionary of National Biography* entry for Prynne.

Chapter Eight: THE BAR CLERKS TALE

If I had not read John A. Flood's interesting pioneer work on *Barristers' Clerks,* published in 1983, this chapter would not have been written.

Although one has to hunt carefully across centuries of history for a mention of Bar clerks here and there, they are central to the life of the Bar, and throw a light upon its history which justifies the effort. For a general account of the position of Roman scribes: *Oxford Classical Dictionary* (1949) p. 817.

p.123: Romilly and his clerk: his *Memoirs,* Vol. 1 p. 76. His letter to Dumont: Vol. II p. 36.

p.124: Roman short-hand writers. Quintilian VII.ii.24.

Erskine and the short-hand writers: Lord Campbell's *Lives of the Chancellors* (5th Ed.) Vol. IX p. 78.

"Climaxes and trees": *Lives of the Chief Justices* Vol. IV p. 182.

Servius Galba prepares a case: Cicero's *Brutus* xxi. 85, p.

p.125: Licinius tootles the flute: Cicero's *De Oratore* III. Ix. 225.

A contract with Shap Abbey. see R.C. Palmer's *County Courts of Mediaeval England, 1150-1350* (published 1982), which gives some fascinating information about the early lawyers. The County Court records are clearly much more important than had been supposed.

Stationery in 1378. see Edith Rickert's *Chaucer's World* (1948).

p.126: Jose the parchment-maker. William Caxton's *Dialogues in French and English,* ed. H. Bradley, Early English Text Society, Series 2, Vol. 79.

These and other mediaeval French Grammars are astonishing in their vivid descriptions, and deserve to be better known. It is a pity that they do not tell us more about the legal profession, It is not known what the "franchin" was, mentioned in this quotation.

A servant in Lincoln's Inn, 1441/2. See *Black Books of Lincoln's Inn.* The lawyers at St Paul's: see J. H. Baker's *The Order of Serjeants at Law* (1984), published by the Selden Society, which must be the definitive work on the subject.

p.127: A servant in Lincoln's Inn, 1520. *Black Books*, "on the morrow of the Purification".

In 1538. *Black Books*, November 17th 1538.

Abusing their positions in 1602. *Black Books*, November 22nd 1602.

Francis North and the skull-caps. *Lives of the Chancellors* IV. 297.

p.128: Sjt. Earl's accounts: *Lives of the Chancellors*, IV P. 286.

Scott's inexperienced young clerk. *Lives of the Chancellors* Vol. IX p. 146.

Scott and the Highwayman. *Lives of the Chancellors*, Vol. IX p. 153.

Charlie Peace's widow: Edward A. Bell, *Those Meddlesome Attorneys* (1939) p. 81.

p.129: The Inn at Kirkby Stephen: Horace Twiss, *Life of Lord Chancellor Eldon* (1844) p. 108.

Lodgings in London: R.S. Surtees, *Handley Cross* (1844) Chapter XIX.

The book is dedicated to "THE RIGHT HONOURABLE LORD JOHN SCOTT.

One of the best of British Sportsmen."

James Parke's Letters, never before published, are in the Northumberland County Record Office, North Gosforth, Newcastle-upon-Tyne. I used some of them in *Foul Bills & Dagger Money*.

p.130: Boswell and Mr.McDougal. His *Journal*, 22nd Feb, 3rd Mar. 1786. Boswell at Lancaster. *Journal*, 6th April 1786.

p.131: Little urchin of a clerk: *A Barrister's Life* (1882).

The crooked half-guinea: J.B. Atlay, *The Victorian Chancellors* (1908) Vol. II. p. 83.

Mr. Pickering: *Black Books of Lincoln's Inn* Vol. III. 473.

p.132: Mike Prendergast. Ballantine p. 35. Other people described Prendergast as a firebrand, who so annoyed a jury that the foreman complained of his verbal attacks upon witnesses. He was made one of the first County Court Judges in 1866.

Huddleston's clerk: Ernest Bowen-Rowlands' *Seventy Two Years at the Bar* (1924).

p.133: Lincoln's Inn Fields in 1729: Duncan Taylor's *Fielding's England*, (1966) p. 17.

Dickens on laundresses: *The Uncommercial Traveller*, Chapter XIV: Chambers.

Mr. Furnival's Chambers: *Orley Farm* (1862) Chapter XII.

Laundresses in Queen Elizabeth's reign. Dugdale's *History and Antiquities of the 4 Inns of Court*, p. 170.

p.134: Laundresses in Lincoln's Inn. *Black Books*, November 22nd 1602.

Sjt. Ballantine's laundress: His *Barrister's Life* (1882) p. 32.

Francis Place's laundress. His *Autobiography* ed. Mary Thale (1972).

p.135: Hawkins' laundress. From his *Reminicsences* (1904).

Laundresses in 1831. J.T. Smith, *The Cries of London*, quoted by M. Dorothy George in *London Life in the 18th Century* (1925).

Lamb's picture of Lovel. His Essay, *The Old Benchers of the Inner Temple*.

p.136: Women at the Inns: J.R. Lewis, *The Victorian Bar* (1982) p. 29.

The Milkman of Gray's: Francis Cowper, *A Prospect of Gray's Inn* p. 97.

Potatoes and gravy: J.R. Lewis, *The Victorian Bar*, p. 18.

p.137: Henry Cecil's *Just Within the Law* (1975).

Obeying the clerk: A.E. Bowker's *Behind the Bar*, (1947) p. 11. His top hat, p. 23.

p.138: Lord Alverstone: A.E. Bowker's *Behind the Bar*, p. 27.

Flybuttons: Flood, *Barrister's Clerks* p. 11.

Refusing a High Court judgeship: Bowker p. 59.

The exam paper: Flood, *Barrister's Clerks* p. 154.

p.139: The case in the House of Lords: Flood p. 94.

Tommy Hughes' memoirs: *Liverpool Daily Post*, February 1961. A copy of them is in the Northern Circuit records.

p.140: Upjohn's clerk: Edward A. Bell, *Those Meddlesome Attorneys* (1939) p. 75.

Norman Birkett's fee, A.E. Bowker, *Behind the Bar* (1947) p. 13.

The Crippen brief: ditto, p. 15.

p.141:The dusty mat: *Tommy Hughes' memoirs.*

The fixed murder: Elwyn-Jones' *In My Time* (1983) p. 175.

Lindon Riley: F.E. Smith led him in the leading case of *Wise* v. *Dunning* (1902) 1 KB 167.

p.142: The Tibetan Temple Defence. *Tommy Hughes' Memoirs.*

Chapter Nine: ERSKINE

It is hardly possible to improve on Lord Campbell's account of Erskine in his *Lives of the Chancellors* 5th Edn. (1838) Vols. VIII and IX.

He saw Erskine in action, and greatly admired him, whilst not being blind to his faults. But the publication in modern times of the *Letters of George IV* has enabled us to see Erskine behind the scenes, in a new light.

Erskine's Speeches, in collected form, is another way of enjoying his advocacy; but Lord Campbell gives copious examples.

J.A. Lovat-Fraser's *Erskine* (1932) is shorter than Lord Campbell, but has much of interest.

The Autobiography of Francis Place ed. Mary Thale (1972), gives an eye-witness account of some of those Erskine defended. When Erskine *prosecuted* one of the radicals, Place was beside himself with fury!

Lloyd Paul Stryker's biography of Erskine, *For the Defence* (1949) is now out of print. Its opening sentence is "Midnight! The clock tower of St. Giles' is echoing the closing hour of a short winter's day." I have not drawn on it.

There are many excellent background books to Erskine's age: Duncan Taylor's *Fielding's England*, Ivor Brown's *Dr. Johnson and his World* (1965), Derek Jarrett's *England in the Age of Hogarth* (1974), and perhaps best of all, M. Dorothy George's *London Life in the 18th century* (1925).

p.144:A midshipman's uniform: Ivor Brown's *Dr. Johnson and His World* (1965).

p.145:The Jeranium: *Memoirs of William Hickey* Vol. II. p. 89, ed. Alfred Spencer.

A poor man's diet, and the spouting-shops: see M. Dorothy George's *London Life in the 18th Century* pp. 166, 273. Also Francis Place's *Autobiography* p. 27.

p.146:The Navy and its tactics in the 18th century: see Michael Lewis' *The History of the British Navy* (1959) and G.J. Marcus' *A Naval History of England* (1961) and *Heart of Oak* (1975). He makes it clear how much Lord Sandwich improved the Navy.

p.150:The age of George III: see John Clarke's *The Life and Times of George III* (1972) and Stanley Ayling's *George III*, both excellent.

p.152:Letters about Erskine: *Letters of George, Prince of Wales* ed. A. Aspinall (1963), at various places.

p.155:Packed juries: see Place's *Autobiography* p. 162.

p.157: Thelwall risks defending himself. See Albert Goodwin's *The Friends of Liberty* (1979).

The Courtship of the Prince of Wales: see Alan Palmer's *George IV* (1972), and *Later Correspondence of George III*, ed. A. Aspinall (1970).

p.160:The rhyme about the affidavit: *Journal of Lady Elizabeth Holland* (1909) ed. Earl of Ilchester.
Painted by Reynolds: see *Diaries of Sylvester Douglas* (1928) ed. Francis Bickley.

p.162: The field of "lavender": see A.M. Sterling's *Coke of Norfolk and his Friends*, Vol. II, p. 172.

p.163:Erskine's sluttish wife: *Joseph Farington's Diary*, ed. James Greig, Vols. IV p. 150, VIII p. 268.
Queen Caroline's indecorous behaviour, various places in the same work.

p.164:Erskine's last speech: 6 September 1820. *The Creevey Papers* (1904) ed. Maxwell, Vol. 1.

Chapter Ten: TRICKS OF THE TRADE.

p.166:Montagu Williams' first case. His *Leaves from a Life* (1890).

p.167:Petronius' *Satyricon*. The very first few sentences in the novel attack the absurdities of young orators, but never return to the subject, unfortunately.

Seduced by Guards Officer. J.R. Lewis, *The Victorian Bar* (1982) p. 16.

Sir Patrick Hastings' *Cases in Court* (1949) p. 9.

Rufus Isaacs. See Denis Judd's *Lord Reading* (1982).

Hastings' first brief. His *Cases in Court* (1949) p. 14.

p.168:Marshall Hall not briefed in scientific case. Geoffrey Lewis, *Lord Atkin* (1983)

The Norwich will case. *Select Canterbury Cases 1200-1301* ed. Norma Adams, (Selden Society Vol. 95, p. 18 (1981).

p.170:A Chancery cross-examination. Sir Henry Hawkins, *Reminiscences* (1904) p. 310. Ballantine, in *A Barrister's Life* (1880) p. 103, said "In the equity courts, the notion of cross-examination is ludicrous; it has, however, the merit of being thoroughly inoffensive."

p.171:Charles Mathews QC. Hawkins, *Reminiscences* Vol. II p. 165.

p.172:Edwin James goes too far. Ibid., p. 196.

p.173:Trial of the Seven Bishops. Campbell, *Lives of the Chief Justices*, (3rd Ed., 1874) Vol. I. p. 203.

p.174:Regulations in 1280 A.D. *Liber Custumarum*, p. 280.

The abbess and her pretty nuns. G.R. Owst, *Literature and Puilpit in Mediaeval England* (1966) p. 346.

p.175:Bacon quarrels with Coke. *Lives of the Chancellors* Vol. III p. 28.

A quarrel in the King's Bench. Referred to in *Punch*, March 4th 1908.

A long replication. *Mylward* v. *Weldon*. (1565) Toth. 101. 21 ER 136. Also Lord Campbell's *Lives of the Chancellors* (5th Ed., 1868) Vol. II. p. 318.

p.176:Tearing up a petition. *Lives of the Chancellors* (5th Ed., 1868) II. 382.

An "infant" aged 63. *Lord* v. *Thornton*, reported in 2 Bulstrode 67, 80 ER 695.

7th Replication to 10th plea. Lord Campbell's *Lives of the Chief Justices* (3rd Ed., 1874) Vol. IV p. 341.

Counsel deceived by his brief. *Memoirs of William Hickey*, ed. Alfred Spencer, p. 336.

p.177:Abusing Plaintiff's attorney. Robert Walter, *Random Recollections of the Midland Circuit* (1869).

Giffard's memory. See A. Wilson Fox, *The Earl of Halsbury* (1929).

Sjt. Maynard poorly paid. *Lives of the Chancellors* Vol. IV. p. 287.

p.178:Bethell tries to pass the buck to Archibald. I found this story in a newspaper collection of legal stories; I have not seen it elsewhere.

Pollock reads the correspondence. Viscount Alverstone's *Recollections of Bar and Bench* (1914) p. 11.

p.180: Hodge and the Blue Smell. Sir Henry Hawkins, *Reminiscences* (1904). Despite this ridiculous exchange, Thomas Platt had a most lugubrious countenance. "Spare us that "wife-and-twelve-children face"", Lord Lyndhurst once said to him.

p.181:Particulars of desertion, and of adultery. I heard these stories from the pleaders themselves.

p.182:The actors learning their lines. Richard Du Cann, *The Art of the Advocate* p. 79.

Partial and gradual disappearance. I cannot recall where I read this story, but it is too good to be untrue.

Gaius Carbo's *commata*. Cicero's views on speech-rhythms are set out in his *Orator*, xlix-lxxi.

Chapter Eleven: DISBARRED!

I thought I had finished my extensive researches on this subject until J.R. Lewis' *The Victorian Bar* (1982) appeared, with much material which had escaped me. I strongly recommend it. The *Dictionary of National Biography* gives a useful summary of James' career.

The Benchers of the Inner Temple kindly made available to me such limited material as now remains from their Inquiry in James' conduct, and I have used it, but the main details of the charges against James, and his answers to them, no longer survive.

The *Times* and *Hansard* give much useful information about James.

p.184: Violating a Vestal Virgin: Pliny's *Letters*, IV. 11.
George Barnwell. A highly popular melodrama written by Lillo.

p.185: Palmer's case is told by Robert Graves in *They hanged my Saintly Billy*, and there are many other accounts. The *Times*, May 14th-28th 1856 gives much detail.

p.186: Electoral malpractices: see Charles Seymour's *Electoral Reform in England and Wales* (1915).
The Mayo election. The *Times* 27th June 1857.
Ballantine's tribute to James. *A Barrister's Life* (1882) p. 284. James was one of the few counsel who could manage Lord Chief Justice Campbell when in a bad mood. He once apologised in open court "for trespassing on your Lordship's impatience."

p.187: Petitions in 1857. The *Times* 22nd May 1857.
Mr. Adderley. The *Times* 5th June 1857.
Payments to "screaming women". Ernest Bowen-Rowlands' *Seventy-Two Years at the Bar*. p. 226.

p.188: Toffee and jelly-shops. Seymour's *Electoral Reform* p. 69.
Assault at the Three Crowns. *Pound* v. *Dawson*, The *Times* 17th Jan. 1857.
The Bond Street jeweller's case. *Hancock* v. *Tempest*, The *Times* 24th Jan. 1857.

p.189: Payments into Court. The old practice is described by the *Rules of the Supreme Court*, (1985 edition), Order 22.
The Commercial traveller in butter. *Donelly* v. *Chancellor*, The *Times* 28th Jan 1857.

p.190: The "clinometer" case. *Lyle* v. *Herbert*, heard at Croydon Assizes on 1st August 1857. See J.R. Lewis, *The Victorian Bar*.
Gladstone's letter to the *Times*, and James' reply. August 15th and 19th 1857.

The Bernard case. The *Times* April 13th-17th 1858.

p.193: James' speeches in Parliament. On arrears of divorce cases, The *Times* 24th March 1859. On majority verdicts, The *Times* 30th March 1859.. On javelin men, The *Times* 27 July 1859.

p.194: The Gloucester election. The *Times* 12th August 1859, 26th January 1860.

John Sadleir. See *Hansard*, June 5th 1857. Sadleir's name was often mentioned with disapproval.

Scully v. *Ingram*. The *Times*, 10th and 11th December 1858.

p.195: Garibaldi's campaign. Jasper Ridley's *Garibaldi* (1974). His welcome in London. Andrea Viotti, *Garibaldi the Revolutionary and his Men.* (1979).

On Garibaldi's train. *Illustrated London News*, 13th October 1860.

Ridley's *Garibaldi* p. 484.

p.196: The Anderson case. An excellent account is given by The *Annual Register* 1861, pp. 520-528.

p.197: James' disbarment, the *Times*, 8th February 1862.

Hawkins' astonishment. *Reminiscences* (1904) p. 129.

p.198: The Inner Temple's Inquiry. The *Annual Register* 1862, pp. 140-143.

Mr. Hudson's impudence. The *Annual Register* 1862, pp. 143-144.

Adjourning the hearing. Letters to the Inner Temple. (Not published).

p.199: His lecture in 1872. The *Times*, 18th April 1872.

p.200: Sjt. Stryver's drinking. Dickens, *A Tale of Two Cities*. It has been suggested that Stryver was modelled on another barrister, but Dickens recorded that he went to watch James in action, and had got him off to the life. Perhaps - as may have been the case with his portrait of the judge in Doctors Commons - he deliberately altered one or two details, to avoid the risk of an action for defamation. Trollope may have done the same in describing Mr. Chaffanbrass as dirty.

Chapter Twelve: F.E. IN SILK

There are several good books about F.E., of which I prefer the one written by his son: *F.E.*, by Lord Birkenhead. This chapter, however, had been compiled largely from the newspapers and law reports of the period.

Readers who seek there may find gems which other books have overlooked.

Chapter Thirteen: COURAGE, COURAGE, COURAGE!

Many of the stories in this chapter come from the *Lives of the Lord Chancellors*, written by Lord Campbell or his successors. I am grateful to them for stories which would otherwise have been lost. The memoirs of Sjt. Ballantine and Sir Henry Hawkins, often quoted below, are also excellent reading.

p.224: Judge Parry's list, quoted Richard DuCann, *The Art of the Advocate*. (1964), Penguin Books.

p.225: Maidenhead: quoted by DuCann, p. 46.

Ballantine's start at the Bar. *A Barrister's Life*, p. 32 *et seq.*

p.227: Hawkins' start at the Bar. *Reminiscences* (1904), p. 15 *et seq.*

Abraham Lincoln's start at the American Bar. Carl Sandburg, *Abraham Lincoln, The Prairie Years (1925)*. All the Lincoln stories here come from this admirably well-written book. It is too easy for English lawyers to overlook Lincoln's career, and I make no apology for including them, for comparison's sake, in a History of the English Bar.

p.228: Lord Eldon's leg of mutton. *Lives of the Chancellors* Vol. IX. P. 142

Robert Henley's sprats. *Lives of the Chancellors* Vol. VI p. 311

Eric Crowther's client. See his *Advocacy for the Advocate* (1984) p. 68, a most enjoyable book with much good advice for young barristers.

Juniors waiting in the King's Bench. Lord Campbell's *Lives of the Chief Justices* Vol. III p. 269.

p.230: Adjourning a rape case in the Southern States. William M. Beaney's fascinating book *The Right to Counsel in American Courts* (Michigan 1955) touches on all sorts of aspects of professional practice which have never been discussed in English courts. I have drawn on it for the American cases.

Moore v. *Dempsey* (1923). 261 US 86, 43 S.Ct.265, 67 L.Ed. 543.

Downer v. *Dunaway* (1931) 53 F.2d 586.

p.231: The Arkansas murder. *Garner* v. *State* (1910) Ark. 63, 132 SW 1010. Drunken M-. Jennings. *McDonald v Hudspeth* (1941) 41 F. Supp. 182, 120 F.2d.962.

p.232: The Trailor case. Sandburg, *Lincoln: The Prairie Years.*

p.233: Trespass by the thickness of a string. Bernard Levin, The *Times,* 7th Jan. 1986.

Toothed beasts in the arena. Guillaume Durand's *Speculum Juris.*

Lord Chancellor Shaftesbury. *Lives of the Chancellors* IV. 176.

p.234: Lord Eldon exasperates Romilly. *Lives of the Chancellors* Vol. IX. 226.

Lord Brougham rebuked by Bickersteth. J.B. Atlay's *The Victorian Chancellors*, Vol. I.

Maule and Lord Tenterden. *The Victorian Chancellors,* II. 85.

p.235: Jenkin Jones and Hallett. Lord Elwyn-Jones' *In My Time* (1983) p. 136.

Alexander Wedderburn and Lockhart. *Lives of the Chancellors* Vol. VII p. 371.

p.236: John Clerk and Lord Braxfield. It appears in full in Stephen Tumim's very entertaining *Great Legal Disasters* (1983).

p.238: Sjt. Wilkins and Baron Gurney. Ballantine, *A Barrister's Life* (1880) p. 208.

Sjt. Wilkins discomfited. Ditto, p. 82.

Kermit the Frog. I heard this story on the Midland Circuit. It gets better every time I tell it. I do not know

the real names of the individuals concerned, to whom I
apologise for any liberties taken.

p.239: A man shoots at Giffard. See A. Wilson Fox' *The Earl
of Halsbury* (1929), and R.F.V. Heuston's *Lives of the
Lord Chancellors 1885-1940.* (Published in 1964).

p.240:Lord Finlay's fortitude. *ibid.*, p. 339.

Chapter Fourteen: THE NUREMBERG TRIALS.

There are many good books on Nuremberg, some written by
eye-witnesses. The general reader may choose any of them with
profit. There is only one which belongs in the realms of great
literature - Rebecca West's *A Train of Powder* (1955), which
includes her three articles on Nuremberg. G.M. Gilbert's
Nuremberg Diary (1948) gives a psychologist's assessment of the
trials from the Defendants' point of view. A number of public
libraries own the complete transcripts of the evidence of the
trials. The reader would do well to dip into them several times
at random, and make his own discoveries.

I have drawn upon:-

A.E. Bowker's *Behind the Bar* (1947); he was Birkett's clerk.

R.W. Cooper, *The Nuremberg Trial* (1947).

Eugene Davidson's *The Making of Adolf Hitler* (1977), which
is very helpful on Hitler's rise to power.

Lord Elwyn-Jones' *In my Time* (1983).

R. Fritzsche's *The Sword in the Scales* (1953), giving a
Defendant's impression of the proceedings.

Whitney R. Harris, *Tyrany on Trial* (1970).

H. Montgomery Hyde's *Norman Birkett* (1964).

Lord Kilmiur's *Political Adventure* (1964).

Werner Maser's *Nuremberg, a Nation on Trial* (1979) is a very
defensive account, in which no fault in the proceedings goes
unremarked, and any horror at what the Nazis did is strikingly
understated.

Martin Middlebrook's *The Nurenberg Raid* (1973) spells
out the importance of Nuremberg as a target for bombing,

and the tragic consequences.

Airey Neave's *Nuremberg* (1978).

Robert Payne's *The Life and Death of Adolf Hitler* (1973), a most readable account.

Bradley R. Smith's *Reaching Judgment at Nuremberg* (1977).

Albert Speer's *Inside the Third Reich*. (1970).

Since these books overlap to a considerable extent, I shall give no other references save,

p.241:Mediaeval Nuremberg. Theodor Hampe, *Crime and Punishment in Germany* (1929).

Chapter Fifteen: ALL THINGS MUST CHANGE.

Although many legal historians in the past have had nothing but scorn for Lord Campbell's books, it is now recognised that they have the very great qualities at least of industry and great readability.

I have drawn on them freely.

J.H. Baker's *Order of the Serjeants* (Selden Society, 1984) is even more learned, and also very readable.

p.258:Dyer takes notes. Lord Campbell's *Lives of the Chief Justices* (3rd Ed. 1874) Vol. I. p. 211.

Metingham monitors candidates. 20 Edw.I (1292) 1 Rot. Parl. 84, quoted by W.C. Bolland, *Two Problems in Legal History*.

Saunders talks to students. Campbell's *Lives of the Chief Justices* II. 324.

p.259:Chaloner Chute takes the term off. *Lives of the Chancellors* Vol. IV p. 281, quoting Roger North's *Lives of the Norths* Vol. I. 10.

The long vacation. Robert C. Palmer, *County Year Book Reports*, English Historical Review (1976) pp. 776-801.

The silks' vacation. *A Barrister's Life* (1880) p. 311.

p.260:Atkin selects Scrutton. See Geoffrey Lewis, *Lord Atkin* (1983).

Martial on bribery. *Epigrams* II. xiii. My own translation. "OH, TYRANT CUTHTOM!". *Lives of the Chancellors* Vol. V. p. 254.

p.261: Martial on long cases. *Epigrams* VII. Ixv. My own translation.

The longest pleading. Ballantine, *A Barrister's Life* (1882) p. 9.

Chitty in a murder case: *R v Thurtell, Probert and Hunt.* J.B. Atlay's *The Victorian Chancellors*, Vol. II. p. 91.

Copley in a Luddite case. J.B. Atlay, *The Victorian Chancellors* Vol. I.

p.262: Guillaume Durand on women. His *Speculum Juris* was very highly regarded in mediaeval times. There is a copy in Lincoln Inn's library.

p.263: F.E. Smith on barmaids. From a newspaper report of 1908.

Bertha Cave. Francis Cowper, *A Prospect of Gray's Inn.*

p.264: "What knockers!" *Daily Telegraph*, 25th July 1985.

Bed of roses. See Denis Judd's *Lord Reading* (1982).

Lord Keeper Williams' working day. *Lives of the Chancellors* Vol. III. p. 148.

p.265: Roundell Palmer's working week. J.B. Atlay's *The Victorian Chancellors* Vol. II p. 392.

p.266: The Serjeants' strike. J.H. Baker's *Order of Serjeants-at-Law* p. 43.

Refusing to become serjeants. Ditto, p. 29 *et seq.*

p.267: Decline of the serjeants. Ditto; see the later chapters.

Barrister stops at monastery. For a case involving Shap Abbey, see Robert C. Palmer, *The County Courts of Mediaeval England 1150-1350.* (Princeton, 1982). This was probably a common practice.

Travel by stage-coach. Ballantine, *A Barrister's Life* (1880).

p.268: Barrister arrives by tram. J.R. Lewis, *The Victorian Bar* (1982) p. 9.

Charging for the salt. Robert Walter, *Random Recollections of the Midland Circuit* (1869).

Abraham Lincoln's circuit. Sandburg, *Lincoln: The Prairie Years.*

p.269: The circuit book-van. J.A. Foote, *Pie-Powder* (1911) p. 40.

The ghoulish children. Hawkins, *Reminiscences* (1904) Vol. I.

A cheese-monger's reputation. J.A. Foote's *Pie-Powder* (1911) p. 78.

p.270: Returning from confirmation. Ballantine, *A Barrister's Life* (1880) p. 8.

Like a crocodile. Robert Walter, *Random Recollections of the Midland Circuit* (1869), p. 13.

Arab steeds. Viscount Alverstone's *Recollections of Bar and Bench* (1914).

p.271: Sjt. Arabin. His amazing sayings were first collected by H. Blencowe Churchill in 1843, reprinted in Ernest Bowen-Rowlands' *Seventy-Two Years at the Bar* (1924), and re-edited in modern times by Sir R.E. Megarry under the title of *Arabinesque-at-Law* (1969).

Coffee at the Old Bailey. Ballantine, *A Barrister's Life* (1880) p. 66.

Fewer wig shops. Richard Roe, *Straws in my Wig* (1954) p.54.

p.272: Working on Saturdays. Fenton Bresler's *Lord Goddard* (1977) p.50.

Marshall Hall's debacle. A.E. Bowker, *Behind the Bar* (1947) p.27.

p.273: Crassus and the thole-pin. Cicero's *Brutus*, LI.194.

Crassus works during the siesta. Cicero, *De Oratore* III.v.7.

p.274: Codd's Duck Puzzle. *Reminiscences* of Sir Henry Hawkins (1904) p.108.

Codd questions Anthony Trollope. Viscount Alverstone's *Recollections of Bar and Bench* (1914).

Birkett defends Hatry. A.E. Bowker's *Behind the Bar* (1947) p.254.

p.275: Cicero defends Ligarius. Plutarch's *Life of Caesar* 39.

Index

Payment into court, 189, 300.
Pavimento, quod adhesit, fake
writ of, 130-131, 294.
Peace, Charlie, 128, 294.
Peckham, defending with
Erskine, 147.
Pemberton, Sjt., 173.
Penance, for castration, 95,
289.
Perjury, 102, 130.
Perverter of justice, 22, 30.
Peterloo Massacre, 108.
Petition of Right, 89.
Petty Treason, 40, 283.
Petronius, 166-7, 298.
Philippic speeches, 15-16, 278.
Phillimore, Harry, at
Nuremberg, 247.
Phineas Redux, 200-1.
Picketing, 204.
Pilgrim Fathers, 103.
Pillory, 64, 103, 121, 286.
Pistol fired at Giffard, 239, 304.
Pitt, 151, 159.
Place, Francis, 105, 134-5,
145, 155, 295.
Plague, 57-8, 65, 78, 241, 268,
285-6.
Platt, Thomas, 180-269.
Pleaders, 6, 22, 29, 39, 53, 99,
174, 277.
Pliny the Younger, 7, 10, 13,
184, 276, 277, 300.
Pokrovsky, General, 245.
Poland, Sir Harry, 132.
Pollock, Sir Frederick, 36,
178, 179, 299.
Pompey, 10, 12, 13, 278.
Pope, Alexander, 104, 144.
Pope, of Rome, 19, 25, 71, 94,
95, 121, 150.
Popham, Lord Chief Justice,
79-82.

Portsmouth, 106, 151, 290.
Postea, 39.
Powder-puffs, carried by men,
218.
Pox, the French, 61, 84, 285.
Pregnancy, impossible after
rape, 46, 283.
Prendergast, Mike, 132, 294.
Prerogative Court, 103,
108-109.
Preston, John of, 265.
Prince of Wales, 149-154,
157-9, 161, 164, 195, 297.
Prior, of Cambridge, gratifying
judges, 29, 280
of Coventry, 42, 283
of St. John of Jerusalem, 54
of Winchester Cathedral, 95.
Prioress whose nun was
abducted, 57.
Prison, 39-40, 42-3, 48, 66, 88,
94, 115, 175.
Privy, polluting water, 36, 54,
58, 284.
Privy Council, 77, 85, 88, 210,
221.
Prize jurisdiction, 217, 220.
Prohibition, writ of, 85, 100-1.
Prostitutes, 22, 34, 60, 65-66,
281, 282, 286.
Protestants, 98-9, 150, 211.
Prynne, William, 119-122,
291-2.
Pump, 66, 286.
Puritans, 100, 102, 103, 119, 292.

Quakers Unmasked, The, 119,
292.
Queen's Counsel, 36, 258, 265,
267.
Queen's Pastoral, The, 119.
Quintilian, 6, 13-14, 124,
276-8, 293.